Victoria

A CELEBRATION

THIS PAGE: "THE CATHEDRAL OF WOOD" MADE
FOR THE GREAT EXHIBITION BY BERNARDO BERNARDIS.
OPPOSITE, LEFT: QUEEN VICTORIA IN 1844,
BY ALEXANDER DE MELVILLE..
OPPOSITE, RIGHT: QUEEN VICTORIA IN 1861.
PAGE 4: QUEEN VICTORIA ON HORSEBACK,
BY SIR DAVID WILKIE.
PAGE 6–7: QUEEN VICTORIA WITH MEMBERS
HER FAMILY, 1881.

THIS IS A CARLTON BOOK

Design copyright © 2000 Carlton Books Limited
Text copyright © 2000 Deborah Jaffé

This edition published by
Carlton Books Limited 2000
20 Mortimer Street
London
W1T 3JW

A CIP catalogue for this book is available from the
British Library.

ISBN 1 84222 180 9

Executive Editor: Sarah Larter
Design: Adam Wright, Mary Ryan
Picture Research: Julia Ruxton, Alex Pepper
Production: Janette Davies

Printed in Dubai

CARLTON
BOOKS

Victoria

A CELEBRATION ❖ DEBORAH JAFFÉ

Contents

Introduction

Queen Victoria reigned for over 63 years, longer than any other British monarch. Her reign was a period of unprecedented change in which Britain shed its agricultural, landed gentry-led image and became a heavily industrialized nation. The repercussions of this change were felt throughout the world.

Victoria came to the throne at the age of 18 in 1837, on the death of her uncle, William IV, one of the sons of George III. Lord Melbourne was Prime Minister and Parliament had already embarked on the great series of Reform Acts, leading to parliamentary democracy and independence from the sovereign, which would continue throughout her reign. Industrialization was well underway, effecting enormous social change as people moved from the countryside to the towns to find work in the mills and factories. A rich middle class and a poor working class were evolving.

During Queen Victoria's reign the British Empire expanded enormously as colonies were annexed and whole countries were governed by men from Britain. The Empire was the source of great wealth and strength for Britain and from the beginning of Victoria's reign, wars and skirmishes were fought to protect its boundaries: the Afghan War of 1839 saw the Russians, posing a threat to India, defeated in Kabul. The East India Company became embroiled in the Opium Wars with China, leading to Britain gaining the territory of Hong Kong in 1842. The Crown took over direct rule of India when the East India Company lost control in the Mutiny of 1857. By a stroke of luck the British Government gained a majority share-holding in the recently opened Suez Canal in 1875. Transportation of convicts to Australia, begun in George III's reign, ended and civilian emigration began to the great island continent and to its smaller neighbour, New Zealand, while in Canada the Hudson's Bay Company ceded to Britain. In competition with European neighbours, there were ruthless forays into Africa culminating, at the end of the century, in the Boer War. By mid-century, the United States of America, still a young country, was fighting a Civil War and carrying little political or economic influence in the world.

GEORGE III,
QUEEN VICTORIA'S
GRANDFATHER, IN
A PAINTING AFTER
ALLAN RAMSAY.

An Age of Invention

This was also a great century of discovery and invention. Queen Victoria herself progressed from a young girl of the pre-industrial age to a matriarch adept at using all the latest inventions and conversing with their creators. The most radical invention of the nineteenth century was the steam railway. When George Stephenson designed the *Locomotive* and ran it from Stockton to Darlington in 1825, few could have guessed at the enormity of its impact. Railways not only changed the face of the landscape and created huge numbers of jobs but enabled people like Thomas Cook to organize cheap travel and package holidays. Great stations, such as St Pancras and Paddington, were built, cathedrals to the glory of the new transport.

Isambard Kingdom Brunel took engineering to new heights, with his bridges, railways and ship-building; Thomas Cubitt built massive housing developments; Herbert Minton commissioned

OPPOSITE:
QUEEN VICTORIA
AT THE AGE OF 56.

Pugin to design tiles, which were made in his factory at Stoke-on-Trent and shown at the 1851 Great Exhibition in Hyde Park. The new medium of photography, much enjoyed by the Queen, made this the first reign to be recorded in detail and in the last years of her life she was an eager user of the telephone.

As the new middle classes became more affluent, the workers got poorer. Thousands of people had moved from the countryside to the new towns; at the beginning of the century only 22 per cent of the population lived in urban areas; by the end, the figure had risen to 77 per cent. The roots of the trade union and Labour movements were laid in 1834 when a group of agricultural workers known as the Tolpuddle Martyrs were deported to Australia for making demands for better working conditions.

Public health became a matter of great concern due to the mass housing problems, and campaigns for better sanitation were inaugurated. Florence Nightingale, nursing in army hospitals in the Crimea, set a pattern for cleaner and safer hospitals in Britain. Charles Darwin, questioning the origin of life, provoked serious and angry debate within –and without – the Church. Charles Dickens, Charlotte Brontë, George Eliot, Elizabeth Gaskell and other writers developed a new, analytical literature in prose and poetry to describe the contrasts and contradictions of life in Victorian Britain. Satirists and cartoonists such as George Cruikshank in *Punch* took delight in debunking much that was wrong or unjust in the society. Meanwhile, the *Illustrated London News*, first published in 1842, provided a visual record of national and royal events.

Marriage with European Links

The marriage of Victoria to her first cousin, Prince Albert of Saxe-Coburg, further cemented the relationship between the British throne and the German House of Saxe-Coburg – much to the delight of their uncle, Leopold, King of the Belgians. Through his emissary Baron Stockmar, Leopold was closely involved with the way Victoria dealt with affairs of state. After Leopold's death and the marriages of her own children across the Continent, Victoria was effectively head of the Royal Houses of Europe.

The emotional basis of the marriage, cut short by Albert's early death from typhoid fever, was a mixture of love, passion, argument and depression. Albert, an educated, cultured and formal young man was, at first, frustrated by the frivolity of the British Court and the hostile reaction of Parliament to his marriage. While Victoria liked to spend time listening to light music, playing cards and games and reading little, the intellectual Albert wanted to meet the leading inventors, engineers, industrialists and philanthropists of the day and to have some involvement with state affairs. One of his greatest achievements was to be at the forefront of the planning and execution of the Great Exhibition, an event that Victoria thoroughly enjoyed, visiting frequently with their children and purchasing artefacts, all the time very proud of Albert's achievement.

Perhaps because of the deficiencies and coldness of their own childhoods, family life was extremely important to Victoria and Albert. They found the atmospheres of Buckingham Palace and Windsor Castle stifling so estates at Osborne on the Isle of Wight and Balmoral in Scotland were purchased for their private use.

At Osborne they created an Italianate-style villa, designed by Prince Albert and Thomas Cubitt, overlooking the Solent. This, Albert imagined, could be the Bay of Naples and the building was influenced by his pre-marriage tour of Italy. In the grounds they built a miniature Swiss cottage for their nine children to play in.

A German schloss-style country house was built at Balmoral, in the Scottish Highlands, reminiscent of Prince Albert's childhood home near Coburg in Thuringia. They loved to escape to Balmoral, where they would ride horses and stay in the mountains, often accompanied by John

QUEEN VICTORIA AND PRINCE ALBERT IN 1854, PHOTOGRAPHED BY ROGER FENTON.

Brown, a ghillie. This much-publicized family of adoring parents of nine children became an ideal to be attained by many in the newly affluent middle classes.

Queen Victoria was not only a monarch but also a mother, grandmother and great-grandmother. Pregnancy and childbirth were extremely trying for her, but she was supportive of all her daughters and grand-daughters during their confinements. She herself broke new ground when, for the birth of her eighth child, Leopold, she used chloroform to help ease the pain. This caused fierce religious debates and a medical argument, but changed the prospect of painful childbirth for generations of women. The birth of Prince Leopold also introduced the ghastly disease of haemophilia into the family which, due to various marriages, spread across the Royal Houses of Europe.

Victoria and Albert delighted in their first-born child, Victoria, the Princess Royal, who married the German Emperor Frederick III. In later life, however, the Queen let it be known she was not at all pleased with the actions of her grandson, William, the eventual German Kaiser. Problems with their eldest son, Bertie, the Prince of Wales, concerned both parents from an early age; showing none of his older sister's aptitude, his early predilection for fast women caused them great pain.

Queen, Empress and Imperial Mother

The public sympathy for Queen Victoria that was widespread immediately after the death of her beloved Albert in 1861 could not be sustained. She became a recluse, followed certain rituals relating to Albert, and organized memorials to and biographies of him. However, the public would not believe that he was as good as she portrayed him and were angry at the cost to the country of the Civil List, the amount of money allocated by Parliament for the monarch. As on numerous earlier occasions when the monarchy was out of favour, republicanism, this time in the form of the Chartist movement, gained support.

Mourning, and all its trappings, was a nineteenth-century phenomenon. Queen Victoria was not the only one to suffer loss and grieve. Many families were devastated by deaths at a time of high infant mortality and stillbirths, the result of malnutrition in the working classes (including the devastating potato famine in Ireland), cholera, typhoid, tuberculosis and other diseases; injuries and deaths of the Crimean and Boer Wars and other insurrections; and accidents in the factories and on the railways. Mourning fashions were widespread and companies such as Courtaulds became dependent on the revenues earned by producing black crêpe.

Gradually, Prime Minister Benjamin Disraeli's sympathy and charm combined with the support and down-to-earth familiarity of John Brown, lured Victoria into reappearing in public again. Life in the Highlands remained especially important to Queen Victoria. She would disappear to Balmoral for months at a time, riding with John Brown, sometimes staying in isolated cottages on the estate, painting watercolours of Highland scenes and writing her journal.

When John Brown died, the Queen commanded the announcement of her best friend's death to be placed in the Court Circular of *The Times*. Some years later, his place was taken by Abdul Karim, known as the Munshi. She was delighted to become Empress of India in 1876 and indulged her fascination in the exotic by learning Hindustani, eating curries and even creating the Durbar room at Osborne in rich Indian style. Like many before and since, she was enraptured by the spirit of India.

Queen Victoria celebrated her Golden Jubilee in1887 and her Diamond Jubilee in 1897. Once past 80, however, her health declined and she died at Osborne on January 14, 1901. Although prepared for her death, the nation was, nevertheless, stunned. The Queen had been "there" for such a long time, indeed for more than a lifetime for many of her subjects. Prayers were said, sermons preached and obituaries written in Britain and around the world.

The nineteenth century in Britain was an extraordinary period: a mixture of change and increased stability, progress and tradition, invention and revolution, wealth and poverty, all with Queen Victoria at the head of it. For the historian, hers was an extraordinary reign not only because of its unprecedented length, but because of the amount of documentation recording it. Logged in public records are costings, lists of members of the households and money spent. Queen Victoria kept a detailed diary and wrote hundreds of letters during her long life. Her secretaries, Charles Greville and Henry Ponsonby, also recorded events in their diaries. The diversity of the period had long-standing effects on the twentieth century and the tiny, sheltered, young woman who became queen gave her name to a fascinating and hugely important era of British and world history.

A WATERCOLOUR BY QUEEN VICTORIA, OF GLASSALT SHIELD IN THE SCOTTISH HIGHLANDS.

Chapter *1* Princess Alexandrina Victoria

When Princess Alexandrina Victoria, grand-daughter of King George III, was born in 1819, the monarchy was in disarray, the family on the throne associated more with loose living, mistresses, illegitimate children and madness than with the reputation for following an exemplary family life it would acquire in years to come. The country itself was ill-at-ease with the monarchy, the cost of supporting their antics and expensive lifestyles was being questioned and republican movements were beginning to voice dissent. Parliament was trying to establish its independence from the monarch and, through reforms, was putting Britain on the path to becoming a fully democratic country.

The Duke of Wellington's victory over Napoleon at Waterloo in 1815 had given the governing upper classes and army great confidence and in Europe, Britain was viewed as supreme. There were no great internal civil conflicts, as in France, nor demands for expansion into neighbouring territories. For Britain, any expansion was carried out much further afield, in the existing Empire and in the colonisation of large parts of the continents of America, Africa and Asia and in Australasia. France was embroiled in internal, bloody civil unrest between monarchists and republicans. Germany and Italy were not yet united as single states and comprised many small principalities, each eager to outdo the others or to make strengthening alliances. Expansionist Russia was constantly trying to push its boundaries further outward. Empire building was high on the agenda of many European heads of state.

Although Britain enjoyed a powerful position in the world, its monarchy did not. The first signs of apparent madness had begun to show in George III in the 1780s, in fact he was suffering from a metabolic disease called porphyria. Since then, the fifteen children borne to him and his wife, Charlotte of Mecklenburg Strelitz, had either remained childless or produced numerous illegitimate children who would be unable to inherit the throne. George III's sons had a predilection for mistresses, particularly actresses, none of whom would make suitable wives.

In 1810, with the King's condition incurable and he himself oblivious to much that was happening around him, a regency had been established, and his eldest son George, Prince of Wales, became Prince Regent. Many found the Prince Regent's extravagant and flamboyant lifestyle distasteful when compared with the lives of many of his subjects, working hard at gruelling jobs in the new factories and living in squalid conditions. Parliament too, was ill-at-ease. The Whigs were the party of government and reform was on the agenda. A review of the Civil List, the amount of money given by Parliament to the monarch, was requested after the example set by George III. In 1760 he had agreed to a fixed sum of £800,000 per annum, but his growing family soon used up the allowance putting the King in the demeaning position of having to periodically ask Parliament for more.

There was disarray at court concerning the future of the succession. There seemed to be a very real danger that another Hanoverian, the Duke of Brunswick, a cousin of George III, could inherit the Crown. Hopes of a successful conclusion to the problem were pinned on the marriage of Princess Charlotte, the legitimate daughter of the Prince Regent. She had married the eccentric Prince Leopold of Saxe-Coburg in Prussia. But in November, 1817 all hope of a legitimate succession from the Prince Regent to his daughter ended when Princess Charlotte died in childbirth and her baby was stillborn.

Rather hastily, George III's third son, William, Duke of Clarence, cut his connection with Dora Jordan, the actress with whom he had been living for 20 years and who had borne him ten children, and married a German princess, Adelaide of Saxe-Meningen. They did have two daughters, but both died in infancy.

Meanwhile, the now widowed Prince Leopold remained in England, nurturing new plans for Britain. His determination to build the small Prussian House of Saxe-Coburg into a dominant Royal House of Europe would be an important factor in the survival of the British monarchy. With Leopold was his physician, Baron Christian Stockmar, who had come to England when Leopold married Charlotte. He had refused to give any medical advice during the pregnancy and delivery, saying the experience of an army doctor was no preparation for the role of obstetrician. Enamoured of Court life, he changed his career to that of emissary, aide and negotiator and worked for Leopold in England, Belgium and Saxe-Coburg for 50 years.

The crisis in the succession subsided when Prince Leopold commenced his role as royal matchmaker extraordinaire and introduced his young, widowed sister, Princess Victoria Leiningen of Saxe-Coburg, to the British Court. Princess Victoria's husband had died, leaving her with two young children, Charles, aged 14, and 10-year-old Feodore Leiningen.

The 50-year-old bachelor, Edward, Duke of Kent, fourth son of George III, had had a mistress in France for many years and, like his brothers, was fond of high living. On meeting Princess Victoria he suddenly realized he could resolve the succession problem. The age difference of 19 years did not deter him from proposing marriage to her. Initially, the Princess was repelled by him but eventually, after much persuasion from her brother, she acquiesced and married the Duke on July 11, 1818 in the Hall of Giants at Coburg.

A Future Queen is Born

Soon after the wedding, the Duchess became pregnant, and the Duke was determined this child should be born in Britain to give it unequivocal rights to the throne. So, heavily pregnant, the Duchess and her husband returned to Britain in April 1819, accompanied by a German midwife. Midwives had little status within the British medical profession and their importance at childbirth was underestimated but in Germany they were educated in universities and worked alongside doctors. The Duke of Kent was anxious to avoid a repeat of the fatal result of Princess Charlotte's confinement and employed Regina von Siebold, a midwife trained at the University of Marburg.

The Duchess of Kent gave birth to a healthy daughter on May 24, 1819, at Kensington Palace. The birth of a daughter to the Duke and Duchess of Kent was treated with little enthusiasm by a court still eager for a male heir and a country perplexed at the antics of its Royal Family. In London, the choice of names for the new baby was problematic. Charlotte was deemed inappropriate because of the death of Princess Charlotte. Her parents wanted to call her Victoria after the Duchess of Kent but one of the godfathers, Tsar Alexander I of Russia, wanted her named Alexandrina after him. The baby's other godfather, the Prince Regent, attended the baptism but showed little warmth towards the new baby. In deference to the Tsar and not wishing to antagonize him, the baby was baptized Princess Alexandrina Victoria at Kensington Palace on June 26, 1819. Throughout her childhood she was known as Drina.

Shortly after the delivery of the baby, Regina von Siebold returned to Coburg to assist at the

THE RECENTLY WIDOWED DUCHESS OF KENT AND HER YOUNG DAUGHTER, PRINCESS VICTORIA, PAINTED BY SIR WILLAIM BEECHEY IN 1821.

delivery of a son, Prince Albert of Saxe-Coburg, to the Duchess of Kent's sister-in-law, Duchess Louise who was married to her brother, Duke Ernest.

A consequence of the Duke of Kent's enjoyment of an expensive lifestyle was that he was seriously in debt. During the winter of 1819–20, and trying to be more restrained economically, the new family went on holiday to coastal resort of Sidmouth in Devon. After walking in the bracing sea air, the Duke caught a chill from which he never recovered, dying a few days later of pneumonia. His will stated that his equerry,

Sir John Conroy, should be his executor and his enormous debt was revealed to his wife.

The Duke of Kent was buried at Windsor on January 23, 1820. Six days later his father, George III, died. The Prince Regent now became King George IV and the fatherless, eight-month-old Drina suddenly became the focus of attention as the future of the Crown of Great Britain, Ireland and territories around the world seemed to rest with her. Unless the Duke of Clarence and his wife had another child, there would be a queen on the throne in the not too distant future.

PRINCESS VICTORIA AGED 11, BY RICHARD WESTELL.

Drina's Childhood

Life at Kensington Palace was not easy for the Duchess of Kent, widowed for the second time and now with three children. She was German in a large English family hostile to her. She claimed that the English language was difficult to master. However, the historian Elizabeth Longford has found evidence that she could speak English fluently but gave the impression she did not in order to gain sympathy.

The Duke of Kent's debts had to be settled. The temptation to return home to Coburg must have been enormous, but fortunately for the Duke's widow, her brother, Prince Leopold, remained in London. Wanting the maximum advantage for the baby's future claim to the throne, Leopold settled the financial affairs and advised his sister not to return to Coburg.

Feodore's governess, Fraulein Louise Lehzen, was brought from Hanover to attend to the education of Drina. Leopold stayed to advise her and introduced Stockmar to Kensington Palace, his influence in the life and court of Queen Victoria was to be enormous. Sir John Conroy, now responsible for the Duchess's financial affairs, would also soon become influential in the life of the fatherless family.

The young Drina spent the early years of her childhood surrounded almost entirely by women. German was her first language and she did not speak any English until she was three. Her mother and Louise Lehzen were in no doubt about the importance of their task to prepare little Victoria for her awesome future role. They were determined to do their best. In this, they were not helped by their poor relationship with George IV who disapproved of them.

The Duchess of Kent's repeated demands for an increase in her allowance, the presence of her increasingly eccentric brother Prince Leopold, who had grown out of favour with the court, and the Germanic way in which the young princess was being brought up did little to recommend Kensington Palace to Buckingham Palace. As the years passed, the relationship between the Duchess and the King deteriorated further as gossip and suspicion began to grow about the nature of the relationship between her and Sir John Conroy.

In early childhood Princess Victoria was very close to her mother, the Duchess rarely letting her daughter out of her sight. They even shared a bedroom until the day of Victoria's accession. Maybe due to her Germanic upbringing or because of shortage of money, the Duchess brought up her daughter frugally by royal standards. In the early part of her childhood, Drina had the company of her much older half-brother and sister, Charles and Feodore. However, Feodore married in 1828 when Drina was nine and went to live in Germany.

Apart from her half-siblings, Victoria spent much of her childhood isolated from other children of her age and oblivious of events outside the walls of Kensington Palace. Ostracism by the King's Court also meant she had little contact with other members of the Royal Family and her horizons were firmly fixed on her mother and Fraulein Lehzen in Kensington Palace. As adults Feodore and Victoria would discuss the desolation and isolation of their childhood at Kensington Palace. Victoria was delighted when Feodore visited Kensington Palace with her two young children in 1834, and the 15-year-old Princess enjoyed playing with them.

Uncle Leopold was still an important visitor, regarding himself as a father-figure to the young Princess, planning her future and continuing to advise his sister. He had rejected an offer to become King of Greece, but in 1830 the newly independent Belgium invited him to become their King, he accepted and left London for good. Sir John Conroy was quick to take Leopold's place as advisor to the Duchess of Kent, but Baron Stockmar remained in London as the King of the Belgians' representative, taking instructions and advising the Duchess. On Leopold's instruction, Stockmar also continued to make frequent visits to Duke Ernest's residence in Coburg to see how his young sons were developing.

Drina's education was left to Fraulein Lehzen, who persuaded her young charge to keep a diary. This recommendation has resulted in a fascinating and unique record of the Princess's, and, later, the Queen's life. She was brought up to speak three languages. There were lessons in drawing, painting and singing and the Princess would become a competent draughtswoman. She enjoyed her singing lessons, often finding them a welcome break from the tedium and loneliness of Palace life.

Fraulein Lehzen was instrumental in preparing the Princess for the challenging role ahead of her. Until she was 11 years old, Victoria had no idea of her future. In 1830, the year of

LETTERS WRITTEN BY VICTORIA AS A CHILD.

George IV's death and his brother William's succession, Lehzen decided it was now appropriate that she should know her destiny. Told of the death of her uncle and the accession of his brother as William IV, she also learned that she was now first in line of succession. One day she would be Queen of Great Britain and Ireland. On realizing this, Drina is reported to have said "I will be good."

Perhaps due to her isolation and because she was surrounded by adults, Princess Victoria

PRINCESS VICTORIA AT THE ROYAL OPERA HOUSE.

built roads to Regent's Park, where the new Zoological Gardens had opened in 1826, or across Wimbledon Common and Richmond Park. There were visits to the Royal Opera House in Covent Garden to see operas including *The Barber of Seville* and *Fidelio*.

There were also visits to other households around the country, both Whig and Tory, her mother having decided she should be brought up as politically unbiased as possible. On her accession she would regard herself as a Whig, partly because her father had been the only one of George III's sons to support the Whigs, and also because they were the government in power at the time.

In 1835, the family stayed at Canterbury en route to Ramsgate, where they were joined by Uncle Leopold and his new wife Louisa, whom Victoria adored. They stayed in a small house overlooking the sea, with the coast of France visible in the distance. Uncle Leopold and Aunt Louisa stayed a short distance away at the Albion Hotel. There was a formal welcome by the town for the royal visitors and Victoria herself was delighted to see her fatherly uncle after his four-year absence. Victoria was enthralled not only by her new aunt's charm and friendliness but by her elegant and exquisite Parisian clothes and well-styled hair. She would try to emulate both once she was Queen and able to order her own clothes from France.

developed her own independent inner world with her collection of 132 dolls. Each doll had a grand name and exquisite clothes. They were often involved in the Princess's fantasy plays. She also had a pet spaniel called Dash who had been given to her mother by Sir John Conroy but adopted by Victoria. Dash was, like many childrens' pets, her confidante and was regularly washed and groomed and dressed up in dolls' clothes. He even sat for Sir Edwin Landseer, who painted many portraits of the young Victoria.

The Princess loved horse riding and treks were made through Hyde Park along the newly

SOME OF VICTORIA'S

COLLECTION OF 132 DOLLS.

The Saxe-Coburg Cousins

Even from afar, Uncle Leopold was still determined to influence Princess Victoria's future and that of his own homeland. Empire building was fashionable among many of Europe's leaders in the nineteenth century. Russia was constantly attempting to expand its boundaries and, consequently, was watched closely by other powers. France was fraught with internal, bloody conflicts as it rocked between being a monarchy and the exclusiveness of the Emperor Napoleon III's conquests until it became a republic later in the century. Germany and Italy were collections of several independent states, though each would be unified by the end of the century.

King Leopold was not unlike his fellow heads of state and the strengthening of the tiny House of Saxe-Coburg and its dominance in Europe remained fundamental to his grand plan. Not only was he closely involved with his niece's upbringing but also with that of his two motherless nephews, the Princes Ernest and Albert of Saxe-Coburg. Stockmar, recently returned from Coburg, reported that Albert, the younger of the two boys, was an intelligent if serious young man who would need to make a marriage which would stretch his intellect. He also reported that he was worried about certain of Prince Ernest's character traits.

King Leopold and Princess Victoria corresponded regularly, so it was no surprise when he suggested his two nephews, first cousins of the Princess, should visit Kensington Palace. Victoria was no doubt oblivious of his plan to marry one of them to her. Leopold and Stockmar must have been anxious about the visit, worried that their plan might not work.

In the summer of 1836 the party from Saxe-Coburg arrived; it included Uncle Ernest, Duke of Saxe-Coburg, brother of the Duchess

of Kent, and his two sons, 18-year-old Ernest and 16-year-old Albert. Victoria was then 17, a few months older than Albert. The boys' mother had brought disgrace upon the family and had been forced to abandon her children. Duke Ernest was a philanderer who, furious on discovering his wife's infidelities, had divorced her because of her affair with Lieutenant Haustein in 1824. Part of the settlement, typical for the time, was that she should leave her two small sons, then aged five and six, with their father. She was heartbroken. She never saw them again and died in Paris in 1831.

For Victoria, no thoughts of such past sadnesses marred the visit, which was a rare occasion for her to enjoy the company of people her own age. The looks and personalities of her two cousins impressed and fascinated her.

A MINIATURE OF A YOUNG AND DASHING ALBERT.

Preparation

As she grew older, the Princess sat at dinner with her mother, Sir John Conroy, Fraulein Lehzen and guests. While those within the confines of Kensington Palace had focused on her future role, there had been an effort to protect her from the broader aspects of the effects of industrialization and other changes in the country. George Stephenson's *Locomotive* ran on the first railway line from Stockton to Darlington in 1825 but Princess Victoria would have to wait until 1837 before she saw her first train. In 1832 the first Reform Act was passed, in 1833 slavery was abolished in the British Empire and the Factory Act limited children between nine and 12 years to working a maximum nine hours a day in cotton mills. Public health and sanitation were appalling, with cholera and typhoid endemic, but steps were being taken to improve it. Thomas Wakley founded *The Lancet* to inform doctors on how to improve their procedures and to oust grave robbers, quacks and poor practitioners.

To protect workers from unscrupulous mill and factory owners, trade unionism was beginning; publication of the People's Charter in Glasgow in 1838 began the Chartist movement. Among the consequences of the wealth created by the Empire and the factories was the emergence of a new, affluent, middle class: the concept of "new" money as opposed to "old" – that is, inherited, usually landed, wealth – had arrived.

Victoria grew up and tensions increased between her and her mother. The relationship between the Duchess and the Court was never anything but strained. However, when George IV died, Princess Victoria did manage to re-establish the relationship, visiting the new king, William IV, and Queen Adelaide regularly. The couple came to regard Victoria as a daughter, becoming increasingly fond of her. By 1837 she was visiting the sick King often, and supporting his wife.

Sir John Conroy continued to annoy and frustrate her. She despised him for his power over her mother and herself; she was disturbed by the rumours that he was the Duchess's lover; and she detested his demands and his inference

ERNEST ... has DARK *hair*, and *fine* DARK *eyes* and *eyebrows*, but the nose and mouth are not good; he has most kind, honest and intelligent expression in his countenance, and has a very good figure. Albert, who is just as tall as Ernest but stouter, is extremely handsome; his hair is about the same colour as mine; his eyes are large and blue, and he has a beautiful nose and a very sweet mouth with fine teeth; but the charm of his countenance is his expression, which is most delightful ...

Victoria found the brothers mature and sensible with impeccable manners. They were good at drawing and playing the piano. Albert was more serious than Ernest and enjoyed talking about "serious and instructive things", but he did have fun with Dash. They enlivened the Princess's household like never before with their wit, fun and energy – so much so that she cried when they left in July after a stay of two months. Stockmar and Leopold were delighted at the success of the visit and all anxieties they may have had dissipated as they planned ways to secure the future of their friendships.

that Victoria would be ill-equipped to fulfil her future duties without his help. The Duchess and Sir John had even tried to have a regency established in the event of Victoria's accession occurring before she was twenty-one. Conroy was no doubt furiously jealous of the role of Fraulein Lehzen, who had long since surpassed her role as governess and attained the position of adviser and friend which he was so eager to assume.

By the spring of 1837, it was public knowledge that the health of William IV was failing. King Leopold was refining his plans for the house of Saxe-Coburg and the Duchess of Kent, Sir John Conroy at her side, remained in total control of her daughter. The relationship between mother and daughter continued to deterioate. For Victoria a waiting game had begun; she knew her apprenticeship was nearly over and, no doubt daunted by her inexperience and feelings of inadequacy, she resolved to try even harder to attain the standard required for her future duties.

On May 24, 1837, Princess Victoria celebrated her eighteenth birthday, in the knowledge that the health of her uncle, William IV, was declining quickly. Prince Albert, now aware, like his cousin, of Uncle Leopold's plans for them both, sent her a letter of birthday greetings to which she replied. She rode in a carriage through the streets of London, crowded with people eager to greet their future queen on her birthday. A celebration ball was held at St James's Palace, which the Princess attended accompanied by Fraulein Lehzen, her lady-in-waiting Lady Flora Hastings, and other members of the Household. She enjoyed dancing quadrilles with many eligible young men, to the pleasure of the establishment eager to see her marry an Englishman.

Victoria's eighteenth birthday was an important point in her progress towards independence from her mother, as she was now eligible to receive her own income from the Civil List. As the King's health continued to decline, the Princess made regular visits to Buckingham Palace, not just to her uncle's sick bed, but also to comfort Queen Adelaide. She was well prepared for his death and grateful for the advice of Uncle Leopold and for the presence of Stockmar, as she wrote to Leopold on June 19, 1837:

MY DEARLY BELOVED UNCLE,- Your *kind* and *dear* letter, containing most WHOLESOME, *prudent*, SOUND and EXCELLENT *advice*, was given me by our good and invaluable honest friend, STOCKMAR … let me tell you how happy and thankful I am to have Stockmar here; he has been, and is, of the greatest possible use, and be assured … that he possesses my most entire confidence!

THE KING'S STATE … is *hopeless* … I feel sorry for him; he was always personally kind to me, and I should be ungrateful and devoid of feeling if I did not remember this.

I look forward to the event which it seems is likely to occur soon with calmness and quietness; I am not alarmed at it, and yet I do not suppose myself quite equal to all; I trust, however, that with good will, honesty, and courage I shall not, at all events, fail …

PEN AND WATERCOLOUR PAINTING OF QUEEN ADELAIDE, WIFE OF KING WILLIAM IV, BY SIR DAVID WILKIE, 1836.

Less than four weeks after her eighteenth birthday Drina's life changed forever and Great Britain had the first Queen Regnant since Queen Anne came to the throne in 1702.

Chapter 2 The Young Queen

King William IV died in the early hours of June 20, 1837. As the death had been expected, William Howley, Archbishop of Canterbury, the Lord Chamberlain, Lord Conyngham, and the King's doctor were all present at Windsor. Their immediate action was to travel to Kensington Palace to inform the young Princess Alexandrina Victoria of his death and her accession.

Travelling through the night, they arrived at the Palace around 5 a.m. They were barred from seeing the Princess by her mother, the Duchess of Kent, who assumed she would still be as closely involved with her daughter now she was Queen, as she had been throughout her daughter's life. For her the day did not progress as she had anticipated.

The Duchess finally succumbed to the demands of the important visitors and woke the Princess. At 6 a.m., the eighteen-year-old Drina, still in her dressing gown and clasping her mother's hand, descended the stairs to meet the Archbishop and Lord Chamberlain who fell to their knees and proclaimed her Queen. "Drina" was a name of the past; from now on, she would be known as "Queen Victoria". She had been preparing for this moment since she had declared "I will be good" when she was eleven years old.

Respects were paid to the dead King and Victoria left to change into a black dress to mourn him and thus begin the first day of a reign which would last for 63 years, longer than any other British sovereign.

The mourning dress, probably worn that day, is now in the Museum of London, and has faded to a dark brown. Rumours that the Duchess of Kent, with her frugal attitudes, had dyed it with black ink are, according to costume historian Kay Staniland, unfounded. There is no reason why the Duchess would have wanted to do this for an event for which she had been preparing for many years. It is an elegant ankle-length dress, well cut with long, pleated sleeves and white lace cuffs and a frill running down the left side from the waist to hem. The style is typical of the formal occasion dress of the period. Much to Uncle Leopold's disappointment, Victoria was less than five feet tall but, at this age, she had a slim figure and marked waistline, very different from the fuller figure of later years. Some months afterwards, Sir David Wilkie, whom Queen Victoria quickly appointed as Court Painter, would portray her with her ministers on this day in a white dress. He requested the dress be white and not black purely to give her figure prominence in the painting.

At breakfast, she discussed the plans for the day with Baron Stockmar, recently returned from a visit to King Leopold with instructions to support her. Shortly after 9 in the morning, her Prime Minister and friend, Lord Melbourne, arrived. Dealing with affairs of state had begun. She received Melbourne alone and later recorded the meeting in her diary:

… of COURSE quite ALONE as I shall always do all my Ministers. He kissed my hand and I then acquainted him that it had long been my intention to retain him and the rest of the present Ministry at the head of affairs, and that it could not be in better hands than his … He then read to me the Declaration which I was to read to the Council, which he wrote himself and which is a very fine one … I like him very much and feel confidence in him.

OPPOSITE: EIGHTEEN-YEAR-OLD PRINCESS VICTORIA RECEIVING NEWS OF HER ACCESSION, JUNE 20, 1837, PAINTED BY FREDERICK SHUCKARD.

THE DRESS PROBABLY WORN BY QUEEN VICTORIA ON THE DAY OF HER ACCESSION.

The Prime Minister, William Lamb, 2nd Viscount Melbourne, was enchanted by Victoria. Melbourne was then a lonely 56-year-old divorcé, he had separated from his wife, Lady Caroline Ponsonby, over twenty years earlier because of her various infidelities, most notably with the wildly attractive poet Lord Byron. Melbourne was a shrewd man who gave the impression of being a relaxed, amateur politician. Although a Whig, he was renowned for his opposition to reforms and intolerance of poverty and saw little reason to change basic social legislation. He was doubtless flattered by

Kensington Palace. Wearing her black mourning dress, she was led by the Dukes of Cumberland and Sussex to the throne to be sworn in as Queen of Great Britain and Ireland. At all times observers were impressed by her; she was tiny and very young but emanated a maturity beyond her years. Confidence, serenity and independence radiated from her; on her own admission, she was never nervous. While most around her were impressed and relieved after the uncertainties created by the royal family in recent years, certain members of her mother's household were aghast at her self-confidence.

the attentions of this young Queen eager to learn everything she possibly could about her future and saw it as his duty to prepare, support and protect her. The close relationship between young monarch and older statesman was to flourish further in the ensuing months.

The Queen presided over her first Council Meeting at 11.30 a.m. in the Red Saloon at

During that first day of her reign, she found time to write several letters. She wrote to her uncle, Leopold King of the Belgians, informing him of the death of William IV. Leopold would indeed be pleased that his niece was now Queen, bringing the fulfilment of his plans near to fruition. She also wrote to her half-sister Feodore in Germany and to the widowed Queen

QUEEN VICTORIA'S ACCESSION DAY SALUTE IN HYDE PARK BY WILLIAM HEATH.

Adelaide whom she would continue to visit. Prince Albert wrote to her again, this time to offer condolences on the death of the King and congratulations on her Accession.

Even at the end of a very busy and most exciting day, the new Queen Victoria found time to write her diary; the consequence of Fraulein Lehzen's training has given us a unique insight into the experience of becoming a Queen, written by the Sovereign herself. In her writings she described her early morning visitors, events of the day and her resolve to do her duty:

Since it has *pleased* PROVIDENCE to place me in this *station*, I shall do my UTMOST to fulfil my *duty* towards my country; I am very young and perhaps in many, though not all things, inexperienced, but I am sure that very few have more real good will and more real desire to do what is fit and right than I have.

The next day, Princess Alexandrina Victoria was proclaimed Queen Victoria to the nation from a window at St James's Palace. Sermons were preached and prayers said in churches, chapels and synagogues around the nation to mourn the dead King and to welcome the new Queen.

The Queen's Household

Eager to reinforce her new position, the Queen quickly made appointments to her own Household. To her relief, she could now act independently of her mother and she informed Melbourne of her feelings about Sir John Conroy. She could not bear the sight of him and was unable to stay in the same room as him. Gossip was rife that the Duchess of Kent was his mistress. With Lord Melbourne's support she was able to make appointments to her Household without including Sir John Conroy, but she was unable to dislodge him from her mother's. Conroy was furious at his demotion, having assumed he would be given the powerful position of the Queen's private secretary.

The relationship between mother and daughter became even more strained as Victoria began to enjoy her authority. It deteriorated further when Queen Victoria discovered her mother was £70,000 in debt, despite Sir John Conroy's financial advice. Lord Melbourne was appalled by this situation and also by the Duchess's assumption that her daughter would help her out. The loyal supporter, tutor and friend, Fraulein Lehzen, was rewarded with a new appointment to the Household as Lady Attendant on the Queen; henceforth she was known as Baroness Lehzen.

On Melbourne's advice, the Household was made up almost entirely of Whigs or Ladies married to Whig MPs, a matter that enraged the Tories in Parliament. An exception was Lady Flora Hastings, a reserved woman from a Tory family who was a Lady in Waiting. Victoria never felt totally at ease with her, suspecting she was an ally of Sir John Conroy. Sir David Wilkie became Court Painter and Dr James Clark Court Physician.

Major appointments also had to be made to the Queen's Wardrobe. The King's Office of Robes was formally closed and a new one opened requiring different personnel and expertise. Kay Staniland suggests that it took the Office some time to get used to the female environment. Now free of her mother's interference, Victoria could indulge herself, albeit for a short period, like any other young woman of her station, in fashion. Remembering the holiday with her new, stylish Aunt Louisa in Ramsgate she bought clothes from Paris.

The Duchess of Sutherland became Mistress of the Robes. Wardrobe maids were appointed to look after the expanding collection of day and evening dresses, underwear, nightclothes, uniforms and riding clothes. Some of Queen Victoria's clothes came from France, although she did request others to be made of silk from the weavers in Spitalfields in East London who had hit hard times.

Other clothes were made by the Royal Dressmaker, Mrs Bettans, and Richard Gundry made the royal shoes. A host of trades and crafts people were employed by the Queen during her reign: glovers, hatters, milliners, bonnet makers, silk and lace makers, providers of stays and corsets, embroiderers, plumassiers, jewellers, florists and perfumiers all made contributions to the Queen's wardrobe. There were also the Royal Robe makers for the Parliamentary and Coronation garments.

One of the Queen's early duties was to fix the payments due to her from Parliament, under the Civil List. The Duchess of Kent would receive £30,000 per annum and for the Queen herself there would be £385,000 per annum and £60,000 from the Privy Purse. She would also benefit from the revenues of the Duchies of Lancaster and Cornwall, although those from the Duchy of Cornwall would pass, in time, to her eldest son.

Buckingham Palace

On July 13, the Queen and Duchess of Kent with their respective Households moved into Buckingham Palace. The Palace, once the London home of George III's consort, Queen Charlotte, had been rebuilt by John Nash to the orders of George IV and completed, more or less, by William IV. Victoria was the first sovereign to live in it. Although building work on the palace was not finished – and indeed, would not be until well into Victoria's reign – it seemed enormous compared to Kensington

OPPOSITE: THE YOUNG QUEEN WITH HER LADIES-IN-WAITING, IN AN IMAGE PUBLISHED BY ACKERMAN, SHORTLY AFTER THE ACCESSION IN 1837.

Palace. Here, for the first time in her life, Queen Victoria was able to have her own bedroom. She ordered that her bedroom be next to that of Baroness Lehzen and quickly had a door put in the adjoining wall. Her mother had assumed they would continue to share a bedroom but Victoria ordered her into a suite of rooms some way away. The Duchess was furious and hurt.

Queen Victoria found the early days at Buckingham Palace hectic but she quickly tired of Windsor Castle, another ancient royal residence, which George IV had extensively rebuilt. Victoria found the castle's atmosphere restrained and boring, and long evenings spent playing cards were not to her taste.

The Duke of Wellington, victor of Waterloo and now an elder statesman, was, along with Stockmar, vital to the Queen in her early days, though neither was as important to her as Lord Melbourne. The Queen and Prime Minister dined together on most evenings and their friendship flourished. No matter how formal the dinner or who the guests were, Queen and Prime Minister always sat next to each other, he on her left. Indeed, the Queen could be jealous if she saw Melbourne talking to another woman.

As well as concerns about affairs of state, the letters from Uncle Leopold and her relationship with her mother, Queen Victoria discussed more personal matters, including her figure and clothing, with the Prime Minister. At almost five foot and with a keen appetite she was prone to put on weight and look rather dumpy; at various times throughout her life she would attempt to diet, but enjoyment of food got the better of her. The question of marriage was also discussed between them. The Queen told her Prime Minister she had no intention of marrying, she was wedded to her job.

Soon Court and Household were becoming uneasy about the closeness of this relationship and many were unhappy. Charles Greville, Clerk to the Privy Council and detailed diarist, reported that they spent at least six hours together each day, in exclusive conversation. For this bachelor it was "more hours than any two people, in any relation of life, perhaps ever do pass together besides." He also noted that the Duke of Wellington, almost an "advisory grandfather", thought Melbourne right to visit the Queen daily to discuss affairs of state, but even he disapproved of the length of time spent together and the intimate nature of the relationship. Gossip about this new Court and its Queen's relationship with the Prime Minister reached the public, satirical cartoons were published and the name "Mrs Melbourne", first muttered by angry Tories, became part of the general parlance.

Uncle Leopold's influence, constantly felt through Stockmar, did not always please Melbourne. Slowly, Victoria realized that Uncle

"A CABINET LECTURE". LORD MELBOURNE, THE PRIME MINISTER, ADVISING QUEEN VICTORIA IN 1840.

THE ARRIVAL AT THE PAVILION IN BRIGHTON WHEN QUEEN VICTORIA DROVE THROUGH THE AMPHITHEATRE AND BENEATH THE TRIUMPHAL ARCH, PAINTED BY G.B. CAMPION.

Leopold's influence was not to her liking, either, or to her need, and she tried to act independently of him. Very early on, Victoria became aware that her position as head of state required her to tread very delicately when it came to dealing with Parliament. Unlike Leopold in Belgium and other European Monarchs, her role, demanded by Parliament, was developing into that of a constitutional monarch. Parliament was slowly becoming accountable to a democratic electorate rather than to the whim of the Sovereign. During the early part of her reign both she and Parliament had much to learn about how to accommodate each other's role. Within the country there was great interest and hope that this young woman as Queen would prove better at the job than her predecessors.

In October the Court went on a progress to Brighton, which had become a fashionable seaside resort patronized by George IV while Prince Regent. Here, in 1815, he had commis-

sioned John Nash, the architect of the magnificent, classical terraces in London's Regent's Park, to renovate a pavilion for him. The Queen stayed at the holiday pavilion but greatly disliked its flamboyant and lavish oriental design, so typical of her uncle.

Victoria's first year in her new role was hectic. Each day was filled with meetings, receptions, paperwork, discussions and discoveries. Dignitaries from around the world were received, meetings were held with her ministers and Privy Council, troops were inspected, and she had to acquaint herself with the workings of Parliament and the preparations for her Coronation. She described the year as a happy one, the happiest she had ever experienced. Observers found her diligent and polite and were amazed at her ability to tackle the tasks, given her youth and inexperience. During this year, the immature and sheltered eighteen-year-old became a respected adult.

Chapter 3 The Coronation

Queen Victoria celebrated her nineteenth birthday on May 24, 1838, four weeks before her Coronation. In her diary she describes her enjoyment of the preceding year and is especially grateful at having found a friend in Lord Melbourne.

> … .I can NEVER be *thankful* enough for the TRUE, *faithful*, HONEST, *kind* one [friend] I've GAINED since last year, which is my excellent Lord Melbourne, who is so kind and good to me …

A huge, state ball to celebrate her birthday was held at Buckingham Palace. To Victoria's disappointment, Lord Melbourne declined to dance with her and chose to go home early. The ballroom was packed with guests, many from abroad. Society's eligible young men danced quadrilles with the young queen. Larger groups of seventy-two couples danced English country dances, each one lasting an hour. With youthful spirits, she danced the night away, left the ball at 4 a.m. and went to bed at dawn.

Lord Melbourne believed it his duty to prepare Queen Victoria for her Coronation. The Coronation of a sovereign is the formal acceptance of the duties invested by the title. In England, coronations can be traced back to the eighth century and have been held in Westminster Abbey for more than 900 years. The ceremony has been developed and adapted with successive sovereigns but each aspect of its stages – Recognition, First Offering, Litany, Communion Service, Sermon, Oath, Anointing, Spurs, Offering of the Sword, Investing with the Mantle, the Orb, The Ring, The Sceptres, the Crowning, The Holy Bible, the Benediction and Te Deum, Homage and Holy Sacrament – is steeped in tradition, history and symbolism.

Plans for the Coronation of Queen Victoria were much debated and argued over because, despite the formalities of the procedures, there was no precedent for the modern coronation of a Queen Regnant. While kings would disrobe in front of the congregation, it was felt inappropriate for such a private procedure to be carried out publicly by a young woman. Eventually, it was decided she would use St Edward's Chapel as her robe room.

The form and length of service had to be considered and the Earl Marshal, the Duke of Norfolk, had to prepare a guest list. Invitations had to be printed, honours bestowed, robes and other clothes designed, crowns and rings fitted and banquets organized. The Government would be paying and the Treasury insisted that cost must be considered. The flamboyant and lavish pageantry, including a circus horse, introduced by George IV in 1821 was considered expensive, distasteful and inappropriate for the times. This was to be a more modest affair.

Unlike modern royal events, rehearsals for Queen Victoria's Coronation were kept to a minimum. The day before the ceremony she visited Westminster Abbey with Lady Lansdowne, Lady Barham, Lord Conyngham and Colonel Wemyss to inspect the preparations. It had already been decided that, for the first time, the Coronation procession between the Palace and Westminster Abbey should be more accessible to the general public to enable them to catch a glimpse of the young queen. Already people were beginning to line the streets. The party was met at the Abbey by Lord Melbourne. Victoria tried two different thrones, remarked that they were too low and walked around the Abbey but she felt relieved and confident about the following day's events. Later she wrote:

> The PREPARATIONS for *fairs*, BALLOONS, &c. in the *Parks*, quite changes all, and the encampments of the Artillery, with all their white tents, has a very pretty effect.

OPPOSITE: QUEEN VICTORIA IN HER CORONATION ROBES IN 1838, BY GEORGE HAYTER.

THE CORONATION PROCESSION PASSING THROUGH TRAFALGAR SQUARE, JUNE 28, 1838.

Vivat Regina!

At 3.17 on the morning of Thursday, June 28, 1838 the Queen was awoken by the sound of a 21-gun salute announcing the dawn of the her Coronation Day. Sightseers were already assembling in Green Park. *The Times* reported that

the whole metropolis was literally awakened, and presented a scene of bustle and excitement rarely if ever equalled. At four o'clock, the streets were so thronged with carriages and pedestrians that they were in many places impassable, and the whole population seemed to have poured out in the direction of the Parks and of Westminster Abbey … even so early as six o'clock the Green Park, the Mall and the enclosure in St James's Park, were filled with persons of all ranks, and at that early hour the struggle for places commenced.

Meanwhile, the Queen was busy preparing herself. She had a light breakfast and dressed in silk stockings and white satin pumps before putting on the heavy kirtle, a ceremonial robe worn for State Parliamentary occasions, over a gold and white satin brocade dress. At 10 o'clock she was ready to board the State Coach for the magnificent procession from Buckingham Palace to the West Door of Westminster Abbey.

The procession was enormous and included trumpeters, a squadron of the Life Guards and the carriages of ambassadors and representatives from Mexico, Portugal, Sweden, Saxony, Hanover, Greece, Sardinia, Spain, the United States, the Netherlands, Brazil, Bavaria, Denmark, Belgium, Prussia, Austria and Turkey. The Count Stroganoff represented Russia and Marshal Soult the King of France. The Duchess of Kent rode with her attendants in a carriage drawn by six horses and an escort of Life Guards, followed by similar carriages bearing the Duke and Duchess of Cambridge and Duke and Duchess of Gloucester. Duke Ernest of Saxe-Coburg was also present, but not his sons, whom Queen Victoria had deliberately not invited as she refused to raise any speculation over the possibility of marriage.

Finally, came eleven carriages, each drawn by six horses, carrying the members of the Queen's Household. They led the way for the Mounted Band of the Household Brigade and the State Coach carrying the Queen, accompanied by the Duchess of Sutherland and the Earl of Albemarle. The beautiful coach was drawn by eight cream-coloured horses and eight walking grooms. A Yeoman of the Guard walked by each wheel and two footmen were at the door. Viscount Combermere, the Gold Stick and the Earl of Ilchester, Captain of the Yeomen of the Guard, rode on either side. Behind them rode, on horseback, the Captain General of the Royal Archers of Scotland and the Silver Stick, Colonel Richardson, followed by a squadron of Life Guards.

The route of this spectacular, long and vibrantly coloured procession was not the most direct from Buckingham Palace to the Abbey, a much longer one having being devised to let as many spectators as possible have a good view. On leaving the Palace, it turned left up Constitution Hill and along Piccadilly to St James's Street, Pall Mall, Cockspur Street, Charing Cross, Whitehall, Parliament Street and the West Door of the Abbey. The journey took exactly one hour.

By the time the State Coach arrived, Westminster Abbey was filled with the invited guests. Peers had been commanded to wear their robes and their wives had to wear court dress without feathers, lappets or trains. Others had to dress in full court dress or uniform; nobody was allowed to wear black mourning clothes. The lavish jewels of the ladies and coronets of the peers sparkled as the tiny figure of Queen Victoria entered. She was met by noblemen carrying the ancient coronation regalia and the Bishops, holding the Patina, Chalice and the Bible, who would form part of the procession to the Transept.

All were enthralled as they watched the Dean and Prebendaries join the procession to lead the young nineteen-year-old along the Nave to the Transept where the thrones and chairs had been placed on a dais. Above, the Duchess of Kent, Charles and Feodore Leiningen and the Baroness Lehzen looked down at her as the choir sang, the orchestra played and the ceremony continued, led by the Archbishop of Canterbury.

After the Recognition and Oath, the Queen retired to St Edward's Chapel to remove the kirtle and mantle, which, had she been a king, would have been done in full view of the congregation. For modesty's sake, retirement was chosen and St Edward's Chapel had been made into a dressing room for the occasion. Unfortunately, nobody had thought to tidy up and sandwiches and drinks had even been left lying around on the altar for the Queen to see.

At the disrobing, the sovereign is no longer a secular being and usually, at this point, his breast is anointed but again, for modesty, it was abandoned here. Instead, Victoria reappeared in the main part of the Abbey wearing the splendid gold supertunica which had been especially designed for her. The wearing of the supertunica dates back to mediaeval times, though the one designed for Queen Victoria was more akin to an academic gown.

Orders of Service for the day describe, in detail, the programme of events and what should have happened. Unfortunately, things did suffer from having been under-rehearsed and at times it was chaotic. Sometimes, the congregation forgot to stand or chant "God Save the Queen"; often, the Queen did not know what to do as nobody, except the Archbishop, knew what the fine details, vital to the success of such a pageant, should be. The service required her to move from throne to throne, and altar to chapel for different rituals. Sometimes there was confusion as to where she should go, she sat or stood at the wrong times, an elderly Peer fell over as he tried to kneel at her feet, and others stood with their coronets askew. Although the Archbishop was the only person present supposed to know exactly what to do, even he made mistakes and Lord Melbourne had to offer guidance.

Sitting in St Edward's Chair, Victoria awaited the most important part of the proceedings. Knights held a gold canopy over her while the Archbishop anointed her forehead. Then she put on her dalmatica or imperial mantle, a long, gold cloth robe covered in embroidered thistles and fleur de lys, for the investiture with the Regalia and Crown.

Each item of regalia with which she was invested had great historical symbolism and

A JUG COMMEMORATING VICTORIA'S CORONATION.

OVERLEAF: THE CORONATION OF QUEEN VICTORIA IN WESTMINSTER ABBEY BY EDMUND THOMAS PARIS.

QUEEN VICTORIA IN HER CORONATION ROBES BY CHARLES ROBERT LESLIE, RA.

significance. The Spurs, dating from 1660, symbolized knighthood and chivalry. The jewelled Sword of Offering, containing over 3000 precious stones and made for George IV's coronation in 1820, was laid on the altar before being placed in the Sovereign's hand. The bracelet-like Armills, symbolizing sincerity and wisdom, were placed on the Queen's wrists and the Orb, a symbol of Christianity – the Sovereign being the Head of the Church of England – was laid in her right hand.

Pushing the Coronation Ring on her finger was problematic. The ring, to depict dignity had been specially made for her little finger, because that used by King William IV was too big. Instead, the Archbishop struggled to push it on to her third finger, causing her much pain,

and great difficulty in getting it off later. Finally, the Sceptres, one with a cross, the other with a dove, a mark of her spirituality, were placed in her gloved hands.

The placing of the crown on the Queen's head was successful, even though she found it extremely heavy. At the moment when the Archbishop placed the crown on her head the congregation chanted "God Save the Queen", trumpets sounded, peers waved their coronets and a gun salute could be heard in the distance. The choir sang "The Queen shall rejoice".

Gradually, the ceremony drew to a close. To leave the ceremony and the Abbey, she changed crowns and wore the spectacular Imperial State Crown. All crowns are extremely precious and heavy; this one weighed almost 1kg (2lb 2oz) and contained nearly 3000 diamonds, 17 sapphires, 11 emeralds, five rubies and 273 pearls set into a gold frame. A band of ermine cushioned it on to the head. The procession went up the nave and through the West Door to the awaiting crowds. The newly crowned Queen got into the State Coach for the return journey to Buckingham Palace. Spectators lined the routes and she was delighted at their excitement.

Always a realist, Charles Greville wrote afterwards "… the effect of the procession itself was spoilt by being too crowded … The different actors in the ceremonial were very imperfect in their parts, and had neglected to rehearse." Since then, all royal ceremonies have been rehearsed in detail. Even if the Treasury classified the Coronation of Queen Victoria as "modest", it was still a magnificent pageant enjoyed by thousands who were in the Abbey and lining the streets.

Back at Buckingham Palace, there were more celebrations and dinner with Lord Melbourne and her close family. Despite all the hitches, Lord Melbourne, who had been quite emotional, thought the day had been highly successful. Even though the Queen was exhausted after such an early start and long day, she went, at midnight, on to her mother's balcony to watch the glorious fireworks in Green Park. She then found time to write a long account of her remarkable day which provides a detailed description of what it feels like for a sovereign to be crowned.

The Court

Queen Victoria enjoyed her first year as queen more than any other in her life so far, but by December 1838 she was beginning to tire of court life, especially at Windsor, where there was little fun or excitement. Charles Greville, a frequent visitor, had no inhibitions about recording his observations about Queen Victoria's Court:

The QUEEN is *natural*, GOOD HUMOURED, and CHEERFUL, but *still* she is QUEEN, and by her must the social habits and the tone of conversation be regulated, and for this she is too young and inexperienced ....Windsor is totally unlike any other place. There is none of the sociability which makes the agreeableness of an English country house; there is no room in which the guests assemble...sit, lounge and talk as they please when they please; there is a billiard table, but in such a remote corner of the Castle that it might as well be in the town of Windsor; there is a library well stocked with books, but hardly accessible, imperfectly warmed, and only tenanted by the librarian. There are two breakfast rooms ... but when the meal is over everyone disperses, and nothing but another meal reunites the guests.

THE YOUNG QUEEN VICTORIA BY FRANZ XAVER WINTERHALTER.

The young Queen had coped well with the first eighteen months as monarch and the dramatic changes they had brought to her life. Possibly due to her youth and insular childhood, she lacked the ability of an experienced hostess intent on making her guests comfortable. Court life also meant she was with people all the time in a position of authority and even she, happy as she was, began to show the outward signs of boredom manifested by headaches and short temper. Occasionally, she even stayed in her room and did not attend dinner.

Chapter 4 The Queen's Marriage

With the problems of the accession now consigned to history and the Queen's Coronation successfully, albeit chaotically, completed there remained just one further question hanging over her personal life. This was marriage.

In an early discussion with Melbourne, she had firmly dismissed all possibility of marrying; her position as sovereign was to be her full-time vocation. Major changes had, after all, transformed her life from that of an immature innocent princess to sovereign of a powerful nation, head of the largest empire on earth – all in the space of twelve months. Queen Victoria was barely twenty years old.

However, by 1839, the plans of King Leopold, backed by the Duchess of Kent and their brother Prince Ernest of Saxe-Coburg, had not been dropped; there would be no breathing space granted her from that quarter. Nor would her English relations let the subject drop. Wanting to avoid another German marriage, they paraded eligible young men such as her cousin, the Duke of Cambridge, before her. Finding a suitable partner would be problematic. She was, after all, one of the most powerful people in the world and a woman too. To find a man who would want to take a subservient role to his wife could be impossible.

Perhaps because of this constant barrage from all sides, or because she was beginning to feel a certain loneliness in her elevated position, the Queen relented and agreed to meet her cousin Prince Albert again. Both were now aware of Uncle Leopold's plans for their future. Naturally, she discussed the proposal with Lord Melbourne, who was uncertain of the suitability of the alliance. For an alliance was how it would be perceived. Melbourne thought that the German-speaking Albert might side with his aunt, the Duchess of Kent and Conroy against Victoria, thus weakening her position.

Then there was the problem of Russia. Dealing with Russia was an ongoing task at this time as Tsar Nicholas I was forever trying to expand his boundaries and had recently invaded Afghanistan. The Tsar did not like the Coburgs and Melbourne did not want Britain to get embroiled in European arguments. Lord Melbourne was also concerned that Parliament would oppose such a match, regarding it as further German influence in Britain. In his paternal and caring role, drawing on his own disastrous marital experience, Melbourne also wondered if Victoria was mature enough for marriage. There was, after all, no rush and he was delighted when she hesitated and decided to wait. His delight was short-lived, however, for a few weeks later Melbourne was left feeling desolate and probably jealous at the thought of being usurped in her attentions when she resolved her situation by inviting her cousin, Prince Albert, to visit.

Scandal and Crisis

Before Prince Albert's visit took place, two events in the Queen's household tested her strength to the hilt and compromised her relationship with her people and with parliament, as she found out how intent government was on reforming its relationship with the monarch. The Sovereign's honeymoon was over.

The first of these events concerned Lady Flora Hastings, her long-time lady-in-waiting. Victoria had long mistrusted this pious and demure young woman from an established Tory family, believing her to be a spy from Sir John Conroy's camp. In the spring of 1839 Lady Flora developed a noticeable swelling in her stomach and she complained of pain. Gossip started immediately, in which both the Queen and Melbourne enjoyably participated. Despite Lady Flora's protestations, the presumption was that this unmarried, religious woman must be pregnant, and probably made so by Sir John Conroy, who had long been believed to be having an affair with the Duchess of Kent. Queen Victoria's great dislike of Sir John undoubtedly clouded her judgement. Despite the fact that her own physician, Sir James Clark, found no evidence of pregnancy when he was eventually allowed to examine Lady Flora, the Queen continued to believe she was pregnant.

The gossip in Royal circles became public when the Hastings family published the physician's findings in an attempt to clear Lady Flora's name and also to damage the Whig Queen and Prime Minister, whom they believed to be the perpetrators of the gossip. The popular press loved it all: "Mrs Melbourne" was in trouble. There was one moment of relief for the Queen when Sir John Conroy resigned in June, following pressure from the Duke of Wellington and the offer of a peerage in Ireland.

Although Lady Flora's swelling had decreased, she was still extremely ill and when she died in July, the post mortem revealed she had suffered from a cancerous tumour on the liver. While the Queen's reputation was badly damaged in the eyes of the public, who were appalled at her treatment of her lady-in-waiting, the departure of Conroy at least meant that the gulf between mother and daughter could begin to close again – though not before the discovery of Conroy's misuse of his position as the Duchess's controller of finance. Thousands of pounds due to her had never been paid into her bank account. Queen Victoria was disgusted.

The second event to cause a major crisis in the Royal Household concerned the government. Lord Melbourne's Whig government was severely weakened after its majority was reduced in the General Election of 1837. A majority of the electorate, then a small proportion of the adult male population, clearly did not approve of the Whigs' electoral reform programme, nor did they find the government's attitude to Ireland and Roman Catholic emancipation agreeable. After the splendid boom years, recession was beginning.

The continuing closeness of the Prime Minister and the Queen was also weakening Melbourne's position as he watched his parliamentary majority slide away. By 1839 Queen Victoria was becoming increasingly anxious at the prospect of losing him. Eventually, in May 1839, as the Flora Hastings scandal was in full flow, Lord Melbourne resigned. Queen Victoria wept at losing her best friend and took an instant dislike to her new Prime Minister, Sir Robert Peel, not only for being a Tory but also for brutally pushing her friend out.

The first meeting between Sir Robert and the Queen was frosty, each disliking the other. Sir Robert Peel was a new-style Tory. He was not from the old Tory landed gentry, but from the new wealthy middle classes created by trade and manufacture, his father having made a huge amount of money in cotton manufacture. As a young MP, Peel had reformed the criminal laws and founded the first uniformed police force, the Metropolitan Police, popularly known as Peelers. His distrust of the Whig reforms had made him attractive as a leader to many right-wing traditional Tories.

In her inexperienced naiveté, Queen Victoria had stated that the British Royal Family should always be Whig and let her hatred of the Tories be known. The elder statesman the Duke of Wellington tried to intervene between Queen and Prime Minister and was appalled at her childishness when, unconstitutionally, she asked him to be Prime Minister. He declined. The Queen was distraught and could not eat, nothing was going well. Baroness Lehzen came to the rescue and supported the Queen in her loneliness.

The second meeting between the Queen and Prime Minister was even worse as Peel chose this time to discuss the members of the Household. The Queen, briefed by Melbourne, was prepared for this. In the past, to avoid any political conflict, the members of the Household had changed with a new government. The Queen's Household at this time was made up mainly of Whigs or women married to Whig MPs or Whig peers. Peel naturally wished to appoint some Tories but, like an angry child, the Queen refused to accept any. She could not see how women could, through their husbands, damage parliament.

THE PRIME MINISTER, SIR ROBERT PEEL, READING TO QUEEN VICTORIA, BY SIR DAVID WILKIE.

The affair, as more information from the palace reached the press and public, was very damaging to her. Questions were being asked about her suitability as sovereign, not only among the working classes, jealous of her wealth, but among the upper classes. She was hissed at as she rode in her carriage through Ascot racecourse.

On May 10, in a desperate attempt to rescue her, Melbourne addressed Parliament on the Crisis of the Ladies of the Bedchamber, as it had become known. He gave such an effective eulogy on the Queen's predicament that enough MPs were won over to defeat Peel. Lord Melbourne was back in office and the Queen delighted. That evening she hosted a glorious ball at Buckingham Palace for Tsarevitch Alexander of Russia, whom she knew was being introduced as a possible husband but in whom she had little interest. Since the Bedchamber Crisis, there has never been a change of Royal Household with a change of government.

Already bored with aspects of court life, and bruised by the Flora Hastings scandal and the Crisis of The Ladies of the Bedchamber, the young Queen began to suffer from what we would now call emotional and physical stress. She gained weight, which was difficult for her figure to carry given her lack of height, and tried to diet by drinking less beer and missing meals. She was more alarmed when clothes had to be ordered in a larger size. The colour of her hair was not to her liking, she put off bathing and cleaning her teeth as long as possible in the day, and complained of headaches and feeling sick.

That the Queen might be depressed sent a frisson through the Court; she was, after all, the granddaughter of the mad king, George III, and a careful eye was kept on her for any signs of hereditary insanity. Throughout her reign, if she was at all depressed, comparisons would be made with her grandfather. Modern diagnosis of George III indicates he suffered from porphyria, a disease of the haemoglobin. During theses periods the Queen found solace in riding, especially on her horse Comus, on whom she was mounted for an equestrian portrait by the great artist, Landseer. To canter up Portland Place to Hampstead Heath or south to Richmond Park and Wimbledon Common gave her a terrific sense of freedom.

OVERLEAF: QUEEN VICTORIA AND THE DUKE OF WELLINGTON INSPECTING THE TROOPS, BY SIR EDWIN LANDSEER.

Prince Albert of Saxe-Coburg

By the summer, it was clear that the marriage question would have to be confronted and resolved. Victoria's English relations were unhappy about the possibility of more German influence in the family and did not approve of the forthcoming visit of the Saxe-Coburg cousins. They knew it would provoke the wrath of Parliament and arouse suspicions among the people. Victoria herself was uncertain, and particularly wary of making any commitment to her cousin Prince Albert, whom at this stage she liked more as a friend than a possible husband.

A VIEW FROM PRINCE ALBERT'S BIRTHPLACE HOME, THE, SCHLOSS ROSENAU, PAINTED BY WILLIAM CALLOW.

Having persuaded Leopold to put off their visit as long as possible, she eventually agreed that they should come to Britain in the autumn of 1839.

After the banishment of their mother when they were small boys, the Princes Ernest and Albert of Saxe-Coburg had been brought up in an entirely male household. The Schloss Rosenau, where they grew up, was outside the tiny town of Coburg and stood like a fairytale castle in the wooded mountains of Thuringia. Stanley Weintraub, in his biography of Prince Albert, likened the boys' childhood at Rosenau to stories recently published by the Brothers Grimm, and pictured Coburg as something akin to Lilliput. Their father, Duke Ernest, having divorced the boys' mother, saw little of his sons, the delights of women, shooting and hunting being preferable.

Divorce was rare in the nineteenth century, but when it did happen custody of the children of a marriage automatically went to the father,

regardless of who had been the perpetrator of the breakdown or of the wishes of the youngsters. Little Albrecht, as he was known in childhood, had been very close to his mother; there has even been a suggestion that Prince Albert was illegitimate and the son of a Jew as neither his looks nor personality bore any resemblance to those of his father or brother. Prince Albert always believed in his mother's love for him and never recovered from the trauma of the divorce, although, like many children faced with such upset, he outwardly put on a brave face to disguise it. She died in Paris in 1831 at the age of 31, never having seen her boys again. To their surprise, Duke Ernest remarried in 1832, but this too was unsuccessful. Occasional visits to grandmothers provided almost the only female contact the boys had as children. As an adult, Prince Albert would deny his childhood had been unhappy, recalling it, with the benefit of hindsight, with warmth and excitement.

The education of the princes was more formal and structured than that of their English cousin. Duke Ernest employed the highly capable tutor Christoph Florschütz, a friend of Baron Stockmar, to oversee it. Their first language was German and they learnt French, English, Latin, Mathematics and Science. The brothers loved the outdoor life, playing in the woods and streams and collecting rocks for their studies of geology. Albert was physically a small child and often unwell; but, even from the age of three, he possessed keen intellectual powers far greater than those of his older brother whose character was more like that of their father.

Their Uncle Leopold, even while living in London and then in Brussels, took a close interest in the boys' upbringing and likened himself to a father. Stockmar made frequent reports on their progress. Both boys found Brussels, with a population of 100,000 on their visit in 1832, a bustling lively place the likes of which they had never experienced before. While Prince Ernest's future as his father's heir was decided, that of Prince Albert posed a problem. His great intellect and curiosity meant that he found the parochialism of the tiny dukedom boring but he was a devout Evangelical Lutheran Christian, thus making marriage to a Roman Catholic impossible.

In 1836, after taking the boys on a grand tour of their relations in Berlin, Dresden, Prague and Vienna, which Albert found very dull, Florschütz and Stockmar suggested Albert should attend university in Bonn. Around this time, he was made aware of the possibility of marriage to his cousin, Princess Victoria, whom they had visited in the summer of 1836. Stockmar and Leopold both thought Albert the more appropriate of the two brothers as a possible husband to the Queen. Stockmar had also remarked that for Prince Albert only a relationship where his intellect could be stretched would be appropriate.

While Victoria delayed the marriage question, Leopold encouraged Albert to stand back and usefully spend his time in Bonn. He studied the arts, law, politics and economics; enjoyed philosophy, German literature and the classics; visited museums and galleries and went on another grand tour, this time to Italy, accompanied by Stockmar. He was enthralled by the art and architecture of Venice and Milan. It was an apprenticeship far different from any undertaken by a member of the British Royal Court or Family. The combined experience of Bonn and Italy were vital to his future achievements in Britain and his development into a cultured, European intellectual.

A Proposal of Marriage

Leopold and Stockmar were delighted when Victoria eventually agreed that her Saxe-Coburg cousins should visit her in the autumn of 1839. They were also anxious lest she prefer Prince Ernest, who was definitely unsuitable, having been initiated into adult life in the seedier parts of Paris and Berlin. He was more like his father, whereas Albert possessed many of their mother's qualities. Prince Albert was also uncertain about Leopold's plan. He was unimpressed by the reports he had received about his cousin. That she did not like nature, had an unhealthily close relationship with Lord

Melbourne and was bored with court life all concerned him. What he was eager to discover from this visit was if she was serious about him because he did not want to waste any more time than necessary on the matter.

After a dreadful Channel crossing, during which Albert was sea-sick, the party arrived at Windsor on October 10. Immediately upon seeing Albert, Victoria was entranced and fell in love with the idea of marriage and with him; he was handsome, courteous, intelligent and fun, very different from his brother. For the twenty-year-old Queen, it was the first time she was able to form a friendship with someone her own age or feel the emotional charge of passion. Cautious at first, however, she kept her thoughts private, though she did discuss with Lord Melbourne how Albert should be told of her

ENTERTAINING PRINCE ALBERT ON HIS VISIT TO LONDON IN 1838 QUEEN VICTORIA, AT THE PIANO, IS WATCHED BY THE DUCHESS OF KENT, DUKE OF SUSSEX AND DASH. LITHOGRAPH BY F ELIAS.

feelings. Five days later, she summoned Prince Albert to her rooms and asked him to marry her. Delighted that the tensions were over, he agreed and in German told her how happy he would be to spend his life with her. From then on they became close companions and the passion between them did not go unnoticed. That evening she wrote in her diary of her excitement and delight at having found a husband.

Lord Melbourne was, not unsurprisingly,

very emotional about the Queen's decision and was still concerned lest it should not work out satisfactorily. Baron Stockmar, too, was uncertain about the suitability of the match and its imbalance, which would necessarily involve Albert in sacrificing everything in order to live in Britain. He was also concerned about the powerful and headstrong Queen marrying an introverted intellectual.

The cousins were both very young and immature in relationships; Albert had not had the same initiation as Prince Ernest. They hardly knew one another and their upbringings had been very different. They were two unknown people, from different cultures entering an arranged marriage. For Albert, there was enormous excitement about his future role. To such a capable and cultured young man, London was certainly preferable to spending the rest of his life in the inward-looking and tiny fairyland of Coburg. But, there was uncertainty, too. He was giving up everything for Victoria, and assumed he would get her undivided attention in exchange, naively unaware of her commitment to her job.

The Queen discussed with Lord Melbourne Albert's looks and the fact that he only had eyes for her and no other woman. She was furious when Melbourne hinted that straying would come in the future and made him withdraw the remark. Perhaps because of the devastating effect of the death, in childbirth, of Princess Charlotte, Uncle Leopold's first wife, the Queen also let it be known that she dreaded having children and all the upset they might cause.

Albert began getting hints of his future wife's commitment to her job very early on. In January 1840, he wrote to her suggesting a lengthy honeymoon at Windsor. The reply shows the seriousness with which she took her work and the adjustments he would have to make:

...You FORGET, my *dearest* LOVE, that I am the SOVEREIGN, and that *business* can stop and wait for nothing. Parliament is sitting, and something occurs almost every day, for which I may be required, and it is quite impossible for me to be absent from London; therefore two or three days is already a long time absent. I am never easy a moment, if I am not on the spot ...

Albert left London after his life-changing visit on November 14, 1839. He returned forever in early February 1840, elated at the prospect of living in metropolitan London and not Coburg. London was exciting and prosperous, the centre of a huge empire, full of fascinating people. It was busy and sophisticated, bigger and better than Brussels, and an ideal place for such a man.

The Queen had announced her intention to marry at a Privy Council meeting on November 23, and February 10, 1840 was set for the wedding day. Immediately, rows erupted regarding the union, the prospect of further foreign influence in Britain and Prince Albert's future status, his stipend, role and title. Some Members of Parliament, led by Colonel Charles Sibthorp, MP for Lincoln, were opposed to the Queen's marriage to a foreigner and rejected all possibility of a peerage for him, mistrusting alien involvement in the politics of Britain. Colonel Sibthorp would continue to attack Prince Albert, creating stumbling blocks for him, in the future.

THE YOUNG PRINCE ALBERT BY? SIR JOHN LUCAS.

VICTORIA AND ALBERT VIEWING THE LLAMAS IN THE HOUSE PARK AT WINDSOR WITH THE CASTLE IN THE BACKGROUND. GOURLAY STEEL IN 1845.

Queen Victoria had rejected the idea of a peerage too believing it to be too lowly a status. She wanted Albert to be King Consort and to have precedence over any other member of the Royal Family after her. It was now the Duke of Wellington's turn to act as a child; he rejected this and even suggested "Protestant" be inserted before his name, in the unlikely event that the Lutheran Prince Albert should ever countenance Roman Catholicism. For years, Queen Victoria battled to have her husband made Prince Consort, finally succeeding in 1853, when she titled him herself.

The question of Albert's allowance remained contentious. Many were reminded that Uncle Leopold had received £50,000 per annum on his marriage to Princess Charlotte and still continued to claim it despite her death, his remarriage and relocation to Belgium. There was mistrust of another Coburger doing the same, when suddenly Leopold, realizing the problem and not wanting to jeopardize the marriage, stopped claiming the full stipend.

Arguments for and against persisted among the general public; unsurprisingly, everyone had a view, often based on false premises and gossip. The pseudonym "Fair Play" was used by one author who wrote a "Letter to the People of Great Britain" concerning the Queen's marriage. In the letter, the author tried to dispel the false rumours surrounding Albert's suitability, rumours that he might be a Roman Catholic and that his family were not worthy of the Queen. He pointed out that the Lutheran Saxe-

Coburgers had done more than many in Europe actively to promote Protestantism and that their heritage could be traced back to the thirteenth century. Firmly demanding that the people, unlike Parliament, should not let prejudice colour their opinions, he left the choice for public acceptance of the Queen's husband to the individual:

…we may *either* indulge in SNEERS at the *comparative* INSIGNIFICANCE of the PRINCE'S family in WEALTH and *territory*, – we may gratify an empty vanity by drawing a comparison between the splendid luxury of the English Court and the humbler sphere of a German Principality; we may, because he is a foreigner, circulate or give ear to a thousand idle reports concerning him, which, were he an Englishman, would not obtain a moment's credit; – or … we may remember, that be the selection of our Sovereign, his lot is now cast in England; that … he has now no other home nor happiness to look for, save what he finds among us; and on these grounds we may greet him with a kind and hospitable welcome; thus offering his character a fair opportunity of developing its qualities, and treating him with that consideration which, unless he forfeits it by his own conduct … the Queen's Consort is entitled to expect from her people. Which of these two courses is more loyal – the more just – the more generous – the more worthy of a Great Nation, I leave it for you, my countrymen, to decide.

ALBERT'S NATURALIZATION CERTIFICATE.

Eventually, despite Colonel Sibthorp's protestations, Parliament agreed a stipend of £30,000 per annum to be paid to Prince Albert upon his marriage. This was £20,000 less than the Queen wanted and she was furious at their undervaluing of her beloved Albert, believing his foreignness to be the root of their hatred. At various times throughout her life, Queen Victoria showed herself to be ahead of her times by her instinctive abhorrence of any inkling of racism and mistrust of the foreigner, and her marriage to Prince Albert was the first of many examples of this.

Prince Albert's New Country

Melbourne was still trying to protect Victoria from outside events. Britain was rapidly changing from the genteel Georgian society in which Victoria had been brought up and in which she and her Court still lived into a widely industrialized nation. During the 1820s and 1830s the population of London had increased by 20 per cent. Manchester, Sheffield, Leeds and Birmingham saw rapid change and growth as they became centres for specialist trades and industries, and people flocked from the rural areas to find work in the new factories. There were massive housing developments, resulting in great problems of sanitation and disease caused by huge numbers of people living closely together.

There had been rapid expansion of the railway system since the opening of the first railway line from Stockton to Darlington in 1825. The Liverpool to Manchester line was opened in 1830. By 1838, a main line linked London for the first time with another major industrial area, Birmingham. Euston Station was opened and from Paddington the Great Western Railway already ran as far as

ST PANCRAS STATION – ONE OF LONDON'S GREAT RAILWAY TERMINI.

Maidenhead. The railways not only provided employment for huge numbers of people building the steam engines and carriages, laying the track and running the trains but were fundamental to the success of the country's industrialization, carrying coal, tin, imported cotton and wheat. More of a side line than a main activity for the railways at this time was the possibility, soon to be used by Thomas Cook, a young temperance supporter from Leicester, of transporting large numbers of people.

The newly affluent middle classes were becoming more prosperous while the workers were living in squalid slums. John Bright and Richard Cobden formed the Anti-Corn Law League in Manchester in 1838 to try to repeal the Corn Laws, which kept the cost of home-produced corn and wheat artificially high. The transportation to Australia of the Tolpuddle Martyrs in 1834, ironically enough for attempting to form a union for agricultural workers, did not stop the movements to protect the men, women and children from working in gruelling conditions in factories, mines, railways and dockyards from exploitation by unscrupulous employers, who paid scant attention to health and safety. In 1844 a group of workers would open the first cooperative shop in Rochdale with the purpose of keeping prices low. The foundations of the Labour movement were being laid.

Relationships with Ireland had been difficult ever since the Act of Union in 1800 had created one parliament for the whole of Britain; but Ireland remained a predominately Catholic country and refused to submit to Protestant rule. The Church of England was the country's established church and anyone from another religion was not allowed to sit in Parliament. Lionel Rothschild, the Jewish banker, publicized the situation when he was elected MP for the City of London in 1847 but was barred from the House of Commons; he had to wait until the law was changed in 1858 to be allowed to take his seat.

Beyond Britain's shores, the maintenance and defence of the British Empire, with its increasing number of territories and colonies, were huge responsibilities. In Asia, the East India Company was involved in 1839 in the First Opium War against China and by 1842 Britain would gain Hong Kong. Aden and New Zealand were annexed to the Empire, Upper and Lower Canada were combined into one administrative area, and transportation of criminals to New South Wales was stopped. Russia's active involvement in Afghanistan was threatening India. A military presence had to be maintained and in August 1839 British troops captured Kabul in the First Afghan War.

As the Industrial Revolution moved into top gear, a torrent of observers developed a new form of literature to comment on its effects on Britain and the individual. In 1839 Thomas Carlyle warned of a new slavery, that of being beholden to the machine; Mrs Fanny Trollope wrote *Michael Armstrong, Factory Boy* about Manchester factory children and the "condition of England" became a subject to explore, by writers as diverse as Elizabeth Gaskell and a young politician called Benjamin Disraeli. In contrast, the Sovereign's privileges, her insularity and recent scandals at the palace, were leading to republican demands for the abolition of the monarchy and Chartist demonstrations took place in Manchester, Newport and London.

Increasingly aware of the wider responsibilities of her role and of her position in this rapidly changing nation, Queen Victoria had no option but to agree to the miserable £30,000 stipend for Albert. There were other problems, including appointments to Albert's Household. He wanted this to be a balance of Whig and Tory, but quickly realized he would have no say in this matter either. Lord Melbourne questioned how much this German-educated Prince could know of the meaning of British liberalism. Finally, a Naturalization Bill was passed so that he could become British, marry the Queen and be known as "His Royal Highness". Albert must soon have begun to wonder what his future held, as he basked in the excitement in Coburg. Throughout, Victoria made him aware of her devotion and support for him.

The Six Points
OF THE
PEOPLE'S
CHARTER.

1. A VOTE for every man twenty-one years of age, of sound mind, and not undergoing punishment for crime.
2. THE BALLOT.—To protect the elector in the exercise of his vote.
3. No PROPERTY QUALIFICATION for Members of Parliament —thus enabling the constituencies to return the man of their choice, be he rich or poor.
4. PAYMENT OF MEMBERS, thus enabling an honest tradesman, working man, or other person, to serve a constituency, when taken from his business to attend to the interests of the country.
5. EQUAL CONSTITUENCIES, securing the same amount of representation for the same number of electors, instead of allowing small constituencies to swamp the votes of large ones.
6. ANNUAL PARLIAMENTS, thus presenting the most effectual check to bribery and intimidation, since though a constituency might be bought once in seven years (even with the ballot), no purse could buy a constituency (under a system of universal suffrage) in each ensuing twelvemonth; and since members, when elected for a year only, would not be able to defy and betray their constituents as now.

DOCUMENT OUTLINING THE AIMS OF THE CHARTIST MOVEMENT.

The Wedding

The Coburgers were jubilant that their prince would marry the Queen of Britain. There was great revelry and many farewell parties to demonstrate their warmth of feeling when Albert left Coburg. Accompanied by his father and brother and members of the Queen's Household, they left by horse-drawn carriage on the morning of January 28, 1840 in bitterly cold, snowy weather, redolent, Albert perhaps felt, of the feeling towards him in the British Parliament. Like many emigrants from Europe to Britain before and since, uncertain of their future, the party made its way across the plains of northern Germany, across the Rhine at Cologne to Aachen and on to Brussels, where they stayed with Uncle Leopold. Then it was on to Ostend where they boarded a train to Calais for the ferry crossing to Dover. Never a good traveller, Prince Albert was again seasick. The party eventually arrived in London on February 6, four days before the wedding.

Throughout the arguments of the previous four months, plans for the wedding had continued. Guests were invited and a simple service planned. Suitable clothes were designed and made in a style that befitted a bride rather than a reigning queen, and unlike anything worn for the Coronation. Above all, Queen Victoria did not want her husband to feel subservient to her.

The Queen discussed her dress design with Lord Melbourne, who suggested patronage of struggling English manufacturers rather than the Parisian designers she had been using. The elegant, simple dress, designed by the Pre-Raphaelite painter, William Dyce of the Government Design School and probably made by Mrs Bettans, was made of very fine, pale cream silk woven by the Huguenot weavers, such as Samuel Courtauld, of Spitalfields. The large collar and cuffs were made by lace makers from Honiton in Devon, who had been suffering because of the recent fashion for Brussels lace. Queen Victoria continued to patronize the Honiton lace industry throughout her life.

THE CREAM SILK WEDDING DRESS WITH HONITON LACE COLLAR, CUFFS AND HEAD BAND OF ARTIFICIAL ORANGE BLOSSOM.

In a break with tradition, the Queen refused to wear any tiara or coronet, nor any gold or silver woven cloth. Instead, she wore a band of artificial orange blossom in her hair and a train covered in the same flowers hung from her waist. This was, indeed, not a magisterial outfit but a simple, well-designed, expensive wedding dress. On the day before the wedding Prince Albert presented his future wife with an enormous sapphire brooch surrounded by diamonds which she wore on the front of her wedding dress. She wore it on numerous occasions during her marriage but hardly ever after Prince Albert's death. The other jewellery worn on her wedding day was a Turkish diamond necklace and earrings. Prince Albert wore the uniform of a British Field Marshal and the Insignia of the Order of the Garter which Queen Victoria had been able to bestow on him.

The morning of February 10, 1840, was dull and wet but nothing would dampen the spirits of Queen Victoria and Prince Albert. After breakfast, she had her hair done and then dressed in her wedding gown. Accompanied by her mother and the Duchess of Sutherland, she went by carriage the short distance from Buckingham Palace to the Chapel Royal at St James's Palace. Here, the couple took their wedding vows and the Queen was overjoyed when Albert placed the ring on her finger. After signing the register they returned to Buckingham Palace where the Queen changed into a simple white silk gown and Albert into a Windsor coat; they then enjoyed a wedding breakfast. Clothes were to become an enduring fascination between them, they planned what each was to wear and often complemented each other, she in her large, flamboyant, cluttered outfits, he in simple, suave, well-cut trousers and jackets.

At four in the afternoon, they left the Palace for Windsor, the journey made longer than expected because of the number of well-wishers lining the route. At Windsor, Prince Albert was surprised to see the proximity of Lehzen's room to their suite: just the other side of the Queen's dressing room. A rapturous wedding night was spent during which, it was disclosed by the Queen, they slept little and enjoyed much love and affection.

QUEEN VICTORIA AND PRINCE ALBERT AT THE TIME OF THEIR WEDDING BY F W TOPHAM, ENGRAVED BY S BRADSHAW.

The next morning, the young bride was further enthralled by her husband's romantic appearance when, at breakfast, he wore a black velvet jacket without a scarf to reveal a little more of his neck and chest than usual. This, with his handsome good looks and blue eyes, made her eulogize him even more. They walked in the grounds together and tried to work, placing their desks side by side, but their devotion to one another was unstoppable. For the first time, they had each found unimagined love and happiness; their deeply passionate relationship was established.

In the midst of her married happiness, the bride did find time to write to her two father figures, Lord Melbourne and Uncle Leopold. To Leopold she wrote:

… REALLY, I do not think it *possible* for any one in the world to be HAPPIER, or AS *happy* as I am. He is an Angel, and his kindness and affection for he is really touching. To look in those dear eyes, and that dear sunny face, is enough to make me adore him. What I can do to make him happy will be my greatest delight. Independent of my great personal happiness, the reception we both met with yesterday was the most gratifying and enthusiastic I ever experienced....I was a good deal tired last night, but am quite well again to-day and happy;

Early Days

The first weeks of marriage passed in a haze of adoration and passion, and Victoria and Albert's affection for one another was obvious to everyone present. At balls, they were the centre of attention as they glided across the floor. They walked through the grounds of Buckingham Palace and Windsor Castle where Prince Albert opened his wife's eyes to the wonders of nature. They rode together, she remarking on how handsome he looked astride his stallion. In the evenings they sang and played music together and discussed religion, where the Queen discovered her preference for his Lutheran Protestantism over the Anglicanism in which she had been brought up.

The Queen dreaded the prospect of pregnancy and childbirth. Although contraception was beginning to be explored by the medical profession, it was not something discussed by respectable people. Childbirth, as the sad example of Princess Charlotte had shown, was highly risky and many women, in every stratum of society, died in childbirth or because of complications arising from it. By the middle of March, six weeks after the wedding, the Queen began to feel unwell. She was pregnant. As had become usual with anything that now happened to her, a problem arose. This time, because there was no other heir to the throne, it was a problem of a regency. A Regency Bill was passed enabling Prince Albert to be made Regent for a child in the event of the Queen's dying before the heir reached the age of majority.

Each morning, encouraged by Lord Melbourne, Prince Albert sat at his desk next to his wife as she dealt with state papers, even blotting her signature when necessary. To Melbourne, Albert appeared to lack a sense of humour and was strict and introverted, not aspects of character this roguish, elder states-man would have relished in a friend. But he did consider them appropriate qualities in the husband of this particular queen. His experience allowed him to predict correctly that in time Prince Albert would have immense influence on the people of Britain, different and in

A PENCIL AND WATERCOLOUR SKETCH OF VICTORIA, BY SIR WILLIAM CHARLES ROSS, IN 1841. A PRESENT FROM THE QUEEN FOR ALBERT.

some respects more far-reaching than those of his wife. He encouraged the Queen to show Albert any papers he wished to see but, even though Albert had views and opinions on them, he was not allowed by the Queen to influence her decision-making.

Character differences began to show. Victoria was relaxed and, despite the Flora Hastings affair, still an avid gossip, who liked to listen to light music and sing, whereas Albert was much more formal and restrained. Soon, he was becoming desperate for some intellectual stimulation. Although the Queen regarded herself as informal, the structure of court etiquette was very rigid and Albert began to find it stifling, especially at Buckingham Palace.

Not surprisingly, arguments, in a patois of German-English, developed between the volatile wife and repressed husband as it became apparent that Prince Albert had nothing to do. He had no role, was bored and became depressed. In an effort to accommodate him, she rethought domestic arrangements and agreed to move the Court to Windsor for most of the time, because he found the atmosphere there more agreeable than the strict formalities of Buckingham Palace etiquette.

The introduction of Albert into the Queen's life had also created tensions among those closest to her. The Queen still regarded Lehzen as a faithful confidante and advisor, and it was perhaps not surprising that in this new situation the introduction of a third person caused difficulties. Lehzen and Albert did not get on. Stockmar asked Melbourne for his support in ousting Lehzen. Melbourne refused, stating he had found her most amenable and loyal to the Queen and himself. Gradually, however, Lehzen's position with the Queen weakened as Albert's increased and in 1842 she retired from the Household and returned to Germany.

Relations with Parliament began to thaw and Albert was invited to sit beside his wife at the State Opening of Parliament. The Queen's popularity also took a surprising upward turn as a result of a potentially fatal event, when on June 10 the couple encountered the first of many assassination attempts. In time these became known as reginacide. As they drove up Constitution Hill, eighteen-year-old Edward Oxford, carrying two pistols, fired a shot at them. The watching crowd demanded he be killed and were amazed at the cool way, despite her fear, in which the Queen continued her drive. Oxford was sentenced to 27 years in an asylum before being allowed to emigrate.

Queen Victoria did not enjoy pregnancy, finding it a hindrance to the blissful time she was having with her husband. Her size bothered her and so did the discomfort, she could only discuss her confinement with Prince Albert, and had to continue her full time duties at the same time. There was never any indication that the Queen might be indisposed due to her pregnancy. Prince Albert provided much needed support and as the pregnancy progressed she became more dependent on him for his advice in affairs on matters of state and also on the more personal aspects of her impending delivery. For the conventions of those times, they both manifested a remarkable frankness about childbirth.

REGINACIDE, EDWARD OXFORD FIRES A SHOT AT QUEEN VICTORIA AND PRINCE ALBERT AS THEY DRIVE UP CONSTITUTION HILL.

Chapter 5 Victoria and Albert: The First Decade

The birth of the Princess Royal, on November 21, 1840, ten months after her parents' wedding, completed the three-and-a-half-year transformation of the Princess Victoria of Kent from innocent child to queen, wife and now mother. Where, eighteen months before, the public saw images of their new queen as an immature young woman, they were now shown her in a romantic pose, cradling a tiny baby.

The Princess Royal, baptized Victoria Adelaide Mary Louise, was the first of nine children born to Queen Victoria and Prince Albert in the twenty years of their marriage. The first seven births, between 1840 and 1850, occurred virtually in Victoria's first decade as monarch. The contrast between the present images of this royal family and those of the debauchery of the previous decades was marked. During the decade of the 1840s, Queen Victoria began to bestow security and a more restrained approach to monarchy upon her people. Her Empire already dominated the world and new colonies and territories were added each year; the industrial revolution was rolling on, bringing rapid social changes and technological innovations to everyone; the possibilities for Britain and the Empire seemed endless.

For the newly married Queen Victoria, there were enormous personal changes as the isolation of her past disappeared and, for the first time in her life, she had a companion of her own age – her husband, Prince Albert. While coping with life as a young mother she had to come to terms with her wider, more important role, to which she felt bound by a great sense of duty. Quickly, but at times with great difficulty, she learnt that, although she was Queen, the sovereign was no longer in charge of government; this responsibility was now firmly placed with parliament. The two institutions, parliament and monarchy, still had to learn to coexist. This led to difficulties on numerous occasions when Victoria's and Albert's opinions differed from the course her government wished to pursue.

During the two decades of her marriage Queen Victoria became confident enough to forge her own personal style as sovereign. Prince Albert's support was vital to her in achieving this. Not only was he her husband but also, like Melbourne before him, he was her closest and most trusted adviser. She tried hard not to let her frequent pregnancies interfere with her work as monarch and continued to hold receptions, dinners and presentations as long as possible throughout each one. However, there were, inevitably, times when she was indisposed.

Tensions

With each pregnancy of the 1840s Victoria became increasingly exhausted. Even though Prince Albert could appear on her behalf at many events, he still had no official title and was subservient to her. Undeterred by the protestations of Parliament in the months preceding their marriage, Queen Victoria remained determined and anxious to find a role and title for her husband. Albert, too, was not content to deputize behind the scenes. He wanted an influential role, which at first Victoria rejected. Tensions soon began to appear between them. Baron Stockmar's thoughts about the unsuitability of the union before the wedding suddenly seemed like a prophecy come true.

Prince Albert was bored with court life and his wife, with her lack of formal education, was not his intellectual equal; there were frequent arguments between them which, on occasion, became monumental. While the Queen was

QUEEN VICTORIA AND PRINCE ALBERT ETCHING, BY C DURRAND PUBLISHED IN *THE ILLUSTRATED LONDON NEWS.*

content to play cards, sing or read light fiction, Prince Albert was frustrated at the repetitiveness of it all and needed to meet more stimulating minds. This was no life for such a cultured, learned and eager young man and even George Anson, Prince Albert's private secretary, was despairing at the lack of a role for him. Anson wrote a memo in January 1841, relating statements made by Lord Melbourne, whose perception highlighted the source of the differences between them:

LORD MELBOURNE said, '*The Prince* is BORED with the *sameness* of his chess every evening. He would like to bring LITERARY and SCIENTIFIC *people* about the Court, vary society ... The Queen however has no fancy to encourage such people. This arises from a feeling on her part that her education has not fitted her to take part in such conversation; she would not like conversation to be going on in which she could not take her fair share, and she is far too open and candid in her nature to pretend to one

atom more knowledgeable than she really possesses ... The Queen is very proud of the Prince's utter indifference to the attractions of all ladies ... I think she is a little jealous of his talking much even to me.

Gradually, with Lord Melbourne's support and because of his pregnant wife's need of help, Prince Albert was allowed to make some input into state affairs and the dispatch boxes were opened in front of him. He had, after all, studied politics at university in Bonn and should have been capable of being above political bias, which was necessary because by now Melbourne's Whig administration was finally running its course.

The General Election of 1841 resulted in defeat for Melbourne and a second election victory for Sir Robert Peel and the Tories. Lord Melbourne now became a figure of Queen Victoria's past and although she kept in contact with him, the relationship did not remain at the intimate degree of previous years. In 1842, Lord Melbourne suffered a stroke from which he never fully recovered and he died in 1848, by now completely supplanted by Prince Albert. Queen Victoria even questioned her former closeness to her first Prime Minister, seemingly failing to recognize the guidance and training he had given her. Albert had now filled his place and he started to work closely with Peel.

Conflict also arose between Victoria and Albert over the continuing presence of Baroness Lehzen in their household. Prince Albert and she did not get on, each resenting the other's relationship with Victoria. Stockmar became involved in the matter, advising Albert and threatening to resign himself if Lehzen did not leave. Lehzen had always been there for Victoria and, not surprisingly, probably assumed she would help look after the new babies when they arrived. However, Lady Lyttelton was appointed to care for the royal children.

Prince Albert had also decided to look carefully at the running of the Royal Household, something that had never been done, and he quickly discovered many irregularities: practices which had never been updated or changed; food ordered and paid for even if not needed; appointments made without any semblance of a contract and overspending on entertaining even above that necessary for his wife's sumptuous parties. Much of the responsibility for this he placed, unfairly, with Lehzen whose post had evolved over the years. Now, it was decided, she was not needed. Eventually, Queen Victoria, under pressure from Prince Albert, Stockmar and George Anson, became convinced of the redundancy of her position and in 1841, Lehzen left England and returned to Hanover after 21 years as a member of the Royal Household.

There were no farewells between the Queen and Baroness, who, thinking of Victoria to the last, did not want to cause any unnecessary emotional upset. She disappeared, to start her journey, one evening and the next day Queen Victoria did wonder about the validity of what she had allowed to happen. Maybe it was her youth and the need she felt to develop her own style which enabled Victoria to drop the two people, Melbourne and Lehzen, who had been

responsible for preparing her for her duty in this way. Without Lehzen's guidance over the years Queen Victoria would have been a very different monarch. As Elizabeth Longford points out, she played a crucial part in preparing Victoria to be Queen: "That Lehzen handed over to the nation a potentially great queen, must be to her credit."

On a pension of £800 per annum, Lehzen lived until the age of 86, surrounded by memorabilia of her time in the Royal Court in England. She kept in contact with Victoria, who visited her on her trips to Germany. Once Lehzen was gone, Victoria became much more self-confident and many, Prince Albert included, found the quality of Court Life much improved without her.

Two months after Lehzen's departure, with a new Prime Minister on the scene, disturbances in Egypt and Turkey, and her husband establishing his reforms to her household and life, Queen Victoria gave birth on November 9, 1841 to Albert Edward, Prince of Wales, making the succession secure. She was now the mother of two very young children, for the Princess Royal had her first birthday just 12 days after the birth of her brother.

Despite the tensions, frictions and terrible rows between them, the relationship between Victoria and Albert remained very passionate, more children were born and gradually they learnt to accommodate one another. Prince Albert, as a mark of his devotion, presented his wife with much jewellery. Rather than purchasing jewels for her, he designed his own, including a circlet, earrings and brooch which he had started in 1839 while still in Coburg. He added to this collection for Victoria's birthday presents until 1846. These elegant and modern pieces with leaves of gold, flowers of white porcelain and oranges made from green enamel, were a break with traditional royal jewels. For their third wedding anniversary, on February 10, 1843, Albert gave Victoria a gold Elizabethan-style heart-shaped brooch with a simple crown of freshwater pearls on the top. Queen Victoria was delighted with the pieces and the dedication of her husband.

Prime Minister Peel

After the General election of 1841, Sir Robert Peel formed his second Tory administration, making the Duke of Wellington Minister without Portfolio; in 1843 William Gladstone was appointed Minister of the Board of Trade. The 53-year-old Sir Robert Peel, whom Queen Victoria had loathed and mistrusted at the time of the Ladies of the Bedchamber Crisis, soon became a Prime Minister she greatly respected.

Sir Robert Peel was a reforming Tory, from a family made rich by the cotton trade, and was educated at Harrow and Oxford. He had had a long parliamentary career before becoming Prime Minister. As a supporter of free trade, he angered the more traditional members of the Tory party by his determination to repeal the divisive Corn Laws. This issue became more pressing for him as problems of malnutrition among the working classes were becoming apparent and the first of the many failures of

MEMBERSHIP CARD OF THE NATIONAL ANTI-CORN LEAGUE.

the potato crops in Ireland occurred.

The economic principle of free trade – in which international trade operates without any artificial tariffs to inhibit business or exchange – is extremely difficult to apply but, during the reign of Queen Victoria, the system managed to operate very well, primarily because the trading and investment markets that opened within the vast and immensely strong British Empire became dependent upon free trade for their success. The Corn Law and its amendments, by contrast, were regarded as an artificial incentive to help landowners retain their wealth at the expense of the poor.

The first Corn Law was passed by Parliament in 1815 when Britain's population started to increase rapidly and there was not enough home-produced wheat to supply the population and grain had to be imported. Parliament decreed that wheat could not be imported until home-produced wheat cost 80 shillings a quarter (£4 per 25kg). Over the years successive amendments to the law altered the tariffs but the Corn Law succeeded in artificially forcing up the price of all grain, and the prices of bread and other wheat products were affected. The Anti-Corn Law League started in Lancashire in 1838 with John Bright and Richard Cobden as its leaders and quickly gained support throughout the country. Peel, seeing the depression facing the cotton industry in the mid-1840s, the artificially high cost of wheat and the ensuing hardship, was determined to repeal the Corn Law and all its amendments.

Queen Victoria came to like Peel enormously; he was one of the few people who genuinely

CARTOON OF SIR ROBERT PEEL FROM *VANITY FAIR*.

FELIX MENDELSSOHN PLAYING FOR THE QUEEN AND PRINCE ALBERT ON HIS VISIT TO BUCKINGHAM PALACE IN 1842.

Educating the Queen

befriended her beloved Albert, which no doubt endeared him to her all the more. Peel also helped her find her way through the minefield of diplomacy and politics of these early days of her reign. Prince Albert liked his political style and Peel was happy for him to deputize for his wife, believing that he was essential to the success of Queen Victoria's performance as monarch. The two men got on well for even though Peel was over twenty years older than Albert, they had had similar educations and had adopted similar outlooks on life. For Victoria, Prince Albert became a vital support; he looked through her endless piles of papers, analysed and discussed them with her. They had become a team; but still he wanted more influence in the decision-making.

The cause of one of Prince Albert's frustrations in the early years of his marriage was undoubtedly his view that his wife had received only a very limited education. His broad experiences with the stimulating Florschütz and at university in Bonn were in marked contrast to her many years under the tutelage and preparations of Lehzen at Kensington Palace. To Albert, Victoria seemed to possess a good, quick and intelligent, but untrained, mind; he took it upon himself to educate her and she acquiesced. Often, as Melbourne had noticed, she felt out of her depth, and unable to embark on "serious" discussions, changing the topic to something more frivolous, to the frustration of those around her.

Prince Albert's intervention was timely. Quickly, Victoria became learned in the arts and literature and continued to develop her love of music and the opera. Often she and Albert would play music together. When the composer Felix Mendelssohn arrived in London in 1842, Queen Victoria invited him to Buckingham Palace. Mendelssohn, the composer of romantic music from Berlin, had spent time in Scotland and was enraptured by the country; while at Buckingham Palace he dedicated his *Scottish Symphony* to the Queen. He thoroughly enjoyed his visit and remarked at Albert's ability to play the organ, the way in which Victoria organized the music and her beautiful singing.

Soon, those around Queen Victoria noticed a marked improvement in the conversation at Court. She became more confident and capable of expressing her own views on the arts, naval activities and other world events. Regular visits to the Opera House at Covent Garden enabled her to continue to see the latest productions. Keen thespians, whose children were often photographed and painted in costume, Queen Victoria and Prince Albert became patrons of the newly expanding theatrical industry and in December 1848 hosted the first *Royal Command Performance* at Windsor Castle. This production of *The Merchant of Venice* starred the actor, Charles Kean, son of the great Edmund Kean.

At the beginning of Victoria's reign, the theatre was still the domain of the middle and upper classes. The Theatre Act of 1843 allowed theatres to sell refreshments on the premises and led to the rise of the music hall, a Victorian phenomenon designed for the entertainment of the working classes. Here, the theatrical revue was refined, leading in the twentieth century to the variety show – a mixture of song, dance, satire and comedy.

The Queen's Husband

The British public did not accept Prince Albert easily. He was regarded as stiff and foreign, often appearing arrogant, which was symptomatic of his shyness when having to speak English in public. At formal dinners held in his honour, such as when he was given the Freedom of the City of London, he would often be snubbed by his wife's relations, most notably the Clarences. The first step to Albert's acceptance came in the summer of 1840, when he was made president of the Anti-Slavery Society. Slavery had been abolished in the British Empire in 1833, when £20 million had been given as compensation to owners, but other countries and regimes still carried out slave-trading on a vast scale. Towards the end of the century, Uncle Leopold's son became a slave trader as he colonized the vast area around the Congo River in central Africa.

PRINCE ALBERT ADDRESSING A MEETING OF THE ANTI-SLAVERY SOCIETY.

THE QUEEN ARRIVING AT THE STATE OPENING OF PARLIAMENT, D ROBERTS

Sir Robert Peel, recognizing Albert's abilities, made him chairman of the Royal Fine Art Commission, among the functions of which was to look at possibilities for rebuilding the Houses of Parliament, which had been devastated by fire in 1834. The new building, in a Victorian Gothic style tinged with Italianate classical, was a collaboration of design by Charles Barry and Augustus Welby Northmore Pugin. Prince Albert was quickly recognized for the valuable and knowledgeable contribution he made to these committees.

Other openings appeared for him, most notably at the Society for the Encouragement of the Arts, Manufactures and Commerce, generally known as the Society of Arts. The Society appointed him President in 1843. Here, welcomed by many lively-minded entrepreneurs, Albert found the stimulating company he had so badly craved. He is credited with making the Society focus on its very important role in

marrying the arts and crafts with manufactures and commerce, vital to the success of the new industries. Albert met and worked with people such as Henry Cole, who designed the first Christmas card in 1843; Herbert Minton, owner of the ceramic company in Stoke-on-

Trent; Thomas Cubitt, a new-style master builder; and George Stephenson and Isambard Brunel, engineers and designers of railway locomotives. It was with Prince Albert's support that these men, and the Society of Arts, were able in 1848 to proceed with the planning of the Great Exhibition. Albert also used the talents of these new associates for his personal family needs at Osborne in the Isle of Wight and Balmoral in Scotland, where new royal homes had to be designed and built.

Gradually, Prince Albert developed a unique and highly suitable role, using his education and European perspective to work alongside his wife; but the title of Prince Consort would continue to elude him until just a few years before his death. Indeed, he was so determined in his work that he became, like Sir Robert Peel, what would now be termed a "workaholic" and his extreme commitment at times affected his health. He was a perfect symbol of a Victorian entrepreneur, fascinated by the

changes and possibilities which the machine brought to everybody's life as well as appreciating the importance of new developments in design, manufacture and commerce.

Threats

As the decade progressed, Victoria, Albert and their growing family became established familiar images, captured in the numerous portraits and early photographs which recorded the lives of the royal family. They became accessible and seen as something to aspire to by the newly affluent middle class. There were numerous sittings for huge paintings of the family group by Winterhalter, von Angeli, Landseer and others.

Even though Queen Victoria and Prince Albert wanted to live economically, which no doubt by Royal standards they did, their wealth and position made their lifestyle very different from that of the mass of their subjects. Popular support for the republican Chartist movement was a perpetual problem to Queen Victoria, especially when she began to disappear to Osborne and Balmoral for weeks on end or when she demanded more money from the Civil List. Questions would be asked in Parliament and the people wondered at the need for and cost of a monarchy.

A greater threat to the Queen's position and the safety of her family came, not from republicanism, but from the assassin's bullet. Reginacide, as it became to be known, was attempted twice in 1842. In May, when riding in their carriage along the Mall, Prince Albert had seen a small man aiming a pistol at them. When noticed he had scurried away into the crowd and was not caught. When driving out after this the royal couple took the precaution of having equerries on horseback accompanying the carriage, which was just as well, for the next day the same small man appeared; this time, he fired a shot and was jumped upon and caught. The man, John Francis, was initially condemned to death, but afterwards was reprieved when it was discovered that the pistol was not loaded. A few days later another

"THE BRITISH BEEHIVE" SHOWING THE VARIOUS ELEMENTS OF SOCIETY.

"THE DINNER HOUR AT WIGAN", EYRE CROWE, 1874, DEPICTING A NORTHERN, INDUSTRIAL SCENE.

attempt was made, this time by a disabled young man called John Bean who had loaded his gun with paper and tobacco. Queen Victoria found him a pathetic creature. Attempts at reginacide continued throughout her reign.

Social Changes

Life in the Royal Household was very different from that experienced by the masses of people in the country. The new middle class, created by the wealth of the industrial revolution, was now established; these people were not just mill owners or entrepreneurs of the Empire but comprised an increasingly important group of professionals. Those practising as lawyers, accountants, bankers, architects, teachers, clergy and doctors were increasing in numbers and professional bodies, like the Royal Institute of British Architects, soon became established to represent them.

For millions of other men, women and children, however, there was little representation at an influential level and they continued to live in squalor and to work in appalling and dangerous conditions. The period of social reform and acts of Parliament to protect the weak, rather than promote the lot of the rich had begun. In 1842 a Royal Commission into mining made recommendations, and legislation was subsequently passed to appoint inspectors and prohibit women and children under ten years of age from working underground. Numerous factory acts were passed to reduce working hours and improve conditions. The 1842 Factory Act concerned conditions in textile mills, predominantly in Lancashire and Yorkshire, and stated that women and young people between 13 and 18 years could work no longer than 12 hours a day and children under 13 could work no more than six-and-a-half hours, where previously it had been nine hours. It also introduced the concept of education of three hours per day, but the children's working age was lowered from nine years to eight years. The 1850 Factory Act decreed that women and children could only work between six in the morning and six in the evening, with an hour-long break for rest and meals. In 1853 another act attempted to further restrict the use of child labour.

Fatal diseases like cholera, typhoid and tuberculosis were endemic. Outbreaks frequently reached epidemic proportions, due to insufficient sanitary arrangements and overcrowded housing combined with a poor understanding of the nature of the diseases and the transmission of infection. In 1840 the existence of slums was noted by a Select Committee on the Health of Towns and in 1842 Edwin Chadwick published his important work on the Sanitary Conditions of the Labouring Poor which showed up the dreadful and lethal

BE UNITED AND INDUSTRIOUS

AMALGAMATED SOCIETY OF ENGINEERS, MACHINISTS, MILLWRIGHTS, SMITHS, AND PATTERN MAKERS.

This is to Certify that _____ was admitted a Member of the _____ Branch, on the _____ day of _____ In witness whereof we have subscribed our names and affixed the Society's Seal.

PRESIDENT.   SECRETARY.

sewage and sanitation systems in urban areas. This would have far-reaching effects, not only on public health for everyone in Britain, but on the battlefields of the Crimea thirteen years later. It enabled Queen Victoria to demand a review of the sanitation at Buckingham Palace and Windsor Castle, where, at times, the stench and associated risk of infection, was appalling.

A number of Public Health Acts were passed from 1848 onwards to enforce local governments to improve sanitation and public health; appoint the first medical officers of health; look at conditions in asylums; and create a more amenable system in the degrading workhouses. At the same time, doctors were researching ways of immunizing the population against disease; perhaps the most important breakthrough was by Chadwick and his understanding of bacteria and their part in the spread of disease and infection.

To cope with medical treatment and care for the increasing urban population there was a major expansion in the foundation of hospitals. While St Bartholomew's, Guy's and St Thomas' hospitals had been long-established in London, and were financed by voluntary and charitable foundations, many of the new hospitals were funded by local councils. The Royal Free and University College Hospitals were founded in 1828, Sheffield Royal Infirmary in 1832, the Samaritan Free Hospital for Women in 1847, Poplar Hospital for Accidents in 1855, and many more throughout the country. Poor Laws were passed and one in 1844 enabled mothers of illegitimate children to claim maintenance for their children from the father. Inflated bread prices, a result of the Corn Laws, meant that vast numbers of the working classes were under-nourished and hungry; most meals consisted of potatoes, which were cheaper than bread and grain, and any money left over was used to buy "luxuries" such as tea and the occasional scrap of bacon. Malnutrition caused scurvy and rickets which often led to blindness, diseases of the nervous system and weak bones.

For working-class women, life was very tough. Not only were they expected to work to bring in income but also to do all the domestic chores, and the lack of understanding of contraception, their weakness due to ill heath and their poor diet meant that many thousands died in childbirth, some from complications, others from not being able to afford appropriate medical or midwifery care. The scourge of death in childbirth affected all women, including Queen Victoria, who despaired at the threat of pregnancy, its inconvenience and pain, and the intrusion into her relationship with her husband.

Education for the poor, girls in particular, was rudimentary, but when Lord Shaftesbury set up the first "ragged schools" to provide free education to the poorest children in society in

THE WORKHOUSE IN ST JAMES'S PARISH FROM ACKERMANN'S "MICROCOSM OF LONDON" BY T ROWLANDSON AND A PUGIN.

1844, it was a sign that recognition of the need to educate everyone was beginning.

The Royal Family was not unaffected by the changes. When Queen Victoria demanded an overhaul of the sewerage systems at Buckingham Palace and Windsor, enormous open cess pits were found beneath the structures and new sewers were built. At Windsor Albert also introduced gas lights; Victoria strongly disapproved of them, preferring illumination by candles throughout her life.

On their journey to Scotland in 1842 they travelled on the outdated Royal Yacht, *George III*. The journey took three days and the yacht,

OPPOSITE: THE TRADE EMBLEM OF THE AMALGAMATED SOCIETY OF ENGINEERS, MACHINISTS, MILLWRIGHTS, SMITHS AND PATTERN MAKERS.

BUILDING THE SEWER BENEATH FLEET STREET IN LONDON.

the conductor, "Not so fast next time." Travelling by train meant that during her reign she was able to visit more distant areas of the country and be seen by her subjects more than any other previous monarch.

Trying to Help

Queen Victoria was greatly affected by reports of individual suffering. A wife in desperate depression, or having committed suicide because her husband had lost his job or been killed in action, could make her demand why, to write a letter of support or condolence and even send money to the relatives. Dispatches from the frontiers of the Empire would make her grieve at the suffering and loss of life incurred in these hazardous regions and she was particularly sympathetic to the plight of mothers. In her way, she was even appalled at the conditions in Parkhurst prison; from her inevitably distant perspective she was a very sympathetic and humane person who cared about her subjects.

At times, however, Victoria's sympathetic nature could cause her to act naively and outrageously. In the mid-1840s cotton manufacturing was in great difficulty, demand had fallen and established British companies were suffering from stiff foreign competition. Sir Robert Peel, himself the son of a cotton manufacturer, understood the problems only too well and discussed them with the royal couple. Victoria and Albert wanted to help the British workers, particularly the Spitalfields weavers in East London, who had been suffering for a long time. The couple's theatrical interests meant they were always eager to hold a costume drama and their solution to the cotton slump was to host a grand Plantagenet Ball in which they dressed up – in British woven cotton – as Edward III and Queen Philippa.

The Prime Minister was aghast. Some months previously he had suggested to them both that adopting a more economical lifestyle would help gain public favour; now, he warned them against holding this great

the last sailing boat commissioned by the Royal Family, had to be escorted by two paddle steamers. Seeing these developments in ship design and building, the Queen and her husband commissioned a new yacht, *Victoria and Albert*, which was a twin paddle steamer. Engine design advanced further and the family grew, so by 1855 they had acquired a much larger yacht, *Victoria and Albert II*.

The development of the railway system was much more pivotal in their lives, enabling them eventually to travel to Osborne and Balmoral remarkably quickly. Queen Victoria made her first railway journey in 1842 when, accompanied by Mr Brunel, she travelled from Slough to Paddington, which took 35 minutes. She was delighted; Prince Albert was said to have told

A *PUNCH* CARTOON, "A COMMENT ON VICTORIA'S FIRST VISIT TO IRELAND" BY JOHN LEECH IN 1849.

ball, telling them again it would be very wrong to flaunt their privileges. He was right. The press was appalled at the scale of the ball and the lavishness of Queen Victoria's dress at a time when masses were starving. The plight of the cotton manufacturers was not improved.

Politics and Famine in Ireland

In Ireland, where many people had long been fervently opposed to being ruled from Britain, a renewed republican movement was gaining support under Feargus O'Connor. Many of the peasants lived on land owned by wealthy Protestants who had emigrated to Ireland in the seventeenth century. Problems had arisen as soon as Ireland's parliament was united with that of Great Britain, under the 1800 Act of Union. At this time, Catholics were debarred from holding any official office. The new constitution tried to move towards greater emancipation, but quickly ran into difficulties. Queen Victoria despised the bigotry she felt the Protestants espoused and was sympathetic to the Catholics'

request to practise their religion freely and take an active part in the running of their country.

The Irish were very dependent on their land for a living and the staple foods for most Irish people were bread and potatoes. Disaster struck in the spring of 1845, when heavy rain ruined the potato harvests. Many peasants, unable to pay their rent, were evicted by their wealthy landowners. This cycle was repeated for five consecutive years. Eventually, one million people starved to death in the Irish Potato Famine. A further million left Ireland, starting the first wave of Irish emigration to America, and thousands arrived in England, many settling in Liverpool and finding work in the docks, mills and railways.

Trying to prevent the disaster, Sir Robert Peel succeeded in having the Corn Laws repealed in 1846, but was forced to resign after being defeated on the Irish Coercion Bill. Lord John Russell became Prime Minister. Although Queen Victoria wept at Peel's resignation she did not despair as she had at the loss of Melbourne, realizing that the loss of a prime minister meant the introduction of a new one. The new Prime Minister appointed as Foreign Secretary Lord Palmerston, whose relationship with Queen Victoria would prove to be tempestuous.

Another attempt on Queen Victoria's life, the fourth so far, was made by William Hamilton, an Irishman, on Constitution Hill in 1849. Despite this incident, it was thought safe for her and Prince Albert finally to visit Ireland later that year. They were delighted to be received by both Catholic and Protestant delegations and Queen Victoria found the people charming and beautiful, though she was appalled by the squalor of the conditions in which many lived. On August 6, 1849, she described her reception in a letter to Uncle Leopold, written from Dublin:

The most PERFECT *order* was MAINTAINED *in spite* of the IMMENSE *mass of people* assembled, and a more good humoured crowd I never saw, but noisy and excitable beyond belief ... We drove out yesterday afternoon and were followed by jaunting-cars and riders and people running and screaming ...

This morning ... we visited the Model School (where the Protestant and Catholic Archbishops received us) ... You see more ragged and wretched people here than I ever saw anywhere else ... the women are really handsome ... such beautiful black eyes and hair and such fine colours and teeth.

A major source of trouble was China. The East India Company had been formed in 1599 to trade in spices from the East Indies, where it competed with the Dutch. By 1623, the company had changed its main area of trading operations to mainland India. Here, it grew in strength and prosperity, its main trading partner, China, being vital to its fortunes, and the company retained a monopoly. By the mid-eighteenth century the East India Company had taken on a governmental role in various parts of the Indian sub-continent, and under the terms of the India Act of 1784, it began effectively to rule on behalf of the British government, with India its largest colony.

This period of strength for the East India Company saw a considerable exploitation of the Indian people, but also awakened a fascination amongst the British for the exotic East. The influence on design at home of the British presence in India cannot be underestimated: George IV's Brighton Pavilion embodying many Oriental designs; the Paisley pattern which originated in Kashmir; and the bungalow and the verandah of India which became resplendent in many British suburbs were just a few examples of the way in which Indian culture permeated Britain.

By 1833, the Company had lost the monopoly of trade with China and in 1839 the Chinese tried to break all trading ties by seizing the opium in the port of Canton. In 1842, British troops, supervised by the East India Company, achieved a resounding victory over the Chinese resulting in, for the Chinese, the humiliation of having to cede Hong Kong to Britain. The East India Company became a quasi-British governmental department until the Mutiny in 1857.

THE HONGS OF CANTON AND MACAO HARBOUR, A PAINTING FROM THE CANTONESE SCHOOL.

Beyond Britain's Shores

The British Empire created enormous wealth, but it had constantly to be maintained, protected and, where possible, expanded. Free trade, propagated by Sir Robert Peel, was necessary for the growing band of capitalists. But underlying tensions would sometimes erupt into violence. Incidents escalating into bloodbaths took place in India, China and North Africa during Victoria's first decade on the throne, many of them growing out of Britain's desire to dominate or defeat the ambitions of other potential empire builders. The Tsar of Russia promised to be an almost constant adversary as he wanted to expand the bounds of his empire. Throughout the decade Queen Victoria had to preside over a government intent on expanding and maintaining its rich Empire. She would write to forgotten men supporting the further reaches of the Empire and visit the injured when they returned.

Revolution in Europe

The year 1848 was momentous for Queen Victoria and for Europe, as republican demands spread across the continent. Queen Victoria gave birth to her sixth child, a daughter, Princess Louise, on March 18; soon after, she was offering refuge to the France's last Bourbon

WINTERHALTER'S PAINTING OF QUEEN VICTORIA AND PRINCE ALBERT VISITING KING LOUIS-PHILLIPE IN 1845.

King, Louis-Phillipe who had had to escape with his family from France disguised as "Mr Smith". Later in the year, Victoria found herself at odds with Parliament over the governance of Schleswig-Holstein and watched with alarm as small independent states in Europe tried to form alliances, especially in Italy and Germany. At home, she saw Chartist demonstrations demand her abdication. She took solace in the fact the Britain, Belgium and Russia were able to remain firm but by the time they retreated to Osborne at the end of the year, Victoria and Albert both sighed with relief that it was over and they were safe and Victoria was still on her throne.

After the Revolution of 1789, France remained unstable, despite being one country and not a collection of small states as Germany and Italy still were. Its history, however, from the Revolution to the formation of a republic, was fraught with antagonism and bloodshed, as monarchists and republicans fought each other. Napoleon I represented democracy but stayed beyond his mandate, became an unelected emperor and, like many contemporary European heads of state was intent on expanding his Empire. The Napoleonic Wars across Europe came to a climax with Napoleon's defeat and exile to Elba in 1814.

QUEEN VICTORIA
AND PRINCE ALBERT
ATTENDING A DINNER
HOSTED BY EMPEROR
NAPOLEON III AND
EMPRESS EUGENIE.

The monarchy was restored under Louis XVIII but Napoleon returned, briefly, to be comprehensively defeated at Waterloo in 1815, the Allied army being led by the British Duke of Wellington. Again, the monarchy was restored in France, Charles X remaining on the throne until a revolution in 1830 forced him to abdicate. His cousin, Louis-Philippe, took over. King Louis-Philippe's daughter, Marie Louise, was married to Uncle Leopold; Queen Victoria, on their first meeting at Ramsgate, had found her charming and was impressed by her sophisticated, Parisian style.

Even though Louis-Philippe was an ineffectual monarch, Queen Victoria felt very protective towards him and his family; they were, after all, relations, however indirectly. She and Albert had visited Louis-Philippe in September 1843, making the first State Visit to France by an English monarch since Henry VIII. Victoria regarded the trip as both a state and a family visit and went in the new yacht *Victoria and Albert*. She gleefully noted in her diary that the Tsar would be furious at her fraternization with Louis-Philippe, for whom he had little regard. Now, in 1848, when things got too difficult for them she offered them refuge in England. Victoria was appalled to see the state they were in when they arrived at Buckingham Palace. Everything they owned was lost. They went to live at Claremont, where Leopold had once lived, and here Louis-Philippe died in 1850.

Back in France unrest continued and elections were held when Louis Napoleon, nephew of Napoleon Bonaparte, was elected Prince President of the Third Republic. Napoleon and his wife Eugénie, whom he married in 1853, the year after he became Emperor of the French, became frequent visitors to Queen Victoria.

The states of Schleswig and Holstein caused a conflict that pitted Queen Victoria and Prince Albert against the government and especially the Foreign Secretary, Lord Palmerston, as their family ties dominated their views. Many of the smaller German states were in dire financial straits; alliances and liaisons became more difficult and the strong Prussia, under Frederick II, dominated them all. The opportunity to discuss and plan the future of a unified Germany arose in 1848, when the governance of the two duchies of Schleswig and Holstein came into question. Prince Albert supported the creation of a unified and enlightened German state and wanted Schleswig and Holstein to be part of this.

Victoria and Albert also had personal interests in a German state, recognizing the power of Prussia; plans were already afoot for the marriage of their nine-year-old daughter, Princess Victoria, to the Crown Prince Frederick of Prussia. However, the British Government, advised by Palmerston, believed that the governance of these two northern German states should remain with Denmark. The discord between monarch and government continued, exacerbated by Victoria's insistence on taking her husband's advice and not that of the Foreign Secretary.

In many respects, Victoria had by now become intellectually subservient to Albert as she doted on his every word and he acquired more influence. She even wrote to Uncle Leopold in August 1848:

It is *indeed to me* one of ETERNAL *thankfulness*, for a PURER, *more perfect* being than my BELOVED ALBERT the *Creator* could not have sent into thy troubled world. I feel that I could not exist without him, and that I should sink under the troubles and annoyances and *dégouts* of my very difficult position, were it not for his assistance, protection, guidance and comfort. Truly do I thank you for your great share in bringing about our marriage.

Queen Victoria's determination to stand against her government did lead to Palmerston's temporary downfall; when he was rude about her in the House of Commons he was forced to resign even though she had tried to have him sacked.

Chartism was growing. Queen Victoria loathed the movement, believing that many innocent workers were being forced into it by unscrupulous and militant organizers. The movement gained a lot of ground throughout the 1840s, as the exploitation of workers and the dreadful conditions in which they worked grew more severe. Rallies were held throughout the country, with a large one at Kennington Common in 1848 which the Queen's own Spitalfields Weavers, for whom she had put on the Plantagenet Ball, attended.

The trade union movement was also beginning. In 1848, two German men based in Manchester write a revolutionary handbook. Friedrich Engels had been living in the city for some time, having been sent from Prussia by his father, to work in one of his cotton mills, Ermen and Engels, in Manchester. By day Engels worked and at night, having already met revolutionaries in Germany, he wrote. His *The Conditions of the Working Class in England* was published in 1845. With another German, Karl Marx, who eventually settled in England, he formed the Communist League in 1847 and in 1848 they published the *Communist Party Manifesto*.

The decade had changed much. Undoubtedly, Queen Victoria, greatly influenced by her husband, had brought a stability to the monarchy in her early years. But defining the sovereign's role was still difficult. While Victoria tried hard to be a good and caring monarch she did not always help her own cause and often displayed a certain political innocence. The purchases of estates at Osborne and Balmoral were from private funds and here the couple and their children would disappear for weeks and almost forget about their positions, even though dispatch boxes were attended to and contact with ministers was maintained. A few weeks after the Chartist meeting at Kennington, Queen Victoria went on a shopping trip and spent £1,200 on a diamond and emerald necklace, followed a few months later by the purchase of a diamond necklace, brooch and earrings.

A DAGUERROTYPE OF THE LAST GREAT CHARTIST RALLY HELD ON KENNINGTON COMMON, IN LONDON 10 APRIL 1848.

Chapter 6 The Royal Family

For Queen Victoria the birth of her first child on November 21, 1840, opened a new phase of her life, that of Royal Mother. Initially, she was disappointed that her first child was not the son and heir essential for a smooth succession but she and Albert both quickly became devoted parents to their daughter Princess Victoria; or Vicky as she quickly became known.

Victoria had said that pregnancy was "the only thing I dread" and she was not happy at the prospect of having more babies after Vicky. The spectre of the fatal results of Princess Charlotte's pregnancy had loomed over her childhood and rumours spread that the Queen was terrified of dying like her cousin and thousands of other women. Whatever her fears, Victoria decided to be strong in spirit throughout her first pregnancy and not let it interfere with her life too much; many thought her silly when she danced at parties or stood for too long in the later months of her pregnancy.

Prince Albert was concerned that her health and that of the baby might be in jeopardy when, in her eighteenth week of pregnancy, young Edward Oxford made an attempt on her life in Constitution Hill. Prince Albert, unusually for the times and for their social status, was a supportive husband throughout his wife's confinements and was present at the births of his children. There was no precedent as to how a Queen Regnant should behave while pregnant and, despite her husband's support, she still had a heavy workload and many responsibilities. Affairs of state, international relations, a growing Empire, guests to be entertained and foreign delegations received, changes of prime ministers and governments all had to take precedence over her role as devoted wife and mother.

Her determination to have a trouble-free first pregnancy was, no doubt, helped by her youth and physical strength and by the fact that, unlike the majority of women in Britain at the time, she had the best possible maternity care available. Sir James Clark, the Physician in Ordinary to the Queen's Household, still unnerved by his involvement in the Flora Hastings scandal, had decided that midwifery was not his forte, but agreed to attend the Queen throughout her confinement.

The specially appointed obstetric team consisted of the First Physician Accoucheur, Dr Locock, who recognized the importance of midwifery and practised at St Bartholomew's Hospital in London; Dr Ferguson, Professor of Obstetrics at King's College Hospital and a doctor at the Westminster Lying-in Hospital; and the Queen's Monthly Nurse, Mrs Lilly. These three supported the Queen through all nine of her confinements and deliveries.

Clothing during pregnancy was another problem: in private, the Queen would wear a loose chemise like a dressing gown, but continued to wear her stays when fully dressed, undoing them in stages as the weeks went by. In later years Queen Victoria would voice her disgust at the fashion for pregnant women, usually her granddaughters, to reveal their full shape by wearing tight clothes.

The birth of a royal child, an heir to the throne, prompted a certain degree of checking up on court etiquette. Victoria decided to break with tradition and, instead of a host of officials being present in the delivery room to witness the birth of the heir to the throne, she insisted that they wait in an anteroom with the door open between the two. Here the Archbishop of Canterbury, the Bishop of London, Cabinet ministers and Sir James Clark were asked to wait for the birth. Despite the professionals, the actual labour and delivery was very much dictated by nature and when, two weeks before the expected date, Victoria was awoken in the

OPPOSITE:

A PHOTOGRAPH

TAKEN BY ROGER

FENTON IN 1854 OF

QUEEN VICTORIA

AND PRINCE ALBERT.

night by the first signs of labour, Prince Albert, fast asleep beside her, was alerted and the doctors and Mrs Lilly were called. Once the baby girl had been safely delivered, Sir James Clark walked through the open door from the anteroom and carried her back to the awaiting dignitaries.

Queen Victoria was repelled by the thought of breast feeding and a wet nurse had been arranged. However, due to the early delivery, she had to be hastily summoned. She was a doctor's wife from Cowes on the Isle of Wight and received a payment of £1000 and a life pension of £300 per annum for her services. Dr Locock received £1000 and Dr Ferguson £800. Mrs Lilly and Queen Victoria developed a close bond and kept in touch for many years, eventually seeing each other for the last time when the nurse was 80.

SIR CHARLES LOCOCK, FIRST PHYSICIAN *ACCOUCHEUR* TO QUEEN VICTORIA.

Looking after the new baby was the domain of nurses and she was brought to her mother twice a day; by the time her daughter was six weeks old Victoria had only seen her bathed twice. The initial disappointment that she had not given birth to a boy was soon overcome and Queen Victoria wrote on December 15, 1840, to Uncle Leopold:

I am *very* PROSPEROUS, *walking* about the house *like myself again*, and we go to WINDSOR on the 22nd ... which will quite set me up ... Your little grand-niece is most flourishing; she gains daily in health, strength and, I may add, beauty; I think she will be very like her dearest father.

Leopold was delighted at the safe delivery and good health of his niece, very different from the tragic outcome of Princess Charlotte's confinement. He flattered himself, he wrote, "that you will be a delighted and delightful Maman au milieu d'une belle et nombreuse famille ..."

Despite the ease of her first labour and childbirth the experience was, as for many new mothers, a shock to Victoria. The death at this time of her beloved dog, Dash, who had been a vital companion during the isolation of her childhood, was made more distressing by her post-natal emotions. As befits a close friend, Dash had his burial, beneath a marble memorial, organized by the Queen herself.

Possibly because of her exhaustion and the still unresolved question of a role for Prince Albert, there were tensions between the couple. These were not helped by the presence of Baroness Lehzen and her assumption that she would be required to look after the new baby as she had its mother. As Lehzen and Albert resented one another, it is not surprising that once she had retired the relationship between he and the Queen improved.

The use of the wet nurse by the upper classes meant that new mothers were not protected from frequent conceptions by the contraceptive effects of breast feeding. This, added to the passion that Victoria and Albert undoubtedly felt for each other, meant that by the spring of 1841, just four months after the birth of Princess Victoria, the Queen found herself pregnant again.

Possibly the Queen was suffering from what we know as post-natal depression, or perhaps it was a combination of exhaustion and fatigue or shock, but she was unhappy about being preg-

A DRAWING BY QUEEN VICTORIA OF PRINCESS VICTORIA, AGED THREE.

THE BAPTISM OF PRINCE ALBERT EDWARD, PRINCE OF WALES, 1842.

nant again so quickly, and anxieties persisted throughout the pregnancy. She was terrified the baby would be premature and was also very concerned about the health of her daughter, who was often sickly.

On the morning of November 9, 1841, after a long and painful labour, Victoria gave birth to a large, healthy boy. The absence of the Archbishop of Canterbury and other dignitaries in the anteroom may have been due to Prince Albert's having sent a message to them too late. Because the baby, Albert Edward, Prince of Wales, but always called Bertie by his family, was a male child, he supplanted his sister as the heir to the throne.

The birth of two children within a year, still only twenty-one months into her marriage, was a cause of great distress to Queen Victoria. Neither she nor Albert had wanted a large family and the Queen had let her abhorrence of pregnancy and childbirth be known. This time exhaustion and depression meant that her return to normal health took quite some time.

The Young Family

In the following nine years, there would not be a period longer than eighteen months in which Queen Victoria was not pregnant. Between November 1840 and May 1850 she gave birth to seven children. All were normal deliveries and the children all survived childhood, not a common feat for any nineteenth-century mother. The first seven of Queen Victoria's children were:

HRH Princess Victoria (Vicky), Princess Royal, born November 21, 1840

HRH Prince Albert Edward (Bertie), Prince of Wales, born November 9, 1841

HRH Princess Alice, born April 25, 1843

HRH Prince Alfred (Affie), Duke of Edinburgh (1866), Duke of Saxe-Coburg-Gotha (1893), born August 6, 1844

HRH Princess Helena (Lenchen), born May 25, 1846

HRH Princess Louise, born March 18, 1848

HRH Prince Arthur, Duke of Connaught and Strathearn (1874), born May 1, 1850.

QUEEN VICTORIA WITH HER YOUNGEST CHILD, PRINCESS BEATRICE, IN 1860.

All these children were born without any of the aids women later in the century and in the future have been able to enjoy almost as a matter of course. Queen Victoria took chloroform as a pain relief during the birth of her eighth child, HRH Prince Leopold, Duke of Albany (1881) on April 7, 1853. The Queen thus played a part in bringing into the open the terrible pain women endured during labour, for her action caused a huge public debate. Victoria and Albert's last child, HRH Princess Beatrice, was born on April 14, 1857.

This enormous, healthy family provided both parents with the happiness and security that had eluded each of them in their own childhoods. Victoria had decided that her husband was the head of the family and as such his words and actions were paramount. Together, they took great care to employ the right staff, equip nurseries and, later, oversee the education of their children, and no expense or detail was missed. In a fascinating account of life with Queen Victoria written in 1898 by "One of Her Majesty's Servants", these attentions were described in some detail:

> When her MAJESTY'S *own children* began to arrive in the world, NO TROUBLE *was spared* from the birth of each to make it *fit*, PHYSICALLY and MENTALLY, for the position to which it was born; for, with all her deep love for her children, the Queen began at once to exercise the strictest discipline in her nurseries, and one of her oldest friends and most valued advisers always remarked: "The nursery gives me more trouble than the government of a kingdom would do"

The nurseries were the domain of the Dowager Lady Lyttelton, who had replaced Baroness Lehzen. She supervised a large staff of nurses, who would now be called nannies, and later, of governesses. Often, the Queen and Prince Albert would be absent or busy and unable to see their children, but they remain devoted to them. So, too, did the reinstated Duchess of Kent, who since the departure of Sir John Conroy, had managed to rebuild her relationship with her daughter. She now lived at Frogmore House, close to Windsor Castle, and rapidly became a loving grandmother to a hoard of young children. When the apartments were redesigned at Windsor, Queen Victoria insisted that the schoolroom should be close to her sitting room. Sanitary arrangements were not so sympathetic; when a new lavatory was plumbed in above the Queen's bedroom, the waste ran into the open drain pipe.

Even though Victoria and Albert wanted their children to grow up aware of their positions, they also wanted them to live privately, away from the curiosity of the Court. Victoria was happy for her children's education to be organized by Albert, who along with Stockmar, employed governesses and tutors for the young princes and princesses. However, they had agreed that each child should be brought up aware of his or her destiny, especially Bertie who, as heir to the throne, would one day be king. Victoria and Albert also wanted their children to be brought up with a degree of freedom and not to be bigoted or narrow-minded.

Victoria and Albert began planning very early the marriages of their children, seeking prospective wives and husbands for them throughout Europe. When she was only four years old tentative arrangements were already being made for the eventual marriage of the Princess Royal to the son of the King of Prussia. The planning bore fruit, for suitable marriages to eligible wives and husbands in royal houses across Europe were found for all their children except Princess Louise, who chose instead to marry into the British aristocracy. Her husband was the Marquis of Lorne, later the Duke of Argyll.

THE DOWAGER SARAH, LADY LYTTELTON.

OVERLEAF: VICTORIA AND ALBERT AND FIVE OF THEIR CHILDREN.

Friction

Due to the almost constant stream of pregnancies, there was, by the late 1840s, equally constant speculation and gossip as to the Queen's condition – was she or was she not pregnant? – which annoyed her immensely. Gradually, Albert's reserved character was beginning to affect the Queen's more extrovert nature and she would be furious at speculation of such a personal nature. Also, despite all the help from her staff, Prince Albert's support and her own youth, she became distressed that she could not enjoy her marriage fully without the threat of pregnancy. This, and the lack of a fulfilling role for Albert, again created tensions between the couple.

Often, the Queen would be depressed or exhausted and rows would erupt between them. As had happened after her accession, people at Court watched her carefully to make sure that a legacy of King George III's mental state had not been bequeathed to her. Fatigue and depression due to childbirth was little understood in those pre-Freudian days and the fact that this woman was not only a mother but a working sovereign was given little consideration.

As the years progressed, Prince Albert, generally wanting peace rather than argument, learned how to accommodate his wife's outbursts; after the initial loud arguments in their Germanic English, often in front of their servants, Albert would respond by writing to his wife. But his toleration could be stretched as when, on occasions, she would summon him away from a public dinner he was attending, in the capacity of its patron or president. Guests would watch, amazed, as up to three different footmen might appear, through the evening, with successive notes from the Queen demanding he return home immediately, all of which he ignored. Despite, or maybe because of, all the frictions, their marriage remained a very passionate and faithful affair, but Prince Albert, in the early years, was very lonely. Maybe as a reminder of Coburg he built a small, wooden pavilion in the grounds of Buckingham Palace in 1842, the design of which was based on a log cabin from Thuringia. He commissioned artists to decorate the interior.

PRINCE ALBERT'S BROTHER, DUKE OF SAXE-COBURG.

Apart

When Prince Albert's father, Duke Ernest of Saxe-Coburg, died in February 1844, Albert returned to Coburg; it was his first visit to the Schloss Rosenau since he left to get married. It was also the first time Victoria and Albert had spent a night apart since their marriage, and they missed one another tremendously; they wrote to each other daily, unable to contain themselves, and looked forward to being together again. By now, not only did they share a bedroom but their desks stood side by side both at Buckingham Palace and at Windsor.

Duke Ernest's death meant that mourning had to be observed at Court and copious amounts of black crêpe appeared, at times seeming rather excessive to those around who could not understand the depth of grief experienced by Albert and Victoria. The Duke had not been a loving father. Having divorced his wife, his children were rendered motherless while he continued his debauched life in the seedier parts of large cities and, when Albert married Victoria, he had even asked her for money as a settlement.

Prince Albert was not particularly close to his father and Queen Victoria, even though he was her uncle, hardly knew him. The new

Duke, Albert's brother, was not in the same mould as Albert, having already copied his father's lifestyle. However, both Albert and Victoria cried incessantly at Duke Ernest's passing. Maybe this episode, as described in a letter from Victoria to Uncle Leopold, gives clues to the future attitude of Queen Victoria to the loss of those nearest to her:

GOD has *heavily* AFFLICTED *us*; we feel *crushed*, OVERWHELMED, *bowed down* by the loss of one who was so deservedly LOVED, I may say adored by his children and family … his like we shall not see again; … The violence of our grief may be over. I have never known real grief till now … And indeed one loves to cling to one's grief … if you knew the sacrifice I make in letting Albert to go … I have never been separated from him even for one night, and the thought of such a separation is quite dreadful …

Chloroform and Outrage

After the birth of Prince Arthur in 1850 there followed a break of nearly three years before the birth of another baby. This was Prince Leopold, a fourth son, born in April 1853. For the Queen, Leopold's birth was significant because it was the first delivery during which she took chloroform.

Even after seven deliveries the Queen still found childbirth extremely painful and was not looking forward to another. From 1842 doctors had been using the inhalation of ether as a form of anaesthetic for surgery and tooth extractions. Until then the pain of labour had had to be endured by women, without drugs for pain relief. In 1847, Dr James Simpson, in Edinburgh, had realized the positive use of ether to relieve pain but was concerned at its effect on the throats of patients. Experiments were being done by other doctors who themselves inhaled chloroform and found it relieved pain without hurting the throat. Dr Simpson then used it on a woman in labour and was impressed by the way it reduced her pain.

Three years later, in 1853, Queen Victoria decided to have chloroform administered during her eighth labour. There was a public outcry, with religious moralists arguing that a woman's pain in childbirth could only make her into a better mother. Within the medical profession itself there was lengthy debate and argument. *The Lancet*, in which its founder Thomas Wakley had always campaigned for safety and improvements in medical procedures, argued that the use of chloroform had led to deaths, indeed it was much later found to be toxic to the liver, and should not be used. *The British Medical Journal*, in contrast, opposed *The Lancet* and was in favour of anything that could alleviate pain. The journal described to its readers how the substance had

A LETTER FROM WRITTEN BY VICTORIA DISCUSSING THE USE OF CHLOROFORM, DECEMBER 21, 1859.

During the last hour of the LABOUR a small quantity of CHLOROFORM was placed on to a *handkerchief* for her to inhale, she was never unconscious but received an appropriate amount to relieve her of the pain of "the most agonizing trials of humanity."

The Queen's use of analgesia in childbirth brought into the open the trauma suffered by women. She herself was undeterred by the outcry and used chloroform again in her last delivery, that of Princess Beatrice on April 14, 1857. "*Anaesthesia à la Reine*", as it became known, was now used widely. So public was the knowledge of the Queen's use of chloroform that Charles Dickens mentioned it in his essay, "The Best Authority", published in *Household Words* in June 1857. Elizabeth Longford, Victoria's biographer, states that "It might well be claimed that Queen Victoria's greatest gift to her people was a refusal to accept pain in childbirth as woman's divinely appointed destiny." In Edinburgh, the Simpson Memorial Maternity Pavilion still remains in honour of Dr Simpson's pioneering work.

Haemophilia

Prince Leopold was always a weak and sickly child and his parents worried greatly about him. At times they were irritated by his clumsiness, found the numerous times he fell over quite trying and put his screaming down to a bad temper. As he grew he fell, sprained limbs, bruised more easily and screamed more often than most children. By the time he was four he had become embarrassed at his falling and getting into trouble with his parents, who would sometimes hit him as punishment for his behaviour. Stiffening of his joints meant that sometimes he was unable to walk after a fall.

Although his parents and those around him

SIR EDWIN LANDSEER'S
PORTRAIT OF
PRINCE LEOPOLD.

were worried by Leopold, their early concern was more for his behaviour than for any physiological problems he might have. It was not until he was six years old that the ghastly spectre of haemophilia was raised. At the time, haemophilia was a little understood disease, only having been studied during the previous twenty years and mainly in Germany. This potentially life-threatening disease, which renders the blood system incapable of clotting, is caused by an inherited defective chromosome which in 1853 had manifested itself in the Royal Family.

Modern genetic research has told us that haemophilia is carried on the x chromosome, one of a pair which determines sex and females can be carriers although only males suffer from it. A female carrier stands a fifty per cent chance of passing it to her children, either to her son as sufferer or daughter as carrier. Research suggests that Queen Victoria herself introduced it by a mutation in her own cell structure as there is no sign of it in her ancestry. All that was known about haemophilia in the mid-nineteenth century was that it was hereditary, and that girls did not get it but seemed to pass it on to their sons. Charlotte Zeepvat in her biography of Prince Leopold say that Queen Victoria was kept ignorant of this devastating news as her daughters were approaching marriageable age, but Prince Albert may have been told. Victoria and Albert's daughters did, indeed, unwittingly introduce haemophilia into the ruling families of Europe.

For Victoria and Albert, the shock of discovering what was wrong with their son, and the long-term prognosis, was devastating. Its effects on their family in the ensuing generations would be drastic. By 1860 the future for any haemophiliac boy was bleak, with a fifty per cent chance of his dying before he was ten, and only a small chance of his surviving into adulthood. Caring for the haemophiliac, in this age before blood clotting treatments, was also very problematic; bleeding could be life threatening and had to be controlled by tight bandaging, but the real danger was in falling and incurring damage to the internal organs, which could be fatal.

Queen Victoria found it hard to come to

A DRAWING BY QUEEN VICTORIA OF A SCENE FROM "THE TRAGEDY OF ATHALIE".

terms with her son's illness and at times would still be angry with him for falling or limping. He was the most intelligent of all her sons and outshone his eldest brother, the Prince of Wales, but her disappointment that her child could be anything but perfect was enormous. When the cold of winter was too much for him his parents agreed that he should spend time abroad, and even as a young boy he would travel to the South of France accompanied by a tutor to oversee his education and help him exercise and get strong. Accommodating his illness and intellectual needs were complex operations but Leopold did grow up, marry and have two children of his own.

The effect of haemophilia within Victoria and Albert's immediate family was devastating and its repercussions lasted for generations. Of their nine children, Prince Leopold was a sufferer and his daughter a carrier, and both Princess Alice and Princess Beatrice were carriers. Princess Alice had seven children, born during her marriage to Louis IV, Grand Duke of Hesse-Darmstadt; two daughters were carriers and one son a sufferer. Alix, the younger of the two daughters, married Tsar Nicholas II of Russia; their son, Alexis was crippled by haemophilia and it is not known if any of the four daughters was a carrier as the entire family was shot during the Russian Revolution in 1918.

Princess Beatrice had two haemophiliac sons

and one daughter, Victoria Eugénie, who was a carrier. Victoria Eugénie married King Alfonso of Spain and of their five sons, one died in early infancy, possibly of haemophilia, and Alfonso and Gonzalo died, as a result of it, in young adulthood. Thus, in total, Queen Victoria and Prince Albert had seven grandchildren who were either haemophiliacs or carriers.

Family Life

Despite the rigours and disruptions of pregnancy, their rapidly expanding family brought security and joy to Victoria and Albert and a model for the increasing ranks of the middle classes to emulate. Aided by developments in printing and photography and the rise of the popular press, news of the royal family was constantly published in newspapers and journals, making them the first royals to be photographed and to live their lives publicly; sometimes this could be detrimental to them as the public caught glimpses of the rich style in which they lived. Victoria and Albert also commissioned many regal, family and individual portraits from the great artists of the day and others to adorn the walls of the family home.

For Victoria, producing nine children in seventeen years would in the future make her the matriarch of the royal houses of Europe as her children, grandchildren and great grandchildren married across the continent: an increase in British power and influence achieved without any bloodshed or conflict, but overshadowed by the threat of haemophilia. But a growing family, and the staff needed to support it, required space and by 1843 they were feeling constrained by the limitations of the accommodation at Buckingham Palace and Windsor.

Parliament was asked for an increase in the Civil List to extend and change the buildings. This did not help their popularity at a time when many people in Britain were affected by a cotton slump and Ireland was seeing the beginnings of the potato famine. It was not until 1846 that Parliament agreed to give Victoria £20,000 for improvements to Buckingham Palace, where nurseries and schoolrooms had to be found and changes made to the sanitary arrangements, following Edwin Chadwick's report on public health.

The Queen's own living accommodation was always a mix of the lavish and cosy for she was a prolific hoarder. Pictures of her rooms show her sitting among a myriad paintings and photographs, sculptures and ornaments. In later life she would spend time cataloguing her possessions. She was also developing her own, feminine style of dress, with lots of flounces and pleats and, in private, she wore dressing gowns of flimsy ruched material. Her love of bonnets was legendary as she wore them in all colours for different occasions. Often it would appear that Albert had become taller and more suave as his wife grew plumper and her clothes flouncier.

The Queen and Prince Albert often gave each other specially commissioned paintings and photographs for their wedding anniversaries, birthdays and at Christmas, and the children would make things for their parents. Balls would be held for special birthdays and tables were always set out to display gifts. While Henry Cole, a friend of Prince Albert at the Society of Arts, had designed the first Christmas card in 1843, the decorated Christmas tree, while popular in Germany, was rare in Britain. In the mid-1840s Prince Albert introduced a conifer tree at Christmas, to be decorated with candles and trinkets, and thus started a new, fashionable, trend in Britain.

The family's Christmas dinner would consist of roast turkey, goose and beef. By 1860, when children and grandchildren celebrated together, the kitchen staff would be busy preparing food in vast quantities, not only for the family but for the household as well. Up to fifty turkeys and a baron of beef weighing 350lbs (160kg) would be roasted on large spits over an open fire and "Windsor Mincemeat" was made containing 82lb (37kg) of currants, 60lb (27kg) of orange and lemon peel and 24 bottles of brandy.

A typical Christmas dinner, influenced by the influx of French chefs into Britain in the 1840s, included Roast Turkey à l'Anglaise – a turkey stuffed with seasoned veal, trussed and covered with streaky bacon, wrapped in buttered paper and spit roasted – served with stewed chestnuts, pork sausages and sauce, accompanied by turnips, sprouts and tomatoes. Goose à l'Estouffade might also be served: a stuffed goose pan-fried in a lavish amount of butter with parsley, onions, celery, carrots and sherry. Desert would be plum pudding served with German custard sauce.

The kitchens at Windsor and Buckingham Palace were enormous to cope with such vast family meals, state banquets and the feeding of the staff. One of Her Majesty's servants described the kitchen at Windsor:

THE ROYAL FAMILY GATHERING AROUND THE CHRISTMAS TREE IN 1848. FROM *THE ILLUSTRATED LONDON NEWS* CHRISTMAS SUPPLEMENT.

The first effect that strikes the eye on entering is that made by some hundred brilliantly burnished coppers, each of different shape and all as big as a sponge bath. They are hung round the walls, and blaze like a million suns through a sulphurous London fog.

The next object that claims admiration is the enormous "dishing-up" table, which is a good deal larger than the gardens of many suburban houses …there is ample elbow-room for the army of white-capped and aproned men-cooks who bustle about, as also for six meat-chopping blocks, each as big as a good-sized dining table.

A large, open fire was used to roast the huge side of beef for Christmas dinner and for poultry and game especially for the Queen. In the middle of the room a large steel table stood, with hollow legs into which steam was pumped in order to heat the top; this acted as a hot food server for the quantities of dishes needed. Later, gas stoves were introduced on which the chef would cook the main meals, while the pastry cooks worked in another kitchen, vegetables were prepared in the "green room" and desserts were made by confectioners in another kitchen. The whole enterprise was like a huge army operation as feet trundled backwards and forwards, metal clashed, heat and steam billowed and mouthwatering smells hung in the air. As the reign progressed, advances in preservation techniques – salting, canning and refrigeration – meant that foods were brought from all over the Empire to feed the Queen, her family and Britain.

The small woman at the heart of all these preparations enjoyed her food but was often distraught at her billowing size and would try, usually in vain, to reduce it by cutting down on her consumption of quantities of pastries and beer.

New Family Homes

To go away from home and enjoy oneself was something unheard of, except for the upper classes who went on Grand Tours around Europe or to house parties, until the development of the railways and Mr Thomas Cook's excursions. For centuries, monarchs had gone on "progresses", when the entire court and household would go from one large house or castle to another, often staying for a few months at a time. In this way the sovereign could be seen by the people.

In 1842 Queen Victoria and Prince Albert decided to visit Scotland. As the train line was only opened part of the way, most of the journey had to be completed in the old yacht, the *Royal George*, accompanied by two paddle steamers, making a journey of three days. When the party finally arrived, the people in Scotland were delighted by her visit as few from the south ventured so far north. Queen Victoria was the first sovereign, apart from her uncle George IV, since the Stuarts to spend time there.

The royal couple stayed in the Highlands, to which they instantly took a great liking; Victoria loved the freedom and openness, the fresh air and colour, while for Prince Albert the countryside was reminiscent of his beloved Thuringia, covered in fir trees and with a similar rough terrain. This time, they did not stay long, but later visits would cause both Victoria and Albert quickly to develop a great fondness for Scotland, especially as the people seemed friendly and relaxed away from the bustle of London. When they returned to England they found that the British public were showing their displeasure at the sovereign's absence in Chartist demonstrations.

Undeterred, the following year they went to the Isle of Wight, which Queen Victoria had visited with her mother in the 1830s, when she

had enjoyed playing in the sea, walking along the narrow lanes and revelling in the general relaxed atmosphere of the island. On this visit, Victoria and Albert put plans into motion to buy an estate with a ramshackle house called Osborne.

Whereas Scotland reminded Albert of Germany, the Isle of Wight was reminiscent of the Mediterranean; together he and Victoria would recreate here both Thuringia and cultured Italy for their family. Here, at a relatively short distance from London and Windsor, they would be able to have the privacy to relax and enjoy what they perceived as a "normal" family life with their children, away from the pressures and constraints of court life at Buckingham Palace and Windsor Castle. But first they had to secure the finances themselves; the Government had given money for improvements to Buckingham Palace but would not support such luxurious, personal investments as two country retreats.

Osborne

The Osborne estate belonged to Lady Isabella Blachford, who put it on the market for the amount of £30,000 in February 1844. Victoria, once again pregnant, left the negotiations and pre-purchase visits to Prince Albert, who proved to be a tough businessman. They both quickly realized that the existing house was too small for their family; it contained sixteen bedrooms, much too small for the family, court and guests, and would have to be extended or demolished and a larger one built. Albert, now very friendly with the leading designers and builders in London, was eager for his own building project and had in mind a large villa overlooking Cowes bay and with the Solent beyond: his own version of the Bay of Naples, in fact. Designers and clients who had made the grand tour to Italy greatly influenced Victorian architecture, introducing clean lines, colonnades, pillars and arches into villas and squares.

At the same time, Queen Victoria decided to liquidate some of her capital; she loathed the Pavilion at Brighton, which had been built by George IV. On her visit in 1837 she had found

BOATS CROSSING TO THE ISLE OF WIGHT.

the oriental style of its architecture and furnishings too extravagant and flamboyant for her taste. Its presence had helped Brighton to become a thriving and sophisticated holiday resort but now, as buildings were constructed around it, the Pavilion no longer had a view of the sea. Queen Victoria decided to close it up and sell the contents, the proceeds of which went towards the purchase of the 200 acres at Osborne. When, in 1850, she suggested demolishing the Pavilion, the inhabitants of Brighton protested and it was purchased for the town at a cost of £60,000. Osborne was bought from the Queen's own funds, not from public money.

Negotiations were under way for the purchase of Osborne, but rather than pay the full asking price they agreed with Lady Isabella to rent the property for one year at a cost of £1000 and then buy it for the reduced sum of £28,000. By October 1844, they had moved in. Victoria was delighted with her new, cosy home which she described to Uncle Leopold in glowing terms as "a very comfortable little house, and the grounds and place are delightful, so private – and the view so fine."

But it was also cramped and the kitchens were not large enough; the pastry cooks had to use the ovens of the baker at East Cowes, nearby. Over the following months, plans were considered for changes and extensions to the house, but eventually it was decided that it would be cheaper to demolish the existing house and start again. Victoria and Albert also decided to buy more land surrounding the estate in order to have farms to make the whole thing more economical. In the end, they owned 1,500 acres on the Isle of Wight.

To the annoyance of the recently formed Royal Institute of British Architects, the Queen and Prince Albert did not employ an architect for the design of their project but the master-builder, Thomas Cubitt. Cubitt was a Victorian entrepreneur, responsible for vast areas of elegant housing in central London and Brighton. By introducing the concept of speculative building he was able to lay out whole streets and squares upon which his houses were built. His other innovation was to employ all the trades and professions himself, making it a complete package.

Cubitt's grand, huge terraces of white stucco homes in Belgravia, Pimlico and Clapham in London, on land owned by the Duke of Westminster, and in Kemp Town in Brighton are still elegant and sought-after properties. By the time he was employed to work at Osborne, Cubitt was well-known and respected for his knowledge, courtesy and ability to build on a grand scale. Prince Albert's desire to create a Mediterranean retreat was not unusual, as the Italian classical was quickly becoming a highly fashionable architectural style for the mid-nine-

courtyard; the Pavilion, the main part, was a three-storey building with large windows and a flag pole on the top overlooking the bay. From the Pavilion, the Grand Corridor led to the Household Wing.

Trying to emulate the Italians, the house had flat roofs, and squat, almost Venetian-type towers with simple arched windows. In Italy, windows in houses were small to keep out the heat and sun; here in dark, cold northern Europe they were made large to let in the maximum amount of light and gave fantastic vistas of the

DESIGN FOR AN INTERIOR WALL AT OSBORNE BY W.H HOMANN.

teenth century, the houses of the upper classes being echoed in the new suburbs where villas were swiftly built by property developers trying to emulate Cubitt's success.

Work began quickly to renovate some of the cottages on the Osborne estate for members of the household and plans began on the main house, which had to include state rooms, private apartments, children's rooms and kitchens as well as heating and sewage systems. Queen Victoria laid the foundation stone of the new building on June 23, 1845, and building then began in earnest. Cubitt oversaw the work and bricks were made on site; carpentry and metal work were made in London and brought down to the Isle of Wight. The house was built around a

sea and estate around. In order to look even more Italian the house, though built of brick, was rendered in sand-coloured cement to make it look like Bath stone. Portland stone was used in the main entrance hall. Cubitt was determined to make the building fireproof and made the skirtings out of cement and not wood, and the wooden floors rest on metal and brick. A central heating system was incorporated as the open fires would not have been sufficient to heat such a building; pipes were placed beneath the ground floor and were filled with hot water and the warm air thus generated passed through grilles and flues to heat the rooms.

The huge hallway and landings to the upper floors contained a magnificent and elegant staircase to please Queen Victoria. She had stressed how much she liked the huge staircase at Claremont, which had been Uncle Leopold's home while he lived in England. Albert had asked Cubitt to copy it exactly and in March 1846 it was installed in the Pavilion.

The Queen, now pregnant with her fifth child, Helena, was delighted with it all. She was also anxious to get it finished as people were already suggesting they would visit and stay. Others living nearby, like Queen Adelaide lived at Norris Castle, also hinted that they would visit. House parties were already being planned. The Queen was certainly going to have plenty of splendidly-decorated space for them all.

As the house took shape decorators moved in to paint. Designs for the Grand Corridor were created by Prince Albert, and Ludwig Gruner from Dresden in Germany was called in to emulate Italian Renaissance decoration. The delicate blues and oranges, with simple geometric patterns in reds, dark blues and gold, along the cornices gave a feeling of height and airiness and took over ten years to complete. At the entrance to the Grand Corridor a tiled floor designed by Matthew Digby Wyatt and manufactured by Minton, greeted the visitor with the Latin word *Salve(*Greetings). Along the corridors, arched niches were made, which over the years provided space for numerous statues of Victoria and Albert and their children. As the Privy Council had to meet here and the Queen receive official visits, a Council Room and Audience Room were built in the main wing, accessible from the Pavilion via the Grand Corridor.

In the Pavilion the three main rooms were inter-linked to provide a billiard room, drawing room and dining room. Each was lavishly decorated with marbled pillars, floral friezes and coloured borders. From the huge main window of the drawing room Albert's vision of the Bay of Naples was complete as the vista down the gentle slope and across the bay and the Solent towards Portsmouth, which was then a small town, came into view. From here, Victoria could watch her naval ships leave the harbour and see them at anchor at Spithead.

Many paintings, which they both bought and commissioned, were hung in the rooms; on Queen Victoria's thirtieth birthday in 1849, a vast painting of the family by Winterhalter was hung on the dining room wall. The large dining table could accommodate family and guests and heavy sideboards were used for laying out and serving the food. Usually, if the weather was good, breakfast was taken outside on the terrace, and all other meals in the dining room. The billiard room contained an enormous table with "marble" painted legs and a frieze and lamp above, all designed by Prince Albert. This room was used as the gentlemen's retiring room, although Queen Victoria would often play billiards there with members of the Household.

Upstairs, suites of rooms provided accommodation for the expanding family, with nurseries, bedrooms and schoolrooms and a kitchen specifically for the children. Small armchairs and tables were commissioned and brought here. Victoria had her own sitting room, where Albert also had his desk, and a dressing room; Albert also had a dressing and writing room and separate bathroom. Edwin Chadwick's report on sanitary conditions led Prince Albert

A FAMILY PHOTOGRAPH AT OSBORNE IN 1850.

THE CHILDREN'S SWISS COTTAGE AT OSBORNE.

to look at lavatories and running water in the house. Water closets had been used but had to be emptied daily. Wanting to avoid this, Albert decided to instruct Cubitt to build a drain to take the waste out to sea. Later, Prince Albert had other ideas to build cess pits and use the waste for fertilizer in the fields. Bathrooms were new and they each had a deep, rectangular copper bath painted to resemble white marble. Albert's bathroom also had a shower and a water closet Queen Victoria's WC was hidden in a huge cupboard in her dressing room. All their rooms contained pictures of the children and even plaster casts of their babies' feet. The Queen's bedroom, which she shared with Albert, contained their large bed, couches and chairs and more of their painting collection. The letters V and A were entwined and carved above each door.

The family finally moved into the completed Pavilion in September 1846. In his serious, Germanic manner, Prince Albert blessed it with a prayer by Martin Luther. They were all entranced at everything so very new; by 1851 all remnants of the old house had disappeared and the new wings were completed. Queen Victoria loved Osborne and spent much of the following fifty-five years there, but others found the building ugly and the interior stuffy and claustrophobic.

ALFRED, LORD TENNYSON BY JULIA MARGARET CAMERON.

Royal patronage of the Isle of Wight helped it to become a fashionable holiday retreat for many, as villas and houses were built in the countryside. The Poet Laureate, Alfred, Lord Tennyson, purchased a house at Farringford in Freshwater Bay, and the photographer, Julia Margaret Cameron, lived opposite. Tennyson, whose poetry was much admired by Queen Victoria, was a regular guest at Osborne.

For the Victorians, sea bathing became very fashionable, especially once the railways had made getting to the seaside so easy. In 1847 Queen Victoria tried sea bathing for the first time, when for modesty's sake, a bathing machine was built especially for her. She would enter it and undress, then the machine was rolled down into the sea for her "to swim", which was, in fact, more of a paddle. The children, under their father's direction, did learn to swim in the sea.

Gradually, over the years, Osborne changed; lifts were installed, a new wing – the Durbar Room – was added in 1890 and more of the trappings and clutter of family life brought in until it seemed to be filled to overflowing. In the grounds, Victoria and Albert truly indulged themselves on behalf of their children when, in 1850, they began work on a Swiss cottage as a playhouse for them.

Built on a scale slightly smaller than full size, the Swiss Cottage measured 25 x 50 feet (approx 8 x 15 metres) and was constructed of logs, like similar cottages in Coburg. The Queen and Prince Albert wanted it to be of educational value to the children to encourage them to learn about farming, housekeeping and the lives of ordinary people. Prince Albert, still a keen naturalist, also wanted them to build a museum of nature and one room in the cottage soon contained samples of rocks. Unlike the rock collections of other children, the Royal children's were acquired from around the Empire. The cottage was equipped with a kitchen and dining room in which were alpine-style furniture and china tea sets. Outside, a miniature fort was built by the children in the 1850s.

Balmoral

In 1845 Prince Albert took his wife for a holiday to the Schloss Rosenau for the first time. Here, she could see where he had grown up, which would be important in the planning of their second holiday home at Balmoral in Scotland. In Bonn, en route to Coburg, they enjoyed a rare musical treat, when they heard Jenny Lind sing in a concert conducted by Franz Liszt.

The building of railway lines up the east and west coasts of Britain made the idea of a Scottish retreat possible. In 1848 they finally agreed on the purchase of a small, rundown, fifteenth-century castle, Balmoral, on the River Dee near Blair Atholl where they had stayed during their second visit to Scotland in 1845. By 1852 they had found the finances to buy it. As at Osborne, plans were immediately put in place to demolish the castle and build a new one. The Balmoral estate comprised 11,000 acres of hills and forests inhabited by numerous tenant farmers living in isolated cottages and by deer and other game for hunting – another of Prince Albert's delights.

Prince Albert decided to use a local architect for this project. John Smith, who had made initial changes to the castle for Sir Robert Gordon, its previous owner, was commissioned but he died soon afterwards and his place was taken by his son William Smith, City Architect and Superintendent of Work in Aberdeen. The castle had to have accommodation for the household and court, guests and state rooms, as well as private apartments. A trained architect who had travelled in Europe, Smith, like Cubitt at Osborne, worked well with Albert, recognizing his visions and putting them into practice.

The site was chosen close to the original castle to make the most of the views along the valleys and up into the mountains. Prince Albert's ideas for Balmoral were undoubtedly influenced by the Rosenau; he made sketches from which William Smith drew up the plans for the building. With its facades of castellations, turrets and apex roofs and its fabric of white granite stone, Balmoral was redolent of the Rosenau and Thuringia. Work began on the site in spring 1853 and the foundation stone was laid in the following September.

Problems arose with the workmen, who camped in wooden huts around the site which caught fire. The work was very physically hard, and the builders went on strike on numerous occasions. After the fire, Victoria and Albert immediately recompensed them for their lost possessions and ordered new accommodation to be built. As Balmoral took shape, Victoria referred to it as "paradise" and viewed it as all

THE ROYAL FAMILY IN THEIR OWN RAILWAY CARRIAGE, C.1848.

A VIEW OF BALMORAL IN 1880.

the creation of Prince Albert – for her, his talents were boundless. However, others had helped create this wonder, not only William Smith, but also master craftsmen and stone masons, plumbers, bell hangers and even Mr Cubitt from London, who supplied the baths. All the granite used in the building came from the estate and the roof slates from a quarry at Strathbogie. Around the gables, above the windows, coats of arms were placed, not only those of Victoria and Albert but also some from Saxe-Coburg and Gotha and the crests of England and Scotland. In 1855 the family was able to move in, but the household still had to live in the old house until the rest of the new castle was finished. Queen Victoria described their arrival:

SEPTEMBER 7 1855. At a *quarter past* SEVEN o'clock we *arrived* at dear BALMORAL … The new house looks beautiful … An old shoe was thrown after us into the house, for good luck, when we entered the hall. The house is charming; the rooms delightful; the furniture, papers, everything perfection.

When she returned to Balmoral a year later, "On arriving at Balmoral … we found the tower finished as well as the offices gone! the effect of the whole is very fine."

Once the building was completed, plans for the grounds were put under way. A public road passed through the estate and, foreseeing public interest in their presence, especially as carriages could now be hired in nearby Ballater, Prince Albert decided to alter the course of the road. By enacting the Highways Act of 1835, he succeeded in detouring the road along the south bank of the Dee and built a bridge across it at Crathie, making this the entrance to the estate. Poplars and roses were planted just like those at the Rosenau and gradually plans were put in place to modernize the outdated farm buildings and build a dairy.

At Balmoral Victoria and Albert firmly embraced everything Scottish; she read and enjoyed the works of Sir Walter Scott including **The Heart of Midlothian**, **The Bride of Lammermoor** and the **Waverley** novels. Scott, the early nineteenth-century novelist and poet, wrote prolifically and his work epitomized the ruggedness, harshness and beauties of Scotland.

He recounted fascinating stories, some clearly influenced by eighteenth-century German literature, and he in turn influenced the Brontë sisters and George Eliot.

Lodges were built along the riverside for fishing and hunting and cottages rebuilt for the ghillies who would accompany them on their treks. They enjoyed the sounds of bagpipes serenading them. But it was the furnishings that proved the most remarkable aspect, combining the influences of Thuringia and Scotland. Prince Albert, by now on a roller coaster of creativity, had designed family tartans: not only did he and their sons wear tartan kilts and his wife and daughters tartan dresses but the walls of many rooms at Balmoral were covered in it. Often they would start on treks in what Victoria referred to as "'Highland state' – Albert in Royal Stewart plaid and I and the girls in skirts of the same."

Days and nights were spent in the hills accompanied by family and friends and often by an experienced ghillie, John Brown, who attended Prince Albert. They trekked and the men went shooting deer and game, parties drove along the rivers and up the mountains, they popped in to see the tenant farmers to watch as the women coped with looking after maybe nine children in a tiny cottage. There were picnic parties, during which Queen Victoria developed her watercolour techniques, producing many fine landscapes of the estate. She wrote enlightening accounts of their pursuits in her diary, which she named "The Highland Journal". Sometimes, even as early in the year as September they encountered snow, but no matter how inclement the weather Victoria thoroughly enjoyed it.

The Prime Minister, Lord John Russell, assumed they would tire of Scotland, finding it too isolated even for their tastes, but he was quickly proved wrong. Both began to find the Scottish Presbyterianism to their liking, especially Albert to whom it was more akin to the teachings of Martin Luther; an attitude endorsed by his wife. Queen Victoria, mistakenly, assumed that she was head of the Church of Scotland, but no one corrected her until some years later. They enjoyed their relaxed life at Balmoral, with the Queen travelling around talking to local people and even popping in to see her tenants in their cottages. Security was at a minimum as Victoria and Albert enjoyed what they assumed was "normal" life.

At Allt-na-Guinhsaich, isolated in the hills, they found two ghillies' huts which they made into one, a covered walkway linking them. In one the Queen and Prince Albert would stay, and in the other their servants, as they retreated further from the world. It was here in 1852 that, two days after the event, Queen Victoria received news of the death of the Duke of Wellington and went into mourning for him.

Surrounding castles and estates were occupied by friends and relations; Deeside had become an upper-class playground. However, as at Osborne, members of her government and

PRINCESS LOUISE (LEFT) AND PRINCESS HELENA, WEARING TARTAN, PHOTOGRAPHED BY ROGER FENTON AT BALMORAL IN 1855.

Court who had to visit, loathed the place, finding it desolate, cramped and a long way from anywhere. Nevertheless, for Victoria and Albert it was the achievement of their own, idyllic kingdom.

Chapter 7 The Mid-Century

The new decade saw a monarch confident in her role. Acceptance of her husband was more widespread, particularly within the circle of designers and industrialists who were making their mark on the century and to which he contributed. In sharp contrast to their own childhoods, Victoria and Albert were at the centre of an expanding and happy family, whom they doted on. In their public lives, the occasional attempt on their lives by single assassins or the threats to their position from the Chartists and their rallies, were nothing compared to the bloodshed and dangerous instabilities experienced by many of their European contemporaries.

In 1850, thirteen years after her accession, Queen Victoria was the mother of seven children. The births of Prince Leopold in 1853 and Princess Beatrice in 1857 had completed the family during the decade. But already the older children were growing up and demanding more of their parents' attention and Victoria was made unhappy by having so little time to spend with her husband. Bertie's behaviour was already problematic and as the decade progressed he caused his parents, particularly Albert, much anguish because of his choice of friends and his lack of interest in learning. The Princess Royal, however, was always a joy to both her parents — especially to her father.

For Prince Albert, this was the decade in which he proved himself to the nation and, in the long term, made his greatest contribution to it. He was constantly working on new and numerous projects, not only overseeing the building of Balmoral and putting the finishing touches to Osborne, but as a working and influential president of various committees, most notably the Society of Arts. His interest in design and architecture, science and nature, housing and health was much admired and he made friendships with the leading entrepre-

neurs, engineers and designers of the age, as he had always wanted to do, so intent was he on improving the lives of individuals. Albert continued to work hard and was often ill — the result of a combination of his weak constitution and his serious, perhaps over-conscientious temperament — but to Victoria it seemed nothing was unachievable by him.

This was Queen Victoria's "Heyday", as the post-Victorian writer, J. B. Priestley, called it, the decade in which she established her position as matriarch of her family and of the nation. It was also, for her, the pinnacle of her marriage to Prince Albert, when she felt secure and confident.

Nation and Empire

The expanding Empire and the advances of the industrial revolution had made Britain leader of the world at the mid-century. In the remarkable decade of the 1850s lay the essence of the Victorian era. The railways continued to weave networks across the country and the major industries of cotton, wool and steel manufacture, shipbuilding and coal mining brought new opportunities for entrepreneurs, ready and eager to adapt, develop and market every new technical innovation. Developments in photography and telegraphy changed the way news was reported, and the age of the mass, popular journal arrived. Literature and the arts moved into new areas, tackling subjects once ignored or little considered.

The mid-century also witnessed an enormous and permanent shift in population in Britain. Where in 1801 only twenty-two per cent had been urban dwellers, by 1851 the proportion was now fifty per cent. The total population of the United Kingdom and Ireland was 27.3

OPPOSITE: QUEEN VICTORIA AND PRINCE ALBERT AT THE OPENING OF THE GREAT EXHIBITION.

million. Figures from the 1851 Census included:

Royalty, baronets and squires		53,000
Senior doctors and other professionals		20,000
Paupers, vagrants, prisoners and lunatics		1,900,000
Domestic servants	134,000 m	905,000 f
Cotton workers	255,000 m	272,000 f
Seamster/ress (inc milliners)	494 m	340,000 f
Coal miners	216,000 m	3,000 f
Printers	22,000 m	106 f

At the beginning of the decade, Lord John Russell was still Prime Minister. Lord Palmerston was Foreign Secretary, intent on pursuing policies independent of the Crown's wishes, particularly in Germany, so that Queen Victoria at the outset detested him. Palmerston and, therefore, Britain opposed her and Albert's wishes for the governance of Schleswig-Holstein in 1848 and the moves towards the unification of the German states. The plans for the Princess Royal to marry the son of King Frederick II of Prussia were underway and her parents did not want them jeopardized. On December 3, 1850, she wrote to Uncle Leopold about the situation in Germany, condemning Palmerston's role in it:

The *state* of GERMANY is indeed a *very anxious one*. It is a *mistake* to think the SUPREMACY of PRUSSIA is what is *wished* for. General Radowitz himself says that what is necessary for Germany [is] that she should take the lead ... Unless this be done in a moderate and determined way, a fearful reaction will take place, which will overturn thrones; Prussia is the only large. ... and really German Power there is, and therefore she must take the lead ... Unfortunately, Lord Palmerston, had contrived to make us so hated by all parties abroad, that we have lost ... our influence, ... which ought to have been immense ... This is what pains and grieves me ...

Palmerston eventually resigned a year later, partly because of reaction to his incivility towards the Queen and partly because of his failure to keep Crown and Cabinet informed of his activities. Queen Victoria was much relieved.

Early in the decade Queen Victoria mourned the deaths of Sir Robert Peel, who died, unexpectedly and tragically, after falling from his horse in 1850, and of the Duke of Wellington, who died in 1852. Wellington was given a State Funeral, reserved for national heroes, which his victory at Waterloo in 1815 had certainly made him. As women at that time did not attend funerals, Queen Victoria watched the cortège pass by Buckingham Palace from the new balcony at the front.

THE FUNERAL CARRIAGE OF THE DUKE OF WELLINGTON.

THE NEWLY OPENED ST PANCRAS STATION AND HOTEL.

Benjamin Disraeli, who had entered Parliament in 1837, the year of the Queen's accession, and had headed the radical "Young England" group of Tories, had become leader of the Conservatives in the House of Commons and in the General Election of 1852 the Whig administration of Lord John Russell was defeated but formed a coalition with the Peelite section of the Conservative Party, under Lord Aberdeen.

The Railway Revolution

In 1852 there were 6,600 miles of railway track criss-crossing Britain. The main routes, emanating from London, went south to the Channel, up the west and east coasts and into Scotland, and out to the west country; many smaller branch lines led off them.

Each town or city required a railway station, which prompted great architectural debate. Opinions varied about whether these great buildings be equivalent in scale to the great cathedrals of the past or designed and built in the classical tradition. Others felt the influence of the Italian Renaissance or the northern European gothic tradition, were more suitable.

The great railway entrepreneurs tried them all.

In London, Euston Station, designed in 1839 by Philip Hardwick, had been given an enormous Grecian-style pediment and columns, redolent of the Parthenon, at its entrance; in Newcastle, John Dobson, between 1846 and 1855, designed and built a station based on Italian classical architecture with arches and colonnades, and with a curved roof – the first of its kind – to cover all the platforms. In the next decade, George Gilbert Scott and the engineer W. H. Barlow chose splendid Victorian gothic for St Pancras Station. Built in 1868 with a hotel at the front, St Pancras was a red brick building with great turrets and pointed arched windows and a ticket hall resembling a chapel; the train shed of metal and glass was, at the time, the largest ever built.

Railway stations had to be built quickly and for many different purposes; they needed to be enormous structures to accommodate goods storage, passenger platforms, storage of coal for the engines, maintenance areas and sidings. Using the new possibilities of working in metal and glass, great shed-like structures were built over the platforms and tracks, while in the front, passenger terminal design was left for the architect to continue the debate of classical versus gothic. Sometimes the metal and glass structures became important elements in their own right, making the use of new materials and techniques obvious in the end result, as at Paddington in West London where Brunel was not afraid to expose his great, fin-like structure over the platform. He used metal in fine formations, creating a landmark building for the future.

Out in the country, track layers used the Roman aqueduct as a basis for their design, spanning valleys with long viaducts, which carried the lines over a series of arches and on to their destinations. Bridge design also had to be considered because many rivers, canals and other waterways, from the great, like the Tamar between Devon and Cornwall, to the small had to be crossed.

The writers of the age quickly picked up the idea of the railway journey as a metaphor for romance or escape to a better or different lifestyle. In *Villette*, Charlotte Brontë described the railway journey through England to London and on to Brussels as her heroine escaped to a very different life of unrequited love. But for many young girls, the railways epitomised leaving home and poverty to escape to the drudgery – but reflected glamour – of domestic service in a large house.

There were disadvantages, of course. The railways brought even more dirt to towns and cities already polluted by the smoke from factory chimneys and domestic coal fires. Steam engines were run on coal and men stood behind the driver stoking the fires as the trains sped along, great plumes of smoke, steam and ash billowing out of their funnels, all of which helped to create thick, heavy fogs. In 1853 a Smoke Abatement Act was passed for the Metropolitan Area in an attempt to control the air quality in the capital.

Working on the railways was hard, dirty and dangerous. The trains travelled fast, at 30mph, which gave many what they thought was the sensation of flying. But tracks, engines and carriages could be unsafe and Michael Freeman describes the arrival of the technological accident. The more advanced the technology, the more horrendous the accident could be.

MR W H SMITH, THE NEWSAGENT.

Sometimes, however, accidents were more the fault of the passenger than the technology. Pranksters would climb on carriage roofs or jump from carriage to carriage even out of the train, so sometimes the operators locked the carriage doors to contain them.

These disadvantages were far outweighed by the advantages. Investment in the railways was highly lucrative and by 1850 there were over 200 railway companies. Three dominated: the London and North Western, the Midland, and the Great Western. Investors were usually the captains of the new industries and dependent upon the railways to develop their own businesses; the arrival of the railway in a town could alter and expand an existing business by opening up the possibility of new markets. When the railway came to Carlisle, the already established biscuit-making business of Carrs, for example, could contemplate exporting around the Empire.

The construction of a station could also mean the building of a large hotel, like the Midland in Manchester and the Great Eastern in London, which brought further revenues for the railway investor. There was competition between companies and amalgamations took place, but it was not unusual for an area to be served by numerous railway companies. At one stage Manchester had nine competitive companies working alongside each other. There was great scope for satirists in *Punch*, and other journals, to poke fun at the new capitalists getting richer at the expense of the passenger.

There were certainly many ways in which capitalists and entrepreneurs could become wealthy by way of the railways and its passengers. Mr W.H. Smith, for instance quickly recognized the need for people to take reading material with them on their journeys. While the educated could read and afford books, many of the poorer people were beginning to make use of literacy schemes and the new, popular and cheap mass-market magazines and newspapers. In 1848 Mr Smith obtained permission to sell books and newspapers on stations along the London–Birmingham section of the London

and North Western Railway. Within ten years he was the sole vendor on all their stations and had stalls on many other stations. When, in Anthony Trollope's *The Small House at Allington*, the hero, Johnny Eames, at Paddington Station "laid his foe prostrate among the newspapers of Mr Smith's bookstall, falling himself into the yellow shilling-novel depot," every reader could picture the scene, and the reading matter, exactly. The company of W.H. Smith grew enormously through Victoria's reign and into the twentieth century.

Queen Victoria and Prince Albert were early converts to the new form of transport. They had made their first journey in 1842 when, accompanied by Isambard Kingdom Brunel, they travelled on the first "royal train", when his engine *Phlegethon* pulled a royal saloon and six carriages from Slough to Paddington. The Queen loved the trip and immediately saw the potential of the railways. Indeed, the development of the lines up to Scotland meant that travelling to Balmoral was truly practicable rather than a three-day journey by boat. Several railway stations were named after the

VICTORIA STATION IN LONDON.

Queen; in 1849 Manchester's Victoria Station opened; its namesake in London led to the whole area behind Buckingham Palace being named after her. From London Victoria it was easy to board trains to Brighton and other newly established south coast resorts.

Thomas Cook and the Package Tour

With the railways came the idea of the excursion and holidays by train. These were pioneered by one man, Thomas Cook, whose innovative idea would have far-reaching consequences around the world. The wealthy had gone on Grand Tours in the eighteenth century, however, few middle-class and working-class people had travelled far from their own village or town. The railways changed all this. The Queen had her country retreats and so now could others, albeit on a more simple scale.

George IV's Pavilion at Brighton had made the town fashionable for the well-off in the early part of the century; now the new railway line from London brought thousands of ordinary people to the south coast. Other coastal resorts developed when railway lines linked them to major industrial towns and cities; Blackpool was easily accessible for workers in Lancashire, and the East Yorkshire coast, with resorts such as Scarborough, became popular for those working in the West Riding woollen industries; for many, the novelty of being in the fresh air by the seaside was wondrous.

Thomas Cook, a young printer and lay Baptist preacher, embraced temperance in his belief that all social ills were caused by alcohol excess. In 1841 he hired a train to take a party of people from Leicester to a temperance gathering at Loughborough. He was quick to spot his passengers' enjoyment of the adventure. So successful was the journey and the potential for passenger transport that he hired more trains.

THE SEA FRONT AT SCARBOROUGH, ONE OF A GROWING NUMBER OF SEASIDE RESORTS.

In 1845, he took people on journeys to Liverpool, where they could watch the steamers leaving for America with hundreds of emigrants, many from Ireland, on board, as well as enjoying the beauty of the North Wales countryside.

Cook's major breakthrough was in organizing return rail journeys, with the cost of an overnight stay in London and entrance to the exhibition included in the ticket, to the Great Exhibition in London in 1851. This was the first, all-in package trip and 165,000 people flocked to London with Mr Cook. A true entrepreneur, Cook saw the potential of yet more schemes and in 1855 took people to the International Exhibition in Paris. During preparations for this trip, he encountered refusals from cross-Channel ferry operators to cooperate. So, instead of booking his passengers from Dover to Calais return, he took them on the North Sea route from Harwich to Antwerp and was able to include a longer, sightseeing trip by train from Antwerp to Brussels, Cologne, Heidelberg, Strasbourg and Paris then back to Antwerp and Harwich. He and his son, John Mason Cook, accompanied the trips and both were encouraged by the enjoyment people got from travel and the potential for the business to develop.

In 1863 Thomas Cook ran package trips to Switzerland, when 500 people went with him, and by November that year he was taking parties south, across the Alps to Italy, again on the circular tour route that enabled them to see more of the countries they were visiting. Suddenly, the middle classes had their own version of the Grand Tour. Mr Cook negotiated with inn owners to keep prices down as far as possible, and in 1868 he introduced the hotel coupon, an early form of the traveller's cheque, as a method of payment.

Having opened up Europe, Cook, now joined by his son in their office in Granby Street, Leicester, organized a trip to the United States. In 1869, four years after the Cooks opened their first London office, the opening of the Suez Canal and the British presence there – which, in 1869, included the Prince and Princess of Wales making a tour of Egypt – gave Cook the opportunity to send a holiday

AN ADVERTISEMENT FOR ONE OF THOMAS COOK'S HOLIDAY TOURS.

party up the Nile. So popular were the Nile trips that he soon opened a large office in Cairo. The British government were so confident in the knowledge and abilities of Thomas Cook and Son, that when General Gordon was besieged in Khartoum in 1884, the company organized the transport of the British Army's relief expedition up the Nile.

Telegraphy and the Press

Developments in telegraphy and electric signals via underwater cables revolutionized the transmission of information around the Empire, enabling the British Government to keep closer control of what was happening in its furthest outposts. In the 1830s Charles Wheatstone, Professor of Experimental Philosophy at King's College London, and William Fothergill Cooke had been experimenting with electrical communication and developing the telegraph.

They finally proved the possibility of transmitting and receiving sound in 1837, when they ran a cable along the railway line from Euston to Camden Town. The sound they transmitted along it was audible at the other end. Work on the telegraphic process developed and in 1851 the first undersea cable was laid beneath the Channel and sound was transmitted from London to Paris. In the same year, a German, Baron Paul Julius von Reuter, opened his first news agency in London. By 1865 cables had been laid from England to India and in 1866 across the Atlantic. All this eventually led to the invention of the telephone by Alexander Graham Bell in 1876 and the era of modern telecommunications.

The telegraph not only changed the method but the style of news reporting. No longer could a government file reports of what was happening now or in the future, and embellish them for its own benefit. Journalists on the scene in hot spots around the world, such as the Crimea, where the war broke out in 1854, were able to report back immediately and in a brief, direct style, describe exactly what they had and were witnessing. Previously, reports of atrocities or bloody battles might take weeks and even months to return home and were then usually embroidered into great deeds of heroism. All this changed with the telegraph as the real horrors and distress of war, its failures and injuries, or the stupidities of army officers as well as heroic acts in adversity were reported back to London within days, bypassing government departments and coming directly into the hands of the public via their newspapers and journals.

Although the masses of the working classes were still largely illiterate, education and reading programmes were underway to improve them. In 1850, the first public libraries were opened and a host of mass-market newspapers and journals were founded for this new market. Between 1850 and 1860 local newspapers were founded in Huddersfield, Hull, Halifax, Leicester, Liverpool, Sheffield, Birmingham and Bristol, towns and cities that were located in predominantly industrial areas with a local working population hungry to receive news of events.

The Times, the newspaper of the upper classes, had been established in 1785 and reached a circulation of 34,000 in 1850, the more radical *Manchester Guardian*, founded in 1821, became a journal of the middle-class reformer and frequent questioner of government. Throughout Queen Victoria's reign the *Manchester Guardian* would oppose the imperialism espoused by successive governments, declare itself in favour of home rule for Ireland and be appalled at Europe's exploits in Africa. *The Daily Telegraph and Courier*, founded in 1855, posted reporters to the Crimea and United States and provided a more conservative and traditional perspective. The *Tatler* and the *Spectator*, both founded in the early 1700s, were well-established journals of essays and the *Illustrated London News*, first published in 1842, followed in their footsteps, albeit for a mass market. Charles Dickens' *Household Words*, first published in March 1850, gave space for the contemporary novelist, essayist or observer to express his or her views. For the satirists, such as George Cruickshank, the magazine *Punch* provided a wonderful outlet for their cartoons.

Visual material was first used by the weekly publication, the *Illustrated London News*, initially in the form of woodcuts and engravings; later, it was the first newspaper or journal to use photography. As a journal of British social life, the *Illustrated London News* helped in no small way to promote the image of Queen Victoria, Prince Albert and their increasing number of children as an ideal family, as well as providing a fascinating record of nineteenth-century life, values and attitudes.

Photography

Another major nineteenth-century innovation which really got into its stride in the 1850s was photography. Like telegraphy, photography revolutionized people's lives, changed the course of painting, the visual arts and news reportage. Queen Victoria and Prince Albert were fascinated by this new art form and quickly became eager patrons of the new photographers and of the Photographic Society.

The camera obscura had been used since the sixteenth century as a tracing aid to artists but it was only in the nineteenth century that the process of recording and keeping an image was perfected. The Frenchman Louis-Jacques Daguerre was the first to begin the process when in 1839 he found that by covering a copper plate with silver iodide, exposing it to light and mercury and then fixing it with common salt, he could make a permanent image remain. These "daguerreotypes" quickly became popular and fashionable in Britain and France but they were only single images and could not be repeated.

In England, William Fox Talbot was also experimenting with the business of recording images. In 1841, he began the process of modern, photographic reproduction with his calotype. By exposing paper with a coating of silver chloride in a camera obscura a negative image was produced on the paper and when this was developed, using acid, a positive, black and white print appeared. The beauty of Fox Talbot's calotype was that numerous prints could be made of the same image. By 1851, he had refined his process further by using wet colodian plates. Cameras, however, were large and bulky and used mainly by portrait photographers, for whom a new art form emerged.

Queen Victoria and Prince Albert were willing models for Roger Fenton and other photographers. Fenton also became one of the first war photographers when he went to the Crimea.

Victoria's was the first reign to be photographed and a vast collection of pictures were taken of Victoria and Albert and their children, in various stages and aspects of their lives. Victoria made family albums of life at Windsor and Balmoral, of her grandchildren and of people in her Household. Many of the images provide an insight into these characters redolent of Holbein's drawings of the Court of Henry VIII. Splendid portraits of Victoria and Albert individually and as a couple reveal

A *CARTE DE VISITE* OF PRINCE ALBERT.

details of clothing and interiors of rooms; sometimes when they were photographed together one had an arm or hand on the other's shoulder or they gazed into each other's eyes.

On her own, Queen Victoria could look regal if the photograph was to commemorate an event or anniversary or, if posed in a relaxed mode,

she might be shown clasping a book, knitting, spinning or holding a flower, sometimes surrounded by the clutter of everyday life or in a garden. Later in her life photographs were taken of Queen Victoria smiling with her grandchildren. Prince Albert clearly enjoyed posing for the camera and, if photographed alone, was usually shown holding a book or scroll of paper and sometimes standing by a huge globe, as befits the image of a worldly intellectual.

The children were photographed individually or in groups, ready for long hikes at Balmoral, dressed up to perform a play or quietly enjoying themselves. Official photographs were taken, as at the betrothal of the Princess Royal to the Crown Prince of Prussia. Victoria and Albert also had a series of photographic *cartes de visite* made. In London, Windsor, Balmoral and Osborne local photographic studios were used; in Edinburgh, James Ross and John Thompson; Robert Hills and John Henry Saunders in Eton; and Hughes and Mullin in Ryde, Isle of Wight. Undoubtedly, Victoria and Albert helped to make portrait photography popular among the middle classes.

Women in the Victorian World

The Queen, with her use of chloroform in the deliveries of her last two children, became a champion for all women terrified of the excruciating pain of childbirth; and the prospect of a pain-free delivery became real. Any understanding of contraceptive practices or of the menstrual cycle and its relationship to female fertility was minimal at this time, and Queen Victoria was not unusual in having nine children. Many women had more than the Queen. Through the dangers of infection and haemorrhage at childbirth many families lost not only the mother but children as well, while disease and infection at all levels of societies, plus malnutrition among the poorer classes, meant that many children did not survive infancy.

There was little education for girls and the women's suffrage movement was in its infancy.

OPPOSITE: QUEEN VICTORIA AND PRINCE ALBERT IN AN EARLY PHOTOGRAPH BY ROGER FENTON.

CLASSES AT THE NEW CHELTENHAM LADIES' COLLEGE.

ELIZABETH
GASKELL.

By 1847 women were allowed to become students at London University and in 1850 the first of many foundations for the education of the daughters of the middle classes was formed when Frances Buss opened the North London Collegiate School in Camden Town. It was followed shortly after by the Cheltenham Ladies College and the Girls Public Day School Trust. The education of the poor was left to social reformers like Lord Shaftesbury and the ragged schools.

Even though it had become acceptable to educate girls, women were still barred from most of the professions and a "good marriage" was to be their career. Some, like Florence Nightingale, eschewed marriage. Miss Nightingale, determined to become a nurse, found her opening with the outbreak of war in the Crimea. There, with a small group of other women, she transformed the role of the nurse and irrevocably changed the care of injured soldiers. When the first training school for nurses was opened at St Thomas' Hospital in London 1860, it was given her name.

Women writers found they needed the respectability of calling themselves "Mrs Gaskell" or "Mrs Craik" or stood a better chance of being published if they gave themselves male-sounding names. The unmarried Brontë sisters, unable to publish their works as women, took the pen names of Currer, Acton and Ellis Bell. George Eliot's real name was Mary Ann Evans. Queen Victoria, despite the supremacy of her position, was in no way interested in the move towards women's suffrage, believing a woman should be foremost a wife and mother. The fact that she was Queen was her duty and not necessarily something she would have chosen, even though she enjoyed many aspects of it. On the other hand, she had no hesitation about making it clear that *Leaves from the Journal of My Life in the Highlands*, published in 1868, was solely the work, including the sketches which illustrated it, of the Queen, the nation's most important wife and mother.

Middle-class women, having made a "good" marriage, now had to excel as homemakers and although they did employ domestic staff, could not afford the numerous housekeepers, cooks, butlers and maids of the upper classes. Many nervous young wives, living in new, large houses in the expanding suburbs, away from their families, felt isolated and panicked at having to run a household and oversee dinner menus for husbands and guests. Upper-class menus, always something to emulate on the upwardly mobile social ladder, had become more difficult as French chefs, escaping the turmoil in Paris, had found refuge and work in many British kitchens, introducing their different and sophisticated food to their employers.

A young wife came to the rescue of these many young and inexperienced middle-class women. In 1852, Sam Beeton made a fortune when he published the highly successful novel *Uncle Tom's Cabin*, written by an American woman, Harriet Beecher Stowe. With his money, he began a weekly journal, *The English Woman's Domestic Magazine*. When he married in 1856, his new wife, Isabella, wrote the cookery and household management sections of the magazine. Her reputation was guaranteed when she published her *Book of Household Management* in 1859.

The book, reprinted and published in new edition, many times since, provided advice on menus, meals and recipes to emulate the upper classes; buying food, selecting recipes and making menus; laundering table and household linens; laying tables and serving food; interviewing and hiring staff; and gave remedies for children's illnesses and much more. Mrs Beeton was the saviour of many young wives, who now felt secure with their copy of *Household Management* in the house.

Although Isabella Beeton did not originate recipes, she was excellent at drawing on and adapting well-tried methods from the past and from the French chefs arriving in Britain. But her great knowledge of running households could not save her from a major cause of death among women in her day, and she succumbed, like many others, to the complications of childbirth, dying in 1865 aged 29.

For working class women however, in mid-Victorian Britain, the domestic life described so vividly by Isabella Beeton was a world outside their experience. Working long hours in factories or as seamstresses and laundry-women, if they had work at all, many women found life very hard indeed. Not for them the foods used so lavishly in the recipes of the *Book of Household Management*. Many were greatly undernourished; they and their families, ate meals consisting of potatoes and corn, supplemented by an occasional piece of bacon.

FANTASTIC DESSERTS FROM MRS BEETON'S *BOOK OF HOUSEHOLD MANAGEMENT*.

Literature and the Arts

The nineteenth century proved to be a watershed in writing style, as writers and artists contemplated the enormity of the revolution surrounding them and the new markets that were opening for their work. The "condition of England", first used as a subject by the young Benjamin Disraeli, continued to be a source of study and writing, not only on the way the British now lived but also on the rapidly changing face of the landscape as towns grew and pushed out into the countryside.

While in Manchester, Friedrich Engels and Karl Marx published their call for a workers' revolution, the *Communist Party Manifesto*, in 1848, others were documenting their observations of society in fiction. Many fiction writers of the mid-nineteenth century tackled

THE FIRST EDITION FRONTISPIECE OF *DOMBEY AND SON* BY DICKENS.

its social problems head on. Foremost among them was Charles Dickens who became the great observer and chronicler of the nuances and subtleties of the impact of industrialization on the life of the individual.

The experiences of his own poverty-stricken childhood and of the strikes, poverty, exploitation and greed which he saw all about him, haunted Dickens' imagination. His novels, set in specific towns and using recognizable character types, were all forged in the fire of his own experiences. *Hard Times* was based in the mills of Preston; *The Old Curiosity Shop* in Birmingham; *Dombey and Son* in Camden Town, London; and the misers he had encountered were personified by Ebeneezer Scrooge in *A Christmas Carol*.

Much of Dickens' work had first appeared in serial form as weekly or monthly instalments in magazines. From 1850 he had his own journal, *Household Words*, which he edited and to which he contributed essays, though he also gave space to many of the leading writers and commentators of the day to air their thoughts.

Another writer who wrote with great power about the changes wrought by the industrial revolution was Mrs Gaskell; her novel, *North and South*, published in 1855, compared the lives of a wealthy, Harley Street family with those working in a mill in the north of England.

Where Dickens tackled the industrialization of Britain, the three Brontë sisters, Charlotte, Emily and Anne, writing in a pre-Freudian era, explored the inner world of people. These three remarkable young women, living in the bleak Yorkshire moors at Haworth, developed their own language and people. Their mother had died of tuberculosis when they were children, and grief, loss and loneliness were well known to them. They were not inhibited in exposing and describing their inner thoughts and feelings, often of unrequited love and passion, grief and loss.

Many of the locations of the Brontë sisters' novels were real and based on their own experiences, at school, in others' homes, as governesses, among the harsh Yorkshire moorland and, for Charlotte, in Brussels. Their brother, Bramwell, was an alcoholic and drug addict

ANNE, EMILY AND CHARLOTTE BRONTË PAINTED BY THEIR BROTHER
BRANWELL, WHO REMOVED HIS OWN IMAGE FROM THE PAINTING.

who eventually died of tuberculosis in 1848, followed by Emily and Anne in 1849, leaving Charlotte alone. Eventually, she became a celebrity in London, where she was a contributor to **Household Words**, visited the Great Exhibition and met her hero, the writer Thackeray. During her time in Belgium she saw Queen Victoria drive through Brussels, and commented, approvingly, on the plainness of the Queen's dress. Charlotte died in childbirth, after marrying Arthur Bell Nicholls in 1855. The Brontës and Dickens paved the way for the writings, later in the century, of George Eliot, Thomas Hardy and Arnold Bennett, for whom industrialization was established and fixed.

The Universities of Oxford and Cambridge nurtured a different type of writer, classically educated, more esoteric and more artistically aware men who were, by their background and situation, wealthy. It was here that John Ruskin, William Thackeray, Lewis Carroll and Matthew Arnold mixed and exchanged ideas. Ruskin's attacks on the changes brought by industrialization, his hatred of machines and their exploitation of the individual, coupled with his calls for a return to classicism, made his reputation as a formidable writer and art critic.

The artistic movement known as the Pre-Raphaelite Brotherhood was founded in 1848 with the aim of promoting a new style of painting which sought its inspiration in the art of the early Italian Renaissance before Raphael. Soon, Edward Burne Jones, Dante Gabriel Rossetti and others had amassed many sup-

porters for their style of painting – one not patronized by Victoria and Albert. Their influence was widespread at Oxford, where the Union building was decorated by Burne Jones, Rossetti and William Morris, who later developed his own form of socialism. An awareness of the problems of the working classes was a feature of the Pre-Raphaelites' work, as in Ford Madox Brown's great paintings, **Work** and **The Last of England**, both painted in the 1850s.

Poetry in mid-century Britain was represented by Alfred, Lord Tennyson, who became Poet Laureate on the death of William Wordsworth in 1850, and held the position until his death in 1892. The Poet Laureate is appointed by the Sovereign to the Royal Household and receives a stipend. Tennyson wrote verses to commemorate the Queen's birthday and other important events, such as his "Ode" for the Duke of Wellington on his death in 1852 and the famous poem commemorating the Charge of the Light Brigade in 1854, when Britain was embroiled in the Crimean War. Queen Victoria liked Lord Tennyson very much and he was a regular guest at her Court, both at Windsor and Osborne. Prince Albert was happy to visit Tennyson at Farringford, his house on the Isle of Wight, but Victoria never did, preferring the poet to attend her. In later life she regarded Tennyson's poetry as one of her favourite forms of literature.

"THE LADY OF SHALOTT" BY DANTE GABRIEL ROSSETTI.

"QUEEN VICTORIA'S FAVOURITE DOGS AND A PARROT", SIR EDWIN LANDSEER.

The Royal Art Collection

Patronage of the arts in Britain had been the domain of monarchs through the ages, kings and queens from Henry VIII on demonstrating through their choices their own wealth as well as the strength and heroism of the nation. Queen Victoria's grandfather and uncles had commissioned great works by the leading artists of the day, including Thomas Gainsborough, Sir Joshua Reynolds, George Stubbs and many others. Queen Victoria left the decisions about the purchases to the Royal Collection to Prince Albert.

In a break with tradition, he decided to buy not only the work of current artists, both British and foreign, but also to acquire some early Italian Renaissance, Flemish and Dutch works. It is largely due to Albert that the Royal Collection today contains works by Duccio, Bernardo Gaddi, Gentile de Fabriano and others. Neither he nor Victoria liked the Pre-Raphaelites very much; their attacks on the Royal Academy were not approved of, especially as Prince Albert often addressed the Academy and provoked interesting debates there.

Sir David Wilkie, whom Queen Victoria had appointed Court Painter on her accession, died in 1841. Sir Edwin Landseer, who had painted her and Dash at Kensington Palace, had long fulfilled the role, albeit unofficially, painting the Queen and the children in London and in the Highlands. Queen Victoria was quite enamoured of Landseer, enjoyed her sittings and even managing to tolerate his periodic alcoholic stupors. However, it was Franz Xaver Winterhalter who was summoned to be her official Court Painter in 1841. Born in Münich, Winterhalter quickly made his name as the leading painter of Europe's royal families; visiting Paris in 1834, he stayed on in the court of King Louis-Philippe and managed to retain his position in that of Napoleon III. But it was his paintings of Queen Victoria's family, with their loose brushstrokes and romantic style, that were his most famous.

Albert's patronage of the arts extended to his own houses. He had long been interested in frescoes and when he built the garden pavilion at Buckingham Palace in 1842, he commissioned leading artists to paint frescoes on its walls based on Raphael cartoons in the Vatican. He also extended his patronage of the arts outside his own circle. In 1857, following the success of the Great Exhibition, Prince Albert promoted the Art Treasures Exhibition in Manchester, the largest such exhibition ever held. His interest in the fine arts was matched by his interest in design and this combination was instrumental in his plans for setting up the first School of Design.

The nineteenth century saw a considerable rise in the number of arts patrons in Britain. There were many rich collectors, such as Sir Henry Tate, who had made his fortune as a sugar refiner in Liverpool and used it to collect British art. In the 1890s he gave his collection to the nation on condition that a building was found to house it. Thus the Tate Gallery was built at Millbank, by the Thames.

Religion at Mid-Century

Prince Albert's devotion to the teachings of Martin Luther, in which he was supported by his wife and family, resulted in a more religiously conservative royal family than its immediate predecessor. Throughout the nineteenth century followers of the non-conformist faiths such as the Methodist, Congregationalist and Baptist churches, increased in numbers at the expense of the Church of England. However, religious worship was declining overall and the 1851 census showed that only fifty per cent of people actually attended church regularly.

In contrast, the nineteenth century saw an increase in the founding of charitable institutions, mainly by the middle classes trying to alleviate working class suffering and by missionary societies moving to the furthest corners of the Empire to convert its people to the ways of Christianity, regardless of the merits of their own cultures. Among the missionary societies formed in mid-century were the Presbyterian Church of England Foreign Missions Committee (1847), the South American Missionary Society (1852), the Christian Vernacular Education Society for India (1858), the Universities Mission to Central Africa (1859) and the China Inland Mission (1865).

In 1850 there was an easing of the rift between the Anglican Church and Rome which had happened at the Reformation 300 years earlier. Cardinal Wiseman became the first Roman Catholic Archbishop of Westminster and Catholic bishops were appointed throughout the country. Jews were beginning to be accepted in society, the banker Nathan Rothschild was the first Jew to take a seat in the House of Commons, and synagogues were being built in London, Leeds and Manchester.

The greatest threat to religion in Victoria's reign emerged at the end of the decade. Religious belief propagated the teaching that all life on earth was sacred and was there at God's will. Suddenly, in 1859, this belief was effectively challenged, when Charles Darwin's great work *On the Origin of Species by Means of Natural Selection*, or *The Preservation of Favoured Races in the Struggle for Life* was published. Charles Darwin, a grandson of the renowned potter Josiah Wedgwood, travelled the world in the 1830s as a naturalist on HMS *Beagle*. Already an agnostic, the things that Darwin discovered about nature on this voyage led him to question God's role in evolution. Gradually and privately, as his work would have been deemed blasphemous and illegal, he developed his theory of transmutation and evolution by natural selection. When his work was published in 1859 it sold out within months and was constantly reprinted; most of the attacks he received were from the Church who did not accept his non-Genesis approach. By the end of the decade, even the religious basis for existence was undergoing a form of revolution.

THE NONCONFORMIST PREACHER CHARLES HADDON SPURGEON PUBLISHED IN *THE HORNET*.

"THE *BEAGLE* IN PONSONBY SOUND" BY C MARTENS.

The Great Exhibition

Prince Albert's greatest public achievement was the Great Exhibition of 1851, a defining moment in Britain's advancing ability to embrace the machine in everyday life. It was also the high point in Queen Victoria's public adoration of her husband.

In London in the 1840s, the Society of Arts, following a tradition established earlier in the century by factories in France, had held small exhibitions to show the potential of combining the products of the new industries with traditional craft and artisan techniques. Henry Cole and other members of the Society had visited an exhibition in Paris and had been impressed at it. They began to consider the potential of holding something similar but much bigger in London. They knew that the French were planning an international exhibition, but due to their domestic troubles, it was believed they would be unable to do so for some years to come.

In 1848, the gentlemen of the Society of Arts were determined to hold an international exhibition and invite the world to London, but knew they needed Royal patronage. Henry Cole travelled to Osborne to discuss the possibility with Prince Albert, who was immediately enthusiastic, recognizing the potential of this first step into global marketing. Albert was also insistent that foreign competition could only be beneficial to the output, innovation and profits of British industries. A Royal Commission was set up to look after the finances, organize a competition for the design of a building and find a site on Crown Property. With Prince Albert's patronage the idea became a reality and it was to be his greatest contribution to Britain.

From 1848 until the opening in 1851, meetings of the Exhibition Committee were held at Buckingham Palace, Windsor Castle and the Society of Arts, off the Strand. At one of these meetings, Prince Albert altered the minutes, in his own hand, insisting it be known as *"An Exhibition of the Industry of all the Civilized Nations of the World"*. He was instrumental in deciding the four categories of goods to be received and exhibited: Raw Materials; Machinery and Mechanical Inventions; Manufactures; and Sculpture and Plastic Art. Fundraising dinners were held at the Mansion House and addressed by the Prince, now more confident at speaking English in public.

Eventually a site was secured on Crown Property, in Hyde Park. This caused much consternation among the wealthy residents of Brompton, as the area was then called, who were appalled at the thought of their park housing such an edifice and terrified at the diseases the poor might bring to the area. Others, including Prince Albert's earlier adversary Colonel Sibthorp, questioned the validity of such an enterprise and predicted that it would fail and Albert look a joke.

After rejecting all the entries for the building's design, the competition committee finally settled on a late entry, a rather futuristic building of glass and metal designed by the Duke of Devonshire's gardener, Joseph Paxton. Horticulture had become an upper class hobby and gardeners were employed to look after the newly constructed glass and metal conservatories which had to be built and heated in order to grow the exotic plants arriving from all around the Empire.

Paxton was intrigued that, at Chatsworth, the Duke of Devonshire's main estate, the leaf of the Victoria Regia Water Lily, one of two newly arrived in the country, the other having gone to Kew Gardens, could withstand the weight of his six-year-old daughter. This observation became integral to his design of the strong metal pillars constructed to support the enormous glass roof of the Exhibition building. The use of iron in building construction had developed considerably since its first successful use in the iron bridge across the gorge of the River Severn in Shropshire in 1779; and glass, since the repeal of the window tax, could now be used in abundance. The making of sheets of curved glass had been perfected by the Chance Brothers company in Birmingham.

Paxton's great Crystal Palace was erected in Hyde Park in under two years. It was 1,848 feet (565 metres) long, and 408 feet (125 metres) wide at its widest point. Goods from 13,937 exhibitors were brought from all over the world.

ONE OF THE DICKINSON BROTHERS' COMPREHENSIVE PICTURES OF THE GREAT EXHIBITION SHOWING THE TRANSEPT OF IRON AND GLASS ENCLOSING THE ELM TREE AND THE GLASS FOUNTAIN.

The first public lavatories were built, admission to which cost one penny (about half a new penny), and refreshment areas were organized where visitors could buy Schweppes minerals, Fortnum and Mason hampers and biscuits from Carrs of Carlisle.

The Queen was fascinated by and proud of Albert's palace of glass and visited the site regularly. Her diary was filled with reports of the visits. "The sun shining in through the Transept gave a fairy-like appearance," she wrote once. "The building is so light and graceful, in spite of its immense size". All practicalities had to considered by the organizers. Sweeping the floors, they realized, could be done by the long dresses of the ladies, the dirt falling into the cracks between the floor boards. Testing the strength of the platforms and balconies was left to soldiers who were brought in to march across them, watched by Queen

Victoria. On another visit she saw the arrival of goods, which had arrived at the docks in the East End and come by carriage across London to Hyde Park. She gleefully noted the delays in the arrival of goods from Russia and looked proudly on as huge quantities of articles were unpacked from all parts of her Empire. In fact Britain, the Empire and India took up the majority of exhibitors' space and the United States about two per cent.

Queen Victoria and Prince Albert drove from Buckingham Palace to the State Opening of the Exhibition on May 1, 1851. The Queen, feeling as anxious as she had done before her Coronation, wore a pink and silver dress, a diamond diadem with a small crown and sparkling, diamond jewellery. As they approached Hyde Park, "a little rain fell ... but as we neared the Crystal Palace, the sun shone and gleamed on the gigantic edifice, upon

which the flags of every nation flew." The crowds cheered, the sound of the huge organ and choirs rang through the building as they walked to the dais, set by a gigantic crystal fountain and metal gates from Colebrookdale. The Transept had been built high enough to encompass the huge elm trees growing in the park. Here, the Queen officially opened the Exhibition watched by Prince Albert, ambassadors, Members of Parliament, Members of the Exhibition Committee, Royal Commissioners and other dignitaries. As the ceremony drew to a close there were more cheers and handkerchiefs were waved in celebration.

The success of the Great Exhibition surpassed all expectations. Six million people, of all classes, came from around the country, to wonder and marvel at the new and innovative things they saw in this fantastic palace of glass. Some came to London for the first time by making use of Thomas Cook's excursion ticket. Gustave Flaubert, the novelist, came from France and four other gentlemen came all the way from China. Like the public, Queen Victoria could not keep away, she took the children and other members of the family; even Uncle Leopold came from Belgium, and Buckingham Palace was full of guests wanting to see the Exhibition.

For Queen Victoria there was always another discovery to make on each visit. She was amazed and "bewildered at the myriads of beautiful things, which … quite dazzle one's eyes." There were courts filled with tapestries and brocades, exotic jewellery, cups, hooker bases, swords, shields, saddle bags and writing desks from India; these items, brought to the Exhibition by the East India Company, eventually formed part of the initial collection of the Victoria and Albert Museum. A real marvel brought by the East India Company was the Koh-i-nor diamond. Until 1860, the only diamonds in the world were found in India and the Company had acquired supplies of them. The huge Koh-i-nor was taken from Lahore by the Company at the end of the Sikh Wars, brought to the Great Exhibition and presented to Queen Victoria.

The fine craft of stone cutting was unknown in India and rough jewels would be placed into gold and other metal mounts. In order to be shown at the Exhibition, the Koh-i-nor was crudely cut which, ironically, reduced its weight from 186 to 106 carats. The following year, the royal jewellers, Garrard, set this brilliant, dazzling jewel into a tiara, like a great flower, surrounded by 2000 smaller diamonds, for Queen Victoria. Eventually, the tiara was broken up and its diamonds were put into a crown for the coronation of George VI's Queen, Elizabeth in 1937.

Metal ware – tools, coffin handles and jewellery came from Birmingham; canoes and sledges from Canada; exquisitely carved furniture from Austria and Germany; delicate china from Dresden, book bindings and sculptures from the states of Italy; ribbons and lace from France; embroidery and watches from Switzerland. Queen Victoria talked to Mr Chubb about his latest lock, looked at the children small enough to work the de la Rue envelope-folding machine and marvelled at the fine craftsmanship and design of many exhibits. There was an American "double piano … 2 people playing at each end, which had a ludicrous effect." She made many purchases, including a tea set designed and manufactured by Herbert Minton's company in Stoke-on-Trent. Minton also exhibited tiles it had manufactured to Pugin's designs.

Many countries and companies presented Queen Victoria with exhibits as gifts. One, known as the Cathedral of Wood, now standing majestically in the Victoria and Albert Museum, was presented to Queen Victoria by Emperor Franz Josef of Austria. This collection of a huge sideboard and book case, originally full of books bound in leather by Italian bookbinders, was made out of oak and carved, in great detail, by the best Austrian craftsmen of the day. It was made by the firm of Carl Leister and Son, cabinet makers in Vienna. On its presentation it was taken to Buckingham Palace and then moved to Holyrood House in Edinburgh. Eventually, George V tired of it and gave it to the Forestry Department at Edinburgh University who presented it to the Victoria and Albert Museum in 1967.

The new discipline of industrial design was

just beginning and there was an irony in the style of many of the exhibits. Although they showed off the latest industries and new methods of combining them with the traditional, artisan skills into mass production, the majority of products were over-decorated for their purpose. Only a few Victorians, like Joseph Paxton and Henry Cole, understood that the simplicity of a design was as important as its decoration, and, as Nikolaus Pevsner pointed out in 1952, many of the exhibits were dressed up in full, cluttered Victorian splendour, often disguising their purpose. Machines were engraved with flowers and fauna, and pianos were decorated to look like organs. Perhaps the influence of the Queen herself had something to do with this, for Victoria was not averse to wearing a plethora of frills and flowers and liked living in highly ornamented domestic surroundings.

October 15, 1851, was a sad day for Queen Victoria and Prince Albert. It was the last day of the Great Exhibition, and Albert attended the closing ceremony alone. The Great Exhibition may have closed, but its influence was felt for generations after. The Royal Commissioners for the Exhibition of 1851, set up to manage the profits of the Exhibition, are still in existence, providing grants to post-doctoral research scientists from the Commonwealth, many of whom are Nobel Laureates.

After the closure, the pre-fabricated Crystal Palace was dismantled and moved to Sydenham in south London, where it was re-erected on land belonging to one of its investors, himself an investor in the railway line going from London to the South Coast. Crystal Palace station was opened here. More of Albert's plans were put into operation as the building was expanded and the grounds landscaped to include a natural history section, complete with models of dinosaurs; fountains and streams; and swings. It all offered a Victorian family a splendid day out; indeed, it was visited by Prince Albert's own children. Moving the Crystal Palace to Sydenham enhanced the new suburb as villas and mansions were built around the site.

Prince Albert's vision went beyond the Great Exhibition and the Crystal Palace. After his death his dream for a grand university and museum campus was realized on the area south of Hyde Park between Exhibition Road, Cromwell Road and Queen's Gate. The Science Museum, the Natural History Museum and the Victoria and Albert Museum are all heirs of Prince Albert's dream.

Florence Nightingale and the Crimean War

For much of the nineteenth century, the eastern European region was dominated by the affairs of the failing Ottoman Empire. The Tsar of Russia saw an opportunity to extend the borders of his empire into Turkey. Britain was always wary of Russian imperialism, and the Russians' efforts to expand their empire. Eventually, Russia did invade the region, crossing the Danube in 1853. Britain and France formed an alliance, each sending armies of 28,000 men to the area.

FLORENCE NIGHTINGALE ADMINISTERING TO THE SICK AND INJURED IN THE CRIMEA.

FLORENCE NIGHTINGALE ADMINISTERING TO THE SICK AND INJURED IN HOSPITAL AT SCUTARI.

Quickly the conflict spread to the area of the Crimea along the northern coast of the Black Sea. The allied base was set up north of the Russian camp at Sebastopol and a swift allied victory was claimed at Alma, in September 1854, when Sebastopol was besieged. As winter set in there were skirmishes at Inkerman and Balaclava, where Lord Raglan commanded Lord Lucan to send troops in to stop the Russians getting their armaments, now behind the allied line. It was here that the Light Brigade were ordered to advance to attack the well-equipped Russians. Over 200 British soldiers died in the mistakenly ordered charge that followed. More allied casualties followed and hundreds died because the troops were unprepared for the severity of a Crimean winter.

At the field hospital at Scutari outside Varna, a group of British women including Florence Nightingale had arrived to nurse the injured and dying men. Neither Miss Nightingale nor her colleagues could understand why more men died of illness than of the terrible injuries inflicted on them, despite the care they were given. They found that the hospital conditions were appalling, with no ventilation or heating, men lay on dirty straw mattresses, sanitation was largely non-existent and disease was rife.

These young women also suffered, comforting the soldiers as they died; sometimes they would start a night shift looking after ten men and by midnight they had all died. Correct supplies rarely reached them, British ships would arrive with stretcher frames whilst the canvas bed would be on another ship and supplies of bandages were beneath the huge load of armaments, which were to be deployed further along the coast.

Since this was the first time an army had had to cope with the effects of the now widely used telegraph system, making dispatches by journalists much faster to reach home than ever before, Britain soon learned of the disasters in the Crimea. Queen Victoria and the government were appalled at the losses of men from disease. Newly appointed medical officers of health sent by the government to Scutari and other hospitals were quick to pinpoint the appalling, dirty and infectious hospital conditions as the reason for the deaths. Florence Nightingale and her colleagues tackled them and some lives were saved. This experience was pivotal in introducing the concept of hygiene in the nursing of the sick. Queen Victoria, while eager to defeat the Tsar, was grief-stricken as she got news of the casualties and felt impotent to help. All she could do was write to some of the widows and, when the injured soldiers returned home, visit them in hospital.

The main area of conflict was the Black Sea coast, but naval battles between Britain and Russia also took place along the Baltic coast, with Britain defeating the Russian Navy off Finland. The Crimean War, eventually won by the allies, did achieve its intention of keeping Russia in place, but it was marred by the inefficiency and ineptitude of the army officers.

Ironically, it was due to an act of bravery in the Baltic area of the conflict with Russia that Queen Victoria awarded the first Victoria Cross in 1856. This was the highest of all British honours and, on Prince Albert's advice, it differed from all others, by being awarded solely for an act of notable bravery, to anyone in the army or Royal Navy, regardless of rank. A twenty-year-old Irishman, who was a ship's mate on HMS *Heda* was awarded it for his outstanding courage when he threw a lit and hissing Russian fuse, which had

DESCRIPTION OF THE NEW ORDER, THE VICTORIA CROSS.

landed on deck, into the sea, where it immediately exploded. This act saved the ship and all the sailors on it. All Victoria Cross medals are made of bronze from Russian guns captured by British troops in the Crimea; they bear the crown and the date of the action in which they were won and are worn on a red ribbon.

After the war Florence Nightingale returned to England, where she became a recluse, possibly as a result of what she had witnessed. However she did dine with Queen Victoria at Buckingham Palace and encouraged her to visit the injured soldiers, now returned, at Chatham Hospital, telling her that although she might feel unable to help, her very presence could do much to encourage the sick. Queen Victoria visited Chatham Hospital in 1855, and was sickened and appalled at what she saw, not just the injuries and illness, but the cramped conditions in which the soldiers were being nursed.

In 1855, while the Crimean War was at its height, Victoria and Albert made a state visit to Britain's ally in the war, France, sailing there on board their new yacht, *Victoria and Albert*. Victoria loved the French style and especially the Parisian clothes she had bought from some of their designers. Their hosts, Napoleon and Eugénie, in turn, were enraptured by Queen Victoria's style: she was, after all, born into a royal role and knew by birth all the matters of etiquette which they were having to learn.

However, Victoria was not enraptured by the Prussian statesman, Prince Otto von Bismarck, whom she met in Paris, nor was she happy to discover that Napoleon was already building up an arsenal of weapons and a fleet of warships. In 1857 Napoleon and Eugénie returned the visit, went to the opera at Covent Garden and stayed at Osborne.

Indian Mutiny

The worst crisis to hit the British Empire in the 1850s occurred in India. In 1857, India erupted into disorder and bloodshed when a group of Indian soldiers in Bengal could not hold back their frustrations at the arrogance of their British officers any longer and mutinied. The flash point of the mutiny was the officers' insistence that animal fat, which the soldiers suspected to be fat from cattle, sacred to Hindus, be used to grease new rifles; the soldiers shot the British officers. They then marched to Delhi and tried to restore the deposed Mughal, Bahadur Shah, as emperor. News of the revolt spread and the mutiny developed beyond the army, including many civilians, and affected the area along the Ganges to Agram, Cawnpore and Lucknow and beyond into central India.

Queen Victoria was terrified as she read the dispatches, hoping that the bloodshed and death rate were not as high as reported; but when her worst fears were confirmed her first instinct was to attack Lord Palmerston over the atrocities. But gradually both she and the government had to accept that the mutiny represented the beginnings of widespread distaste and anger at being ruled by Britain, at the East India Company's arrogance over the native people and at their monopoly on trade. The Queen continued to believe that India was an essential part of the Empire – the "Jewel in the Crown", in fact – and did not want control to pass back to the Mughal. Undoubtedly she was relieved when the East India Company was wound up and control passed to the British Crown; she developed a life-long fascination for India and things Indian.

European Connections

Arranging suitable marriages for their children in Europe took up much of Victoria and Albert's time. Throughout the 1850s there were endless discussions and meetings with possible suitors. Since the age of four Vicky, the Princess Royal, had been destined to marry Crown Prince Frederick of Prussia. In 1855 the twenty-four-year-old suitor visited Balmoral and, to the delight of Victoria and Albert, seemed to like fourteen-year-old Vicky. Somehow the press had been alerted of the visit and possible betrothal, much to Victoria's displeasure: spiky relations between the Royal family and the press began long before the twentieth century.

While Vicky's future seemed secure, those of Bertie and of Princess Alice were more complex. Bertie continued to vex his parents and their disappointment, especially Albert's, in him was apparent. He showed little application for learning but a strong aptitude, even at sixteen, for enjoying a lifestyle similar to that of both of his grandfathers and Prince Albert's brother. To other members of the family, Bertie was fun and amusing but remained the despair of his father. To find a suitable wife for him, who would also be queen one day, was proving troublesome. The possibility of Princess Alexandra of Denmark was raised, but Victoria and Albert had opposed Denmark's governance of Schleswig-Holstein. Princess Alice's marriage plans were less problematic and Prince Louis of Hesse-Darmstadt was suggested. So the plan for the domination, by Britain, of the Royal Houses of Europe through marriage was under way.

There were many other changes among the people of Victoria's immediate household in the 1850s, including several deaths, which always involved the Court in going into deep mourning for several weeks. A major departure from the royal household took place in 1857, when Baron Stockmar finally retired and left England, where he had worked tirelessly for the family, and returned to Germany.

The vexing question of a title for Prince Albert still tormented Queen Victoria, eighteen years after her wedding. His position and abilities were, she believed, surely now obvious to all, following the success of the Great Exhibition and his numerous other achievements; but a title still eluded him. She therefore decided to take the matter into her own hands and in 1857 made him Prince Consort.

In January 1858 the royal family and guests gathered at Buckingham Palace for the wedding of the Princess Royal to Crown Prince Frederick of Prussia. Albert's brother, Duke Ernest, arrived from Paris with the news of an assassination attempt by an Italian on Napoleon and Eugénie. To celebrate the forthcoming marriage, dinners and banquets were held where princes and princesses, dukes and duchesses attended, all dressed in the latest fashions, and glittering with jewels. The day before the wedding the young Vicky received a present of sparkling jewellery, including opals and diamonds, from her parents.

In her wedding dress, covered in Honiton lace, the nervous girl knelt in the Chapel Royal in St James's Palace, as her mother had done before her, repeated her vows and became the wife of Crown Prince Frederick William of Prussia; afterwards she walked down the aisle to the sound of Felix Mendelssohn's *"Wedding March"* and returned to Buckingham Palace where the couple appeared on the new balcony to acknowledge the cheers of the roaring crowds.

Whilst Victoria and Albert were delighted that their long-term plan for the beloved daughter had come to fruition there was also sadness that this young and intelligent girl should be leaving them. As she had done so often in the past, Queen Victoria expressed her feelings in a letter to Uncle Leopold, writing on January 12, 1858:

> It is a time of IMMENSE BUSTLE and *agitation*; I feel it is *terrible* to GIVE UP one's *poor* CHILD, and feel very *nervous* for the coming time, and for the departure … Vicky … has had ever since February '57 a succession of emotions and leave-takings – most trying to any one, but particularly to so young a girl with such very powerful feelings. She is so much improved in self-control and is so clever…and so sensible that we can talk to her of anything – and therefore shall miss her sadly.

After a honeymoon at Windsor it was time for Vicky to leave them permanently and go to Berlin. Albert was very upset. In many respects he was closer intellectually to Vicky than to his wife, and on February 3 he travelled with the party to Gravesend, where this shy, repressed man fought back tears as he said goodbye to his daughter. Although Queen Victoria missed her, her daughter's marriage and the consequent separation did give her the opportunity to enter into lengthy correspondence with her daughter,

a correspondence that lasted for the next 43 years. In the letters they disagreed, cajoled and supported each other as well as discussed state affairs and the political differences between their two countries.

In her early letters mother revealed to daughter the difficulties facing a young bride, writing of the problems of trying to fulfil a husband's desires without becoming pregnant. To Victoria's dismay, Vicky was pregnant within the year, and astounded her mother, when she and Albert visited Berlin, by talking openly about the plans for the impending birth.

On January 27, 1859, Prince William of Prussia was born and Victoria and Albert became grandparents. The life of her first grandson, who eventually became Kaiser Wilhelm II, would over the years, be the source of much distress to Victoria.

Victoria ended the decade, sad at the departure of her eldest daughter, concerned at the antics of her son, but delighted at her husband, his achievements and the great happiness that their marriage had brought:

> my BLESSED MARRIAGE, which has brought such *universal blessings* on this country and EUROPE! For what has not my beloved and perfect Albert done? Raised monarchy to the highest pinnacle of respect, and rendered it popular beyond what it ever was in this country!

LEFT: THE WEDDING PORTRAIT OF THE IR ROYAL HIGHNESSES PRINCESS VICTORIA AND CROWN PRINCE FREDERICK WILLIAM OF PRUSSIA, JANUARY 25, 1858. ENGRAVED BY CARL SUSSNAPP. VICTORIA AND PRINCE ALBERT.

RIGHT: PRINCESS VICTORIA WITH HER BABY SON, PRINCE FREDERICK WILLIAM, FIRST GRANDCHILD OF QUEEN VICTORIA.

Chapter 8 Mourning

Even though Queen Victoria was always concerned about her husband's weak constitution, his increasing work load and its effect on his health, no amount of care and worry could have prepared her for the lifelong effect on her of two dreadful events in 1861, the deaths of her mother and her husband.

Ever since 1856, when several of Victoria and Albert's closer relations had died, life at Court had known periods of subdued mourning. The Dowager Queen Adelaide, widow of King William IV, and to whom Victoria had been close, died in 1849. Her death, while sad, did not provoke the outpouring of grief witnessed at the death of Prince Albert's father. However, in 1856, Prince Charles of Leiningen, Victoria's half-brother, died; his death was followed shortly after by that of their cousin, Victoria, Duchess of Nemours. Both these deaths sent intimations of mortality through Victoria's Court.

Prince Albert had never been a strong man and was working harder than ever, with more projects to do and committees to sit on, and refusing to relax or rest. Following the success of the Great Exhibition, he was involved in the planning of another international exhibition due to be held in South Kensington in 1862, for which a new building had to be designed and erected. He was involved in new housing schemes for the poor, the Horticultural Society and the continual building programmes at Osborne and Balmoral, as well as being his wife's unofficial advisor, head of his family and overseer of his children's education. At times he complained to Stockmar that he was so busy and tired that he would be unable to fight death if it loomed.

Both Victoria and Albert greatly missed their eldest daughter, Vicky, now living in Berlin, and were in a permanent state of anxiety about their eldest son, the future king. Bertie was easily impressed, especially by older, powerful men and felt inferior to his father. Prince Albert's expectations of him were frustrated by Bertie's inability to pass an examination or show any inclination to be interested in education. Rumours were beginning to spread in Britain and abroad about his lifestyle.

When it was reported to Albert that the Europeans knew about his son's affairs he was furious, but also upset that his son appeared to be on the same path to "sin" that so many of his relatives, on both sides of his family, had followed. A major concern was that if Princess Alexandra of Denmark heard about his antics she would refuse to meet him, let alone marry him. However Vicky, now the mother of a son and daughter, came to the rescue and arranged a meeting for the young couple in Germany.

Meanwhile, Princess Alice's suitor, Louis of Hesse-Darmstadt, was also proving elusive, but Prince Albert was so exhausted he could not think about this alliance. Vicky wanted her sister to marry a Prussian and only Queen Victoria was intent on the House of Hesse-Darmstadt. Then there was the health of young Leopold to worry about. One consolation for them was the vitality of little Beatrice, who charmed them all. However, by Christmas, 1860 both parents were distraught and exhausted.

Death of the Duchess of Kent

The previous rifts in the relationship between Queen Victoria and her mother had long been healed and the two were in almost daily contact with each other. The Duchess of Kent now lived in a large house at Frogmore, near Windsor and had an apartment at Osborne. Early in March 1861, she complained of an abscess and surgery

OPPOSITE: THE WIDOW, QUEEN VICTORIA IN MOURNING FOR HER HUSBAND.

DAGUERREOTYPE BY ANTOINE CLAUDET OF THE DUCHESS OF KENT, 1856.

was recommended to cure it. Surgery at this time was extremely hazardous and painful, as infections often occurred and anaesthesia was in its infancy. The operation proved unsuccessful and the Duchess's condition deteriorated.

On the evening of March 15, Queen Victoria was summoned from Buckingham Palace to her mother's bedside at Frogmore; both she and Albert were very upset to see the condition of the dying woman. Victoria spent most of the night tiptoeing in to see her mother who died the next morning, clasping her daughter's hand. Queen Victoria was distraught and Albert could do nothing to console her. The Court went into mourning and appropriate black clothes, black ribbons and black-edged writing paper were used by everyone.

Queen Victoria entered an abyss of a deep depression, insisting that she was now an orphan. When she went through her mother's papers, she discovered, to her amazement, that almost everything from her own childhood had been kept. In her mother's diary she read that, all those years ago, during the Conroy period when Victoria had felt nothing but contempt for her mother, the Duchess had loved her daughter. Victoria was devastated, having convinced

herself all those years ago that her mother did not care for her.

The more she read, the more grief-stricken she became. Soon, she had decided to build a mausoleum for her mother's remains at Frogmore. Building a mausoleum for a loved one was not unusual for the upper classes and aristocracy in the late eighteenth and nineteenth centuries. Uncle Leopold had built one for his first wife, Princess Charlotte, at Claremont in 1817 and Prince Albert and his brother had made one at Coburg for their father Duke Ernest, in 1844. In the late 1850s, under Prince Albert's direction, a small circular, stone summer house with a domed roof, designed by Ludwig Gruner who had worked at Osborne, was built for the Duchess in the grounds of Frogmore. Queen Victoria decided to convert this into a mausoleum for her mother. Here, on the ground floor, a full length statue of the Duchess was erected and on the floor below was laid a sarcophagus containing her remains.

Meanwhile, Prince Albert, possibly unable to deal with the raw state of his wife's grief, immersed himself, even more, in his work. Several weeks spent at Balmoral in the summer of 1861 seemed to revitalize Victoria, but not Albert. He grew weaker and was unable to shake off the effects of the frequent chills he caught.

By mid-November, more news of Bertie's escapades had reached the Royal Family, this time concerning an episode in Ireland. Exhausted and deeply upset Prince Albert managed to write a letter of forgiveness to his son. Unbeknown to Bertie, Albert told Victoria about this latest sign of waywardness in their eldest son.

The Death of Prince Albert

From this point, Victoria and the doctors noticed a rapid deterioration in Prince Albert's heath and energy which, in retrospect, they put down to the onset of the incubation period for the typhoid he contracted. Gradually, as the days progressed, his condition weakened and he became unable to attend functions as fever

QUEEN VICTORIA AND PRINCE ALBERT FORDING THE POLL TARF IN THE HIGHLANDS A FEW MONTHS BEFORE HIS DEATH.

set in. In her heart, Victoria knew things were bad but Sir James Clark and Dr William Jenner, who had become Royal Physician after the official retirement of Sir James in 1860, perhaps because they wanted to keep the worst from her, insisted he would improve and recover.

However, by the beginning of December, obviously suspecting typhoid, they advised her that his condition would deteriorate.

Dr William Jenner was well able to recognize the symptoms of typhoid. Jenner was a talented pathologist who had recently discovered the differences between the germs of typhoid and typhus. This was regarded as a landmark in the search to find a cure for these deadly endemic diseases. Jenner found that typhus was a fever contracted from an infected louse that bit the patient's body, spreading the disease through the blood stream; ten days later headaches, fever and rash occurred, followed by a coma and inevitable death.

Typhoid was different. Jenner had discovered that it was caused by contaminated food or water entering the body through the mouth. As good hygiene practice was poorly understood

DR WILLIAM JENNER,
THE ROYAL PHYSICIAN.

and clean sanitation procedures in their infancy, much food and water was unclean. Once the typhoid germ was in the body, septicaemia developed in the blood stream and after a ten-day incubation period the patient developed headaches, fevers, sleeplessness, a cough and diarrhoea. At the beginning of this stage, patients were still able to walk, but after two weeks a rash appeared and the bowel could haemorrhage as the internal organs became infected, mental confusion ensued and death followed soon after.

Victoria was distraught but tried her hardest to keep Albert's spirits up while he became delirious, feverish, bedridden and then, suddenly, ambulant again. Once, he got dressed and Dr Jenner advised Victoria that he was improving. Hope soon turned to despair, however, as she watched him become more delirious and bowel problems develop. After a week, he did not recognize her and spoke only in German.

By December 13, lying in the Blue Room at Windsor, his breathing was shallow and he was delirious. His distraught family gathered around the bed. The exhausted Queen was taken into an ante-room, Princess Alice constantly consoling her. Eventually, on Saturday December 14, 1861, Prince Albert died. Queen Victoria howled, she and her children were stunned; they had been given much false hope by the doctors. She had lost everything – her closest friend, adviser, husband and lover. As she wrote to Uncle Leopold, now referring to him as "father" a few days later, "... The poor fatherless baby of eight months is now the broken-hearted and crushed widow of forty two! My life as a happy one is ended! ..."

The widowed mother of nine children, the youngest only five years old, wanted to die and could see no future for herself coming out of this hopeless situation. She could not sleep in case she dreamed of Albert. She was upset at Bertie's grief but also angry with him, even blaming him for his father's death, thinking that perhaps the shock of the Irish exploits had irrevocably weakened Albert. In letters to Vicky, she described her loneliness, anxieties and insecurities about her work. Albert had sheltered and guided her but she felt she was still the immature nineteen-year-old:

I MUST WORK and WORK, and *can't rest* and the amount of work which comes upon me is MORE than *I can bear!* I who always hated business, have now nothing but that! Public and private, it falls upon me! He, my own darling, lightened all and every thing, spared every trouble and anxiety and now I must labour alone!

The royal children, too, were desolate at the loss of their "dearest Papa". Vicky's letters revealed the desperation that they felt, each having lost a trusted adviser and friend. Bertie was grief-stricken, he had never thought his father would die and had been shocked when he saw him on his death bed. Possibly he had believed that one day he would get his father's approval and now it was too late. A few hours after Albert's death, he comforted his mother by reassuring her that he would try to be good from now on.

Queen Victoria decreed that mourning for her husband should be the full three months and that the Household must wear black for a year. People attending Court had to wear black clothes. She herself took to wearing black for the rest of her life, a period of forty years, though sometimes she would lighten the effect by wearing a white collar and black jet beads. Uncle Leopold arrived and stayed some weeks,

to console his niece, attend the funeral and help with official matters.

Tributes rolled in, Alfred, Lord Tennyson wrote to her and the press lamented the Queen's and Nation's loss, claiming that Prince Albert had changed Britain and the world for the better. It was all very different from the hostile reception he had received when he arrived twenty years earlier: the foreigner was now British. His hard work, dedication and diligence were noted and intimations that he had affected every person's life were made. The tribute published by the *Illustrated London News*, on December 21, 1861, was typical:

The DEATH of his *Royal Highness Prince Albert*, on Saturday last, is the HEAVIEST NATIONAL CALAMITY which has *befallen* this country for many years ... Our *gracious* QUEEN! The hearts of her people bleed with hers. They share her agony of grief. They are overwhelmed with the same sense of desolation. The terrible tidings which...ruthlessly crushed her loving spirit have sorely bruised theirs also. England mourns with her widowed Queen. Every family in the land is smitten with the awe and the sorrow which Death excites when he breaks into the domestic circle and snatches from it its chief pride and joy. For the moment there seems no consolation. It is all dark and mysterious ...

Most of us can recall the joyous satisfaction we felt in common with all her fellow-subjects when the young Prince came hither from his father's Court to claim the fulfilment of what maiden love had promised. Royal marriages had so seldom in this country been a union of hearts as well as hands that this exception to the rule awakened the liveliest interest, ... everything concurred to surround them with an atmosphere of affectionate sympathy, and to diffuse over the whole kingdom the gladness of hope ... The bridegroom became the husband, the husband the father, the father the grandsire, without losing in any degree the hold he had taken upon the esteem and respect of the nation."

The journal continued by commenting that when he arrived, without status or purpose, Prince Albert could have become a man of leisure, but chose not to, finding a role in elevating the humanities and sciences and improving the lives of the people of Britain. The Great Exhibition was, it claimed, his major achievement.

The Prince's Funeral

In the nineteenth century, women did not attend funerals, and Victoria followed established protocol by not going to her husband's funeral. The Prince of Wales was chief mourner, accompanied by his brother Prince Alfred and Prince Albert's brother, Duke Ernest of Saxe-Coburg-Gotha. Prince Albert's funeral was to be, according to the *Illustrated*

THE ROYAL FUNERAL CORTEGE OF PRINCE ALBERT IN ST GEORGE'S CHAPEL AT WINDSOR.

London News, "… by the express desire of his Royal Highness … of the plainest and most private character …". It was held, breaking with royal tradition, at St George's Chapel, Windsor on December 28.

From dawn on that day the Union flag flew at half mast on the Round Tower at Windsor Castle and gun salutes were fired, at five minute intervals, by the Royal Artillery. The town came to a standstill as hoards of people arrived for the funeral. Throughout the country shops and business closed and services were held in churches and synagogues to pay respect to the Queen's late husband. In London, a service for 4,000 people, all wearing black, was held at St Paul's Cathedral and all the ships on the Thames flew flags at half mast. Never before had a royal death affected the nation to such a degree.

At 10.30 in the morning, a train arrived at Windsor station from London, bringing noblemen and statesmen, as commanded by the Queen, and at 11.30 the progress to St George's Chapel began. Politicians of opposing parties attended and sat together. Lord Palmerston, who had been Prime Minister since 1859, was unable to attend because he had been laid low by an attack of gout.

At noon the guns were fired at one-minute intervals as the funeral cortège arrived at the chapel. It was made up of ten mourning coaches, each drawn by four horses, carrying gentlemen closely associated with the Prince, including Dr Jenner, Sir James Clark, valets, equerries, Lords in Waiting, the Lord Chamberlain and the Master of the Bedchamber. The last carriage in the procession carried the State liveries and Earl Spencer, who was Groom of the Stole to his late Royal Highness. Then the Hearse arrived, drawn by six horses and an escort of Life Guards and followed by four more carriages carrying the family mourners. The mourners entered the chapel through Wolsey's Gateway and were followed by the coffin carried by pallbearers.

The Prince of Wales, Prince Arthur and Duke Ernest were very emotional as the lessons were read and German hymns sung, including

Luther's "Great God, what do I see and hear!". As the Coffin descended into the Royal Vault, cries of grief could be heard from the mourners. When the "Dead March" was played, the Prince of Wales returned to the vault to place on it flowers that had been sent from Osborne that morning, at the express wish of his mother.

Prince Albert's death was recorded in the Town Register Book of Windsor, witnessed by the registrar of births and deaths, Mr Towers, and signed by the Prince of Wales, having been present when his father passed away. The cause of death was given as "Typhoid fever; duration, twenty-one days".

The Court in Mourning

Periods of mourning were all too common for everyone in Victorian Britain and the Royal Family was not unusual in having to face up to such grief. Sudden and untimely deaths occurred in most families; mothers and babies died, children and adults succumbed to disease or industrial accidents and wars caused the deaths of thousands of young men. Mourning fashions were advertised in journals and dressmakers adapted existing styles to the mourning requirements of their clients.

When the refugee Huguenot, George Courtauld became an apprentice silk weaver in Spitalfields in London's East End in 1775, little did anyone imagine that his son's company would become responsible for producing thousands and thousands of yards of black crêpe, made to a secret formula, in the 1850s and 1860s, for the middle- and upper-classes to wear in their grief. In 1860, the silk manufacturers of Lyons, in France, had hit difficulties and, fortuitously, British textile dealers bought up huge amounts of their stock at cheap prices, which meant that at the time of Prince Albert's death, mourning fashions were accessible to a greater number of people than ever before.

The fashion for mourning grew greater over the years, with more and more advertisements for the latest black dress, coat and hat designs and jet jewellery appearing in journals and newspapers – even in mourning and grief a woman had to be

MOURNING FASHION BY JULES DAVID IN *LE MONITEUR DE LA MODE.*

fashionable. However, the fashion for black did little to help many struggling haberdashery business whose success was built on producing and utilizing coloured yarns and fabrics.

According to the costume historian Kay Stanniland, the designs for Queen Victoria's mourning dresses, even immediately after Prince Albert's death, followed the latest fashions, where the influences of the new French couture houses were being felt. A British designer working in Paris, Charles Frederick Worth, patronized by Empress Eugénie and Queen Victoria, was particularly fashionable. Victoria wore a fashionable black crêpe dress with a fitted bodice to the waist and full skirt, tuck pleated over the hips, and a small white collar and white lace widow's cap. Her children also donned black: poplin dresses, black stockings and shoes for the girls and black suits and shoes for the boys.

In its issue of December 28, 1861, the **Illustrated London News** published details of different types of mourning dresses suitable for the fashionable woman to wear. The French influence was apparent:

Black Crape and Jet
Dec 28 1861
"FASHIONS FOR JANUARY"
MOURNING

The CORINNE is a dress of *rich glacé silk*, with one flounce, trimmed round the bottom with crape, and finished at each point with rich jet, and silk ornaments, with a fluting of crape eighteen inches from the bottom. Bodice square Pagoda sleeves, showing undersleeve of white tulle; the waist and side of the skirt ornamented with crape poche a la Chatelaine, suitably trimmed.

The MONTE ROSA is a *mantle* circular in shape, large, and falling gracefully over the figure; the style of trimming is the great novelty, and is composed of broad bands of crape, corded with silk, carried round the neck and down the centre of the back and front, terminating at a distance from the bottom of the mantle with handsome tassel ornaments; a fold of crape round the skirt.

HEADDRESS, *coronet of jet flowers*, fullness of glacé at the back, with drooping jet falling over it; rich black ostrich plume on the right side. Bouquet of jet flowers to correspond.

Queen Victoria's Mourning Rituals

On Albert's death Victoria quickly put into effect certain rituals, many of which continued until her own death forty years later. None of his rooms was to be disturbed and portraits of him were pinned on the wall above his bed. Busts and statues were made of him and stood in rooms. At Osborne, in January 1862, she wrote, from his desk, to Vicky, clearly believing Albert to be present:

... writing in *beloved* PAPA'S *room*, at his table, and let me in both our names – for *dear* PAPA does wish you JOY too I know and feel it – wish you JOY our *dear*, darling, little William's birthday ... He loved that dear child so dearly, felt so anxious about him, was so sure he would be so clever ...

A WEDDING
PHOTOGRAPH OF THE PRINCE
AND PRINCESS OF WALES.

At Windsor, Queen Victoria planned to dedicate the Blue Room, where Albert had died, to him, making it a sacred place with busts and sculptures, and some Raphael drawings printed on to china. Mr Gruner was again requested to come and advise her.

Perhaps her greatest ritual, because it was the one that fixed her image so firmly in the minds of her people, was the donning of the widow's cap and black clothes that she wore for the rest of her life. She would never forget Albert and would live forever bounded by her grief for him.

Just over six months after her father's death, in July 1862, Princess Alice finally married Prince Louis of Hesse-Darmstadt. The ceremony was held privately, at Buckingham Palace, and Queen Victoria dominated the proceedings with her depression and her black clothing. She had relented enough to agree to her daughter wearing a white wedding dress but insisted on a black trousseau. The following year, the Prince of Wales married Princess Alexandra of Denmark at St George's Chapel, Windsor. Again, Queen Victoria attended and watched from the gallery, dressed in black and radiating sadness.

Within weeks of Prince Albert's death plans were afoot for many appropriate private and public memorials. The Queen began planning her husband's final resting place and her own memorials to him within days of his death. Following the building of the mausoleum to the Duchess of Kent, Queen Victoria embarked on creating a joint one for her husband and herself, as well as plans for the conversion of a side chapel of St George's Chapel into the Albert Memorial Chapel. She and Albert had, many years before, talked about their burial plans and had decided against the official royal places of rest in Westminster Abbey and St George's Chapel. No doubt influenced by the fashion for mausoleums, they had decided to build one for their own remains.

Four days after his death Victoria found a site in the grounds of Frogmore, near that of her mother. Ludwig Gruner was appointed architect and designer, accompanied by A. J. Humbert, and Queen Victoria and the family, especially Vicky, all contributed to the plans. Work started in the spring of 1862 and was

PRINCE ALBERT'S TOMB
IN THE MAUSOLEUM
AT FROGMORE.

advanced enough to be consecrated the following December. It was nine years before the
building was completed, however, and Queen
Victoria, not the nation, paid all the costs.

The building was of classical and not gothic
design, the ground plan was based on a Greek
cross 70 feet (21.4 metres) wide, and the
central dome built to a height of 70 feet (21.4
metres). The building was constructed of
granite brought from all over Britain and of
Portland stone and the domed roof was of
Australian copper. Statues and medallions
adorned the walls, inside and out, all gifts from

grieving relatives, and paintings, in the style of
Raphael, adorned many of the interior walls.

In 1868, Prince Albert's remains were placed
in a tomb of grey Aberdeen granite in the
centre of the interior Octagon. Space was left
alongside it for those of Queen Victoria.
Effigies were made of both of them by Carlo
Marochetti in 1867, and the one of Prince
Albert was placed on his tomb. Four smaller
chapels radiated from the Octagon. Here, for
the rest of her life, Queen Victoria would visit
her beloved Albert and took solace in being
close to him. In 1863 Baron Stockmar also died

and Queen Victoria honoured him by placing a commemorative cross, the Stockmar Cross, in the grounds of Frogmore. Now, Uncle Leopold was the only one who remained alive from Queen Victoria's early life.

The architect George Gilbert Scott was engaged to convert the chapel at Windsor into the Albert Memorial Chapel, which became a fine example of Victorian gothic decoration within an original gothic building. Here, the high vaulted ceiling was covered in Italian mosaics and marble, and inlaid pictures by Henri de Triqueti, depicting biblical scenes which Victoria felt were reminiscent of the goodness of Prince Albert and his life, covered the walls.

Plans for a public memorial were also soon being discussed. Henry Cole, recalling Prince Albert's ideas for a school of design and a huge campus of the arts, sciences and humanities, suggested that an "industrial university" should be established, like London University, to be known as Albert University. This suggestion eventually became the great centre of museums and colleges of the arts and sciences in London's South Kensington, built from profits of the Great Exhibition. The Victoria and Albert Museum, Science Museum and British Museum Department of Natural History were housed alongside the Royal College of Art, Imperial College of Science and Technology, Royal School of Mines, Royal College of Music, Royal College of Organists and the Royal Albert Hall. This campus became known as the Albertropolis and, although no longer so-called, remains Prince Albert's greatest memorial. Its colleges and museums are still recognized as centres of excellence throughout the world.

A more public memorial, built in Kensington Gardens facing the Albertropolis, was planned in 1862 and took ten years to complete. The idea for the Albert Memorial was first discussed at a meeting at the Mansion House in the City of London, fund-raising for it took place throughout the country, and Parliament gave £50,000. Queen Victoria was very involved in the project and selected the final design, again by Scott.

This splendid Victorian gothic memorial was built on a base 200 feet (61 metres) square and

PAINTING BY EDWIN HOLT OF THE NEWLY BUILT ALBERT MEMORIAL.

a canopy, 180 feet (55 metres) high, rose over the statue of Prince Albert. The whole edifice was covered with friezes and sculptures representing Europe, Africa, Asia and America; steps of granite led up to the statue of Prince Albert, which was surrounded by pedestals of sculpted figures representing Agriculture, Manufacture, Commerce and Engineering, and other figures of painters, poets, architects, musicians, and men of science and the humanities. The huge statue of Prince Albert, wearing his Garter robes and holding a copy of the Official Catalogue of the Great Exhibition, by John Foley was unveiled in 1876. In 1863, the Society of Arts inaugurated its Albert Medal to respect the work of Prince Albert as President of the Society.

By organizing memorial meetings and observing her rituals of mourning, Queen Victoria became completely trapped in her grief and seemed to disappear from public gaze, despite her position as Sovereign. Believing that her country and Empire would understand, since her devastating loss was also theirs, she became a recluse for many years.

Chapter 9 The Widow

Queen Victoria's attitude to widowhood, while extreme by modern standards, was not unusual for the nineteenth century. In the days before women's emancipation, all decision-making was a husband's domain in his capacity as head of the household, while his wife remained loyal to him and respected all his opinions. Like other husbands, Prince Albert had been head of his family and his wife had been subservient to him; even in her dress, she only wore clothes her husband approved of and would not venture out if he disliked her appearance.

But unlike most other men of his age, Albert had been more than a husband to his wife, and Queen Victoria not only grieved the loss of her partner but also the loss of a confidante and, more importantly, an adviser in all things relating to her role as monarch. During her first twenty years as queen he had told her how to react, and what to say and do. Now, he was gone. At first, she was able to anticipate what his response to a specific situation would have been, but as time wore on and perspectives inevitably changed, Queen Victoria had to learn to form her own opinions and make independent decisions.

Personalities had also changed and she could no longer assume that she would have the support and guidance of her prime ministers as she had done with Melbourne in earlier times. Lord Palmerston died in 1865 and his place was briefly taken by Earl Russell, followed by the Earl of Derby, then Benjamin Disraeli, whose first short term as Prime Minister occurred in 1868. The Liberals (Whigs) won an election in 1868 and remained in power, with William Gladstone as Prime Minister, until 1874. Although Gladstone became one of the century's greatest prime ministers, Queen Victoria never liked him, once complaining that "he speaks to Me as if I was a public meeting". Gladstone's reforming nature and his desire to make the British monarchy a truly constitutional one, often to the exclusion of Queen Victoria, enraged her.

Among widows of Victoria's reign, a total absorption in harrowing grief was common, as was the establishing of rituals which might be followed for years, or even the rest of the widow's life. For Victoria, rituals such as leaving Prince Albert's rooms as they had been

PRINCE ALBERT'S PERSONAL SITTING ROOM AT BALMORAL FROM QUEEN VICTORIA'S "LEAVES FROM THE JOURNAL OF OUR LIFE IN THE HIGHLANDS".

at the time of his death and lighting fires in them, and observing his birthday, were vital to keeping his memory alive, for guilt could quickly creep in if that memory waned or was superseded by happier thoughts. Queen Victoria became history's greatest widow, during a period which lasted for 40 years. At times it almost became a cult for her to follow, though it would be wrong to underestimate the depth of her genuine despair, as a letter to Vicky from Osborne on January 22, 1863 describes:

I MUST have *some* days of as much *quiet* as I possibly can. You never will *believe* how UNWELL and how WEAK and *nervous* I am, but any talking or excitement is far too much for me. I must constantly dine alone, and any merriment or discussion are quite unbearable.

OPPOSITE: QUEEN VICTORIA LOOKING MORE THAN HER 48 YEARS IN A PHOTOGRAPH BY W & D DOWNY TAKEN AT BALMORAL IN 1867.

Retreat to Albert's Houses

Essential to Victoria's devotion to Albert was the spending of much time at Osborne and Balmoral. These were homes created by him and his presence could be felt throughout them, making Queen Victoria feel more comfortable, even believing, in her despair, that he might reappear. It was at Balmoral and Osborne that she now lived for most of her time, becoming a virtual recluse for ten years and rarely visiting Buckingham Palace and Windsor Castle.

To many around her, this was a great trial as they could be separated for months on end from their families and London life. At Balmoral, in particular, life could be very uncomfortable. Queen Victoria insisted that heat should be minimal and, even on the coldest of days, the windows were to remain open. Nobody was allowed to contradict the Queen in these matters, or any other. The gloom and despair must have been exhausting and intolerable as the months and years wore on.

At times Queen Victoria contemplated the afterlife and whether she would see her beloved Albert again, and would sit in a room "expecting to see dear Papa every minute!", as she told her daughter. Her clothing, too, became that of an elderly widow as she intentionally dressed to look much older than her years. A photograph of her in 1866, when she was aged 47, showed the image of a woman apparently in her mid-sixties. As she no longer had to dress to please Albert she chose more comfortable dresses and even stopped wearing some of her corsetry so that she appeared plumper.

As the focus of Queen Victoria's life became totally fixed on the loss of Prince Albert, she published anthologies of his speeches and contemplated publishing a biography. Alone, she watched the plans for the prospective marriages of her children, sometimes discussing them with Vicky who had now become her confidante, despite the geographical distance between them. In 1863 she visited Coburg and went to the Rosenau to see the memorial erected to Prince Albert and visited Vicky in Berlin en route.

So immersed was she in her widowhood that Queen Victoria became ignorant of the feelings of her people, mistakenly assuming that they shared the enormity and desolation of her grief. Dr Jenner, fearing her physical and mental health might deteriorate further, often insisted that news of any republican talk should be kept from her. While there had been public shock and many condolences expressed immediately after Albert's sudden death, the mythical proportions of his goodness could not be sustained in the public mind and many wondered how anyone could have been so perfect.

The Queen's subjects looked on as Victoria immersed herself in widowhood and memorials, her grief seeming no nearer to abatement. As the years went by and their reclusive monarch showed so sign of reappearing before her people, there were increasing calls for her abdication and questions were often asked about the cost of this absent queen's Civil List. Queen Victoria did not help the situation by demanding more money from Gladstone's government for herself and her family.

SIR HENRY PONSONBY.

Household Changes

Not everything could stay as it had been at the time of Albert's death, and Victoria had to accept changes in her immediate entourage. Sir Henry Ponsonby, who had been an equerry to Prince Albert, became Queen Victoria's secretary. He was a likeable, humorous man and his relaxed wife was a refreshing change to many of the more formal women in the household. In 1865 came the death of Uncle Leopold, the last of her childhood father figures. Uncle Leopold had helped her after Prince Albert's death and even advised her on parliamentary matters. Victoria was now Head of the Family.

The world that Victoria had retreated from was changing, too. In 1863 the world's first underground railway was built between Bishop's Road and Farringdon Street in London. In 1865, a movement began for women's suffrage, which Queen Victoria would not support, believing that women should be subservient to men. Mr Gladstone was determined to pass another Reform Act and both political parties were realigning. The Whigs became Liberals and the party of reform under Gladstone. The Tories, under Disraeli, became the party of the Empire, capitalism and generation of wealth under a monarchy.

The Queen's Highland Servant

Gradually, Victoria's children married and had their own families, naturally taking more interest in their lives than in that of their mother. Queen Victoria, in her despair and loneliness, formed an unusual and remarkably close friendship with a Highland ghillie, who had first become known to her when she and Prince Albert began to develop the estate at Balmoral twenty years earlier. John Brown had accompanied them on many of their Highland jaunts and Prince Albert had appointed him his personal ghillie. From the outset he seemed an unlikely person to command the Queen's total attention and devotion, but that he did for almost twenty years was astonishing.

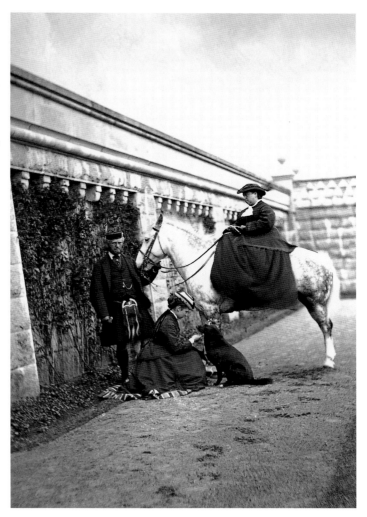

QUEEN VICTORIA WITH JOHN BROWN, PRINCESS LOUISE KNEELING, IN A PHOTOGRAPH BY W & D DOWNY.

In the winter of 1864, Dr Jenner suggested that Victoria take up horse riding again as a way to becoming fitter mentally and physically. John Brown was summoned from Balmoral to Osborne for the winter to be her groom. Where Henry Ponsonby was a sophisticated, educated gentleman, albeit with a wry sense of humour, John Brown was a rough Highlander, who was not averse to a dram of whisky and was not afraid to speak his mind. He seemed oblivious to royal protocol and people looked on askance when he called Her Majesty 'Wumman!', refusing to take "no" from her as an answer. Almost immediately, Victoria responded to Brown's straight talking and cheek; no one had ever

THE QUEEN IN HER PONY AND TRAP ACCOMPANIED BY FIVE GRANDCHILDREN AND JOHN BROWN STANDING AT THE PONY'S HEAD AT OSBORNE.

addressed her so directly and gradually he coaxed her to take up riding again, which she had found so relaxing as a young woman, enabling her to escape from the tedium of life at Kensington Palace.

The relationship with Brown quickly became very close and she began to depend on him for advice, discussing affairs with him. At last, a man whom she could trust had reappeared and they became inseparable. John Brown was not liked in the household, court or family as he had succeeded where nobody else had. He even managed to make her smile and laugh. To the public, their absent Queen became a happy recluse and their disapproval increased. Some even spread rumours that she and Brown had married and gossipmongers called her "Mrs Brown".

Queen Victoria's biographer, Elizabeth Longford, has found no evidence that they were lovers, just very good friends; in John Brown Queen Victoria had found a man she could lean upon once again. The situation with her public was not helped by her creating a new title for him, that of "The Queen's Highland Servant",

in 1865. She also increased his salary, promoted him within the household and gave him a cottage at Balmoral. Weeks were spent roaming

CARTOON, PUBLISHED IN *LE RIRE* OF VICTORIA AND JOHN BROWN.

across the Highlands, visiting Brown's friends and family or being involved in the minutiae of the Highlanders' lives. The Queen recorded many of these moments in her published journals of her life in the Highlands. From *More Leaves from a Journal of our Life in the Highlands*, published in 1884, comes this sad story:

TUESDAY, JUNE 11, 1872.

BROWN came in *soon* after four o'clock, saying he had been DRAWN down to the *waterside*, for a *child* had FALLEN in the *water* … but it must be drowned. I was dreadfully SHOCKED. It was the child of a man named Rattray … with Beatrice and Jane Ely … [we] drove along the north side of the river…Two women told us that two children had fallen in (how terrible!), and that one 'been gotten - the little een' … They were searching everywhere … amongst them was the poor father – a sad and piteous sight – crying and looking so anxiously for his poor child's body …

THURSDAY, JUNE 13.

… [We] DROVE out…to the small cottage called *Cairn-na-Craig* … BROWN went in *first*, and was received by the old grandmother … On a table in the kitchen covered with a sheet … lay the poor sweet innocent 'bairnie" …

Brown went everywhere with her, read her mail to her and discussed state affairs; she even quoted his advice and thoughts. He accompanied her on trips abroad even though, Dr Reid, the newly recruited Scottish physician reported, Brown hated being away from Scotland. As a mark of her appreciation of his devotion to her, Queen Victoria lavished presents on him. At Christmas in 1876 she gave him a large silver teapot with the words "Given by V to J Brown" engraved on the front and her insignia on the reverse. Other presents included a crystal and silver decanter and a silver shaving kit.

THE PRIMROSE WALTZ, A MUSIC SHEET INCORPORATING A PORTRAIT OF BENJAMIN DISRAELI.

Another New Figure

It was with relief that in 1868 Queen Victoria welcomed a new Prime Minister more to her taste than Gladstone and his successor, Lord Derby, had been. Benjamin Disraeli was the grandson of an Italian Jewish immigrant to London and the young Disraeli had grown up in a poor but intellectual family. But his father became estranged from London's Jewish community and when Benjamin was 13 had all his children baptised into the Church of England. This meant that the ambitious young Benjamin Disraeli was able to take a seat in the House of Commons and eventually become Prime Minister.

While John Brown straight talked, Disraeli charmed the Queen, calling her his "faery" and she gave him primroses. Disraeli

GIFTS FROM QUEEN VICTORIA TO JOHN BROWN. A SILVER MOUNTED GLASS CLARET JUG (LEFT) MADE BY MARK ROBERT HENNELL WITH "V.R TO J.B." INSCRIBED ON IT AND A SILVER TEAPOT (RIGHT) MADE BY GARRARD AND "FROM VICTORIA R TO J.B. CHRISTMAS 1876" INSCRIBED ON IT.

QUEEN VICTORIA OPENS THE ROYAL ALBERT HALL, FROM THE *ILLUSTRATED LONDON NEWS*, APRIL 8, 1871.

was fascinated by the Empire, seeing it as a way of enhancing capitalist growth and making many British companies very wealthy by trading with and servicing the Empire. This desire to make Britain a truly Imperial power could only work if he could persuade its reclusive monarch of its validity and the need for her to be more public. Seduced by his charm, and fascinated by his thoughts on the Empire, she agreed, somewhat nervously, to attend the State Opening of Parliament for the first time since Prince Albert's death.

But Disraeli's first premiership lasted only until the end of 1868 and then Gladstone was back for a further six years. While Gladstone had minimal interest in the Empire and did little to abate the reclusive nature of Queen Victoria, he introduced constitutional and other reforming changes in Britain in the 1860s and 1870s; such changes did not help Victoria conquer the absolute loathing she felt for him.

Reappearance

Gradually, from the beginning of the 1870s, ten years after Prince Albert's death, Queen Victoria began to feel stronger and more confident about herself and her place in the world. She received counselling from the Archbishop anxiety to her. She liked his wife Princess Alexandra but did not help Bertie by continuing to make clear to him her misgivings about his ability to be King, delegating few of her responsibilities to him. The Prince's recovery from typhoid brought about a change. In February 1872, in recognition of Bertie's recovery and in some way to mark her own recovery, she attended a public Thanksgiving Service in St Paul's Cathedral. The next day, a sixth attempt at reginacide was made on the Queen. This time, John Brown caught the would-be assassin, Arthur O'Connor, who had pointed an unloaded pistol at her.

The Queen's image was softening, too. Her clothing became a little more relaxed as jet beading and silk frills were added as decoration to her black dresses. But with her white widow's cap and great black dresses she still retained the air of an old woman. Sometimes she wore some of her splendid diamond and sapphire jewellery, though her jewellery purchases were on a more restrained scale, usually consisting of bracelets and lockets, than they had been in the early years of her marriage.

Ever since her coronation Queen Victoria had found her crown very heavy and cumbersome to wear and the arrangements to wear it tiresome; for every wearing, it had to be retrieved from the security of the Jewel House in the Tower of London. In 1870 she commissioned a smaller crown for her personal use. It was made of 1,300 diamonds taken from a large necklace, weighed only just over 5oz (160g) and was just 33/4in (9cm) high. Images of Queen Victoria from this period until the end of her life often show her wearing this tiny crown perched on the top of her head over her widow's cap.

A MINIATURE OF QUEEN VICTORIA WEARING HER SMALL CROWN ON TOP OF HER WIDOW'S CAP.

of Canterbury about the possibility of feeling happier without being disingenuous to the deceased and was strengthened by John Brown's support. One of her first public engagements of the 1870s was to visit the Albert Hall, built on land opposite the site of the memorial to her husband in Kensington Gardens and officially opened in 1871.

There was also a dreadful fright for the Queen in 1871. In the autumn, the Prince of Wales, by now the father of five children, became desperately ill with typhoid. Queen Victoria, fearing a repeat of Prince Albert's death, dashed to his bedside but, fortunately, he recovered. At this time, Bertie was still an

Chapter *10* Victoria's Empires

The death of Uncle Leopold in 1865 and the marriages of her own children into royal houses across Europe made Queen Victoria effectively Head of European Royalty, which was like an empire in itself – less extensive or powerful than the British Empire, perhaps, but influential nevertheless. In 1864 a son, Albert, was born to the Prince and Princess of Wales, followed by another son, George, the next year. Now, not only was Victoria's succession secure, but so was that of her son.

The weddings of her children, the births of grandchildren and their subsequent marriages all took up a great deal of the Queen's time. Not only was the appropriateness of a future husband's or wife's personality considered but also the political implications for Britain in any proposed alliance. At times, Queen Victoria could be appalled by the behaviour of the young, however carefully chosen: engaged couples went out unchaperoned, sometimes a daughter or granddaughter displayed her pregnant shape by wearing fashionable tightly fitted clothes.

Events in Berlin often caused the Queen great worry and the copious correspondence between her and Vicky, the Crown Princess of Prussia, was full of their anxieties. Not only was Victoria concerned on the political front, she was also worried about her grandchildren, especially her eldest grandson, Wilhelm. His birth and early childhood had delighted her, but Wilhelm was born with a weak neck and a withered left arm which, despite attempts to correct it with exercises, never grew to its full size. Correspondence between the Crown Princess and Queen Victoria in April 1863 indicates the degree to which they were prepared to go to attempt to correct the four-year-old's deformities.

In a letter from Berlin, the Crown Princess wrote to her mother:

… they are going to put the *poor child* in a MACHINE on account of his not being able to hold his head *straight* … this machine is sure to EXHAUST him a little … Langenbeck [the doctor] … thinks the turn of the head is serious and the only thing he thinks doubtful about Willie. He wishes to cut the right side of the neck and then the machine to be worn for a short time.

The Queen's reply, written at Windsor Castle, expressed her horror "at the idea of cutting poor dear little William's neck and putting him into a machine".

As he grew up, Wilhelm found his father weak and ineffectual and the devotion of his mother overpowering, especially her attempts to instil in him the values she had inherited from Prince Albert. However, Wilhelm was always intent on forging his own way ahead. Realizing, as political events unfolded in Europe, that a unified Germany would have to be created, he became attracted by the image of himself as a powerful and dominant ruler of its people. This was a very different image of his role from that held by his maternal grandmother, who was outspoken in her despair of her grandson's increasing arrogance and disregard for other people.

Life was complicated for Vicky as she championed the cause of her father. He had wanted a liberal, united Germany, while her father-in-law, the Emperor, wanted Prussia to dominate the nation. Such differences of opinion often led to strained relationships between family members in Britain, Germany and Russia. These family arguments always caused Queen Victoria great personal anguish. Nevertheless, Queen Victoria and her daughter remained close and in their letters discussed every possible problem as it arose, whether it related to the family or to politics.

OPPOSITE: "AN ALLEGORY OF THE BRITISH EMPIRE" BY ARTHUR DRUMMOND.

THE WEDDING CEREMONY
OF PRINCE ALFRED
AND GRAND DUCHESS
MARIE, DAUGHTER OF
TSAR ALEXANDER OF
RUSSIA IN ST PETERSBURG.

Family Marriages and Deaths

Marriages of Victoria and Albert's children into the royal houses of Europe took place at regular intervals in the 1860s and 1870s. The Schleswig-Holstein connection was further strengthened in 1866 by the marriage of Princess Helena, called "Lenchen" by her family, to Prince Christian of Schleswig-Holstein. The couple had four children.

In January 1874, Alfred, Duke of Edinburgh, despite earlier escapades with unsuitable women and the protestations of his mother, who distrusted the Russian royal family, finally married Marie, the only daughter of the Tsar, in St Petersburg. The couple were to have six children, one of whom became King of Rumania in 1914.

In 1878, Prince Arthur, Duke of Connaught, became engaged to Princess Louise Margaret, daughter of Princess Louise and Prince Frederick of Prussia, which at first Queen Victoria found difficult, as Louise's parents were divorced and she herself was not particularly attractive. But by now Victoria had learnt not to get in the way of a couple determined to marry. This marriage produced three children. The marriage of Princess Louise to a British Liberal MP the Marquis of Lorne, who later became Duke of Argyll, was a great relief to Queen Victoria because it meant they would live in England. Sadly Louise, who lived until 1939, and her husband had no children.

The Queen's delight in her children's marriages and the joy which her grandchildren brought her were countered by the sadness of several deaths of relatives close to her. In 1872 her sister Feodore died at the age of 64. By this time, the wider consequences of Leopold's haemophilia were being felt within the extended family. In 1873, Princess Alice's three-year-old son Friederich Wilhelm died of it, because his mother was a carrier.

Then, in 1878 Alice's four-year-old daughter, Marie, contracted diphtheria. Alice herself caught the infection and on December 14, the anniversary of her father's death, she died. Queen Victoria was distraught. Alice had been a vital support to her during Albert's last days and now she was dead. Victoria resolved to become a mother figure to her daughter's remaining five children living in Darmstadt.

Now experienced in the design of memorials, Queen Victoria had a large cross of Aberdeen granite erected in memory of her "darling Alice" at Balmoral. On it were inscribed the words:

TO THE DEAR MEMORY OF
ALICE, GRAND DUCHESS OF HESSE
PRINCESS OF GREAT BRITAIN AND IRELAND
BORN APRIL 25 1843, DIED DEC.14 1878
THIS IS ERECTED
BY HER SORROWING MOTHER
QUEEN VICTORIA

For the Queen personally, worse was to come. In the spring of 1883 she fell downstairs, which caused much pain and the recurrence of previous knee problems. John Brown carried her from the sofa to her pony chair and Dr Jenner and the newly recruited Highlander, Dr Reid, attended her. But Brown himself was not well. He had been overworking and erysipelas, an infection of the skin causing fever and a purple pallor, was diagnosed.

Both the Queen and her companion were ill and neither seemed to recover quickly. John

Brown's condition deteriorated and the Queen was not aware, until it was too late, of its seriousness. On March 27, 1883, John Brown died. Prince Leopold had to break the news to his mother. Not for the first time, Queen Victoria was distraught; once again she had lost a dependable companion. As befits some-one close to the monarch, but not a servant, John Brown's body lay in state for six days and Queen Victoria, breaking with tradition, attended his funeral at Crathie Church at Balmoral. She even announced his death in the Court Circular of **The Times**.

Again memorials were built, including a life-size statue in the grounds at Balmoral and a bust at Osborne. Tie pins, incorporating photographs of John Brown, were made and given to the staff, some of whom refused to wear them, their loathing of him being so great. For Brown's mother, the Queen commissioned a brooch to be made with an oval gilt frame, about three inches (10cm) high, with a photograph of John Brown on one side and a lock of his hair displayed on the reverse. Around the frame were the words "Dear John 27 March 1883". In her concluding chapter of **More Leaves from a Journal of our Life in the Highlands**, Queen Victoria wrote of him in glowing terms:

…The FAITHFUL *attendant* … is no longer with her whom he served so *truly*, DEVOTEDLY, *untiringly* … His LOSS to me … is *irreparable*, for he deservedly possessed my entire confidence; and to say that he is daily, nay, hourly, missed by me, whose lifelong gratitude he won by his constant care, attention, and devotion, is but a feeble expression of truth.

Despite all the accidents and setbacks caused by his haemophilia, Prince Leopold did reach adulthood and married Princess Helen of Waldeck-Pyrmont in April 1882. Queen Victoria attended the ceremony. She was impressed by Helen's devotion to her son, especially as she had informed her future daughter-in-law of Leopold's prognosis and the difficulties of living with such a sick man.

In 1883 a daughter, Alice, was born. Helen became pregnant again early the next year, so Leopold went without her on one of his respite trips to the warmth of the South of France. It was here, while out walking in Cannes, that he fell badly. Messages were quickly sent to England warning that he was failing fast; the fall, as was common with

"DEAR JOHN" – THE MOURNING BROOCH PRESENTED BY QUEEN VICTORIA TO MRS BROWN.

THE TOMB OF PRINCESS ALICE.

MARRIAGE OF PRINCE LEOPOLD TO PRINCESS HELEN OF
WALDECK-PYRMONT IN ST GEORGE'S CHAPEL, WINDSOR.

haemophiliacs, had caused internal swelling. Leopold did not recover and died the next day, the first anniversary of John Brown's death. His son, Prince Charles Edward, was born after his death. For Queen Victoria and his widow Leopold's death was a terrible and devastating shock. After the deaths of Alice and Leopold Queen Victoria always wore a locket with a miniature photograph of each of them on either side. Prince Leopold was buried in the newly transformed Prince Albert Memorial Chapel at Windsor Castle.

A Marriage with Many Consequences

Queen Victoria had to regain her strength quickly because one month after Leopold's death her granddaughter, Princess Victoria of Hesse-Darmstadt, Alice's daughter, was to marry Prince Louis of Battenberg in Darmstadt. Still determined to be the mother figure to her dead daughter's children, she attended the wedding in Darmstadt but not the celebrations afterwards as she was still in mourning for Leopold.

This wedding, in the heart of Europe in mid-1884, was quite a family gathering, and had many repercussions. The Crown Prince Frederick, Crown Princess Victoria (Vicky), Wilhelm and Victoria came from Berlin; the Prince and Princess of Wales and Princess Beatrice from England were there, and many other guests, most of them related in some way or other.

For the tiny state of Hesse-Darmstadt it was a joyous occasion, but there was a great deal of intrigue and excitement in the background as well. Queen Victoria's dead daughter's husband, the Grand Duke of Hesse-Darmstadt, had kept the relationship with his mistress, Madam Alexandrine de Kolémine, a secret, with the excuse that he did not want to defame the memory of his wife. On the evening of his daughter's marriage, he secretly married Madame de Kolémine; three days later it was left to Bertie to tell his mother. She was furious and hurt, insisting the marriage be annulled, which it eventually was. In true regal style, Victoria remained in Darmstadt for the full length of her stay, never mentioning the "misdemeanour" and even returned to England accompanied by the Grand Duke.

Excitements and romances blossomed further at this wedding. Princess Elizabeth of Hesse-Darmstadt, having previously rejected her cousin, Prince Wilhelm of Prussia, announced her engagement to Grand Duke Serge of Russia. Two of the Battenberg brothers, Henry (known as Liko) and Alexander (called Sandro) became very popular amongst the women. Princess Beatrice, the youngest of Queen Victoria's children, was only four years old when Prince Albert died and had grown up a shy child in the shadow of her mother's grief. Even as an adult she was referred to as the "baby" and Queen Victoria was alarmed when, in Darmstadt, a close bond developed between Beatrice and Liko. With Vicky in Berlin and Alice dead, the thought of losing her youngest daughter to Europe was too much.

Then there was the problem of Sandro, Prince of Bulgaria, who had fallen passionately in love with the Crown Princess Victoria of Prussia, Vicky's daughter. Sandro had quar-

PRINCESS BEATRICE AND HER HUSBAND PRINCE HENRY OF BATTENBERG.

relled with the Tsar, and was disliked by Victoria's paternal grandmother, the Empress of Prussia, and by her brother Wilhelm; only her mother and maternal grandmother approved of the match. Sandro's position as suitor became untenable when, some months later, he was unable to repulse a Russian invasion into Bulgaria, was kidnapped and deposed. Victoria eventually married Prince Adolphus of Schauraburg-Lippe.

Alice's third daughter, Alix, married Tsar Nicholas II of Russia in 1894. The marriage caused consternation at the time and was to end in tragedy. It produced five children, the only son being a haemophiliac, and the whole family was shot in 1918 by the Bolsheviks during the Russian Revolution.

The relationship between Princess Beatrice and Prince Henry of Battenberg flourished and Queen Victoria's fears of losing her daughter abroad were ended when he renounced his army career and agreed to live in England. Princess Beatrice was the only one of Queen Victoria's daughters to wear the same Honiton lace as her mother had worn on her wedding dress when she married Prince Henry at Whippingham Parish Church near Osborne on July 23, 1885. The couple's four children, all born in Britain, were a source of great delight and pleasure to Queen Victoria.

Recurring tensions in family relationships were exacerbated by European politics and one state's leader's decision to expand his boundaries. In 1877 Affie's father-in-law, the Tsar of

Russia, caused Queen Victoria to threaten to abdicate over his desire to invade Egypt. The following year he again attempted to move Russian troops into Turkey and the Balkans and a long period of unrest ensued during which British fleets were dispatched. At a conference convened by the German Chancellor, Bismarck, in Berlin the last remnants of the Ottoman Empire were imperially divided by Russia and Britain and Cyprus became a British-occupied territory.

The British Empire

While Victoria's influence grew in Europe as a result of the marriages of her children, it was quite insignificant when compared with the strength of British influence in the world at large. During Queen Victoria's reign the British Empire grew at an unprecedented rate. By the 1880s it had become the largest Empire, in area, that had ever existed, with a population of almost 300 million people. Its rapid growth in the nineteenth century was the result of the expansionism of the capitalist spirit, founded on British industrialization, and greatly helped by Benjamin Disraeli's political desire for the Tory party to develop it.

It was through Disraeli's influence that Queen Victoria began to take a keen interest in the acquisition of new territories and sea routes

AN INVITATION FOR THE COLONIAL AND INDIAN RECEPTION AT GUILDHALL ON JUNE 25, 1886.

as more and more of the world became "British" and "hers". More territories, dominions and colonies became British in her reign than at any other time as Imperial Britain spread around the globe: it was indeed an Empire "on which the sun never set".

British dependent territories, colonies and dominions within the Empire at this time included Aden, Australia, Basutoland, Bechuanaland, British North Borneo, British Solomon Islands, British Somaliland, Brunei, Canada, Christmas Islands, Cocos-Keeling Islands, Cook Islands, Egypt, Fiji, Gambia, Gilbert and Ellice Islands, Hong Kong, India, Leeward Isles, Maldive Islands, Mauritius, Natal, New Zealand, Northern Rhodesia, Nyasaland, Papua, Sarawak, Uganda, Windward Isles. They were all lands a long way from home, many of them had not been heard of by the great majority of Britons and few, apart from the large countries, bore any real interest for the masses of the population.

Being part of the Empire meant rule by white men, but Queen Victoria firmly believed that Britain was offering the peoples of the world safety, security and progress. The British Empire had begun in a very unstructured way, a matter of exploration and discovery unfettered by political ideology. When the exploring British mariners, intent on navigating the world, discovered new lands the British flag was raised, with the indigenous population usually being quite oblivious to its implications.

The Empire grew gradually. Some territories, like Newfoundland in 1623, Canada in 1714, and Australia in 1788, consisted of an enormous land mass and a very small indigenous population. Large swathes of these lands were distinctly inhospitable to people from temperate Europe, so that they were not seen as places for mass emigration. Australia, for instance, began its time in the Empire as a place to send convicts and other undesirable British citizens, although the first sheep, on which Australia's prosperity was to be founded, were sent there as early as the late eighteenth century. India was different. British sailors had first intruded on the sub-continent in 1601, in search of spices and other riches, for even then the

ARRIVAL OF A TRAIN IN INDIA.

country was regarded as a particularly good investment.

Revenues from the Empire could be enormous for investors, merchants and speculators, but it was only late in the nineteenth century that the mass of the British people became aware of its potential as a source of a better life for themselves. Until then the Empire had been the domain of either a few government employees sent to run it or of speculators and investors. The industrial revolution opened great new prospects for such people outside Britain. British coal could be delivered to ports across the globe to provide fuel for British ships; railway tracks and trains, made in Britain, were transported around the world as railways were laid across whole continents – Cecil Rhodes' dream was a railway line from the Cape to Cairo – up mountains and through gorges. Telegraphic cables, invented in the 1850s, were soon being laid across British territories and beneath British seas, ensuring safe and confidential transmission of messages right round the globe. The free trade policies of successive British governments enriched the pockets of many British companies doing business, unhampered by tariffs, throughout the Empire, as the revenues came back home.

Benjamin Disraeli was the Prime Minister most closely associated with the development of Empire, a development which Victoria viewed

LORD CURZON OF KEDLESTON, THE MAHARAJA OF REWA AND CAPTAIN WIGRAM "IN THE JUNGLE WITH HIS BAG OF TIGERS".

in very positive terms. She firmly believed that the being part of the British Empire could only bring good to indigenous populations. She was also always notably devoid of any racist sentiments; later in her reign she employed Asians in her household and supported the Boer War because she did not want to leave the black population of southern Africa at the mercy of the Boers. Her imperial possessions become a source of great interest to Victoria and there was joy when another was added to her collection. She always hoped that there would be no bloodshed involved in these acquisitions and expected that one day Britain would gracefully withdraw when the people were ready.

A STEAMER LEAVES DAWSON CITY IN THE YUKON WITH A CARGO OF GOLD.

Victoria was firmly behind Benjamin Disraeli's two great Empire-building gestures. In 1875 Disraeli, with the help of Rothschild's Bank, bought on behalf of the British Government the shares in the Suez Canal owned by the bankrupt Turkish Khedive of Eygpt. This gave Britain a majority interest in the Canal and therefore control of the quick sea route to India via the Red Sea. Two years later, he was instrumental in having Victoria proclaimed Empress of India.

The Empire grew on a two-way trade. Many goods found their way into Britain on British ships from all over the world, and many aspects of the British way of life found their way to every part of the Empire. British men and women went to work in other countries far from their homes, taking their social habits, their foods – settlers in Australia were not at all sure about the local plants, so had their favourite root crops, including potatoes sent from home – their sports and their language with them.

Animals and plants were introduced to alien environments, not always with happy results: rabbits sent from Britain to Australia and New Zealand became great pests in both countries, threatening the indigenous animal life in Australia and causing erosion in New Zealand. Sheep, on the other hand, were of great benefit to the economies of Australia, New Zealand and the Falkland Islands, developing into huge meat and wool industries. Refrigeration meant that the first frozen meat cargoes from New

Zealand reached Britain in the 1870s. The rubber tree was introduced to Malaya, resulting in a huge rubber trade; and the Royal Botanical Gardens at Kew grew rapidly to make room for the plant samples sent home from the tundra to the Equator and almost to the Antarctic. Botanists gave many of these plants the prefix Victoria, in honour of their Queen and Empress.

In the earlier part of the Empire's development those working in its companies or representing the British government would return home at the end of their tenure of office, rarely settling within the foreign lands. For years the British Empire was of little significance to the masses of people in Britain, the daily toil and changes of their own lives being more than enough to contemplate. Emigration was only attractive to speculators if there was the promise of quick wealth, such as the possibility of gold, diamonds and copper, or enticements such as cheap land. The early development of a colony was usually done as a monopoly by an individual company, like the East India Company in India and the fur-trading Hudson's Bay Company in Canada. Eventually both of these great companies hit difficulties and had to sell out to the government.

The running of the Empire was done by white men and pandered to the British fear of the foreigner. Gradually, professionals other than civil servants were recruited to run the Empire and doctors, nurses, lawyers, bankers and teachers were enlisted. Their descent upon an imperial possession led to the growth of large ex-patriate communities within towns where they were able to keep themselves to themselves, seldom fraternizing with the local population in those countries where the indigenous population was large and socially well-organized. Jan Morris describes how they would even have the same churches, schools and cricket pavilions, chosen from mail order catalogues, packed up and sent out from Home, to be assembled on the spot, around the Empire. The same applied to their clothing, for many stores in Britain, such as London's Army and Navy Store, specialized in providing clothing and other gear for all climates and all situations.

By the 1890s things had changed considerably. The possibility of settling in one of the "white" colonies – Canada, Australia or New Zealand – had become a realistic prospect for many middle and working-class people, holding out the chance of a better standard of living in a good-sized house sitting on its own land, perhaps on a road called "Queen Street" or "Victoria Road", and in a society marked by a much greater equality than they knew in Britain. Cheap passages on emigrant ships were widely available, so that travelling to the other side of the world became possible for many people who could only have dreamed of it earlier in Victoria's reign. The great difference between them and the colonial administrators and their wives of earlier generations was that the men and women of the 1890s were going away for good, to start a new life in a new land that they did not expect to return home again.

Queen and Empress

By the mid-1870s Queen Victoria was aware of an anomaly in her position: the heads of state of Russia, Germany and France were all called emperors whereas she, the head of the biggest empire of them all, was not. When Disraeli became Prime Minister again in 1874, he immediately jumped at the idea of making Queen Victoria Empress of India; this fitted in with his plans for the Empire. A Royal Titles Bill was put before Parliament and became law in 1877; under the Delhi Proclamation, Queen Victoria became Empress of India. From now on she signed herself VRI: *Victoria Regina et Imperatrix*.

India had always held a special place in the Imperial mind; it was a vast, heavily populated country with an enormously rich culture. The largest imperial possession, it stood on one axis of the Empire, Great Britain on the other. After the Indian Mutiny of 1857, control of the colony had passed from the East India Company to the British Crown. By the mid-1860s the miracle of telegraphy meant the British Government was just a few days' communication away.

The romantic exoticism of India and the Orient had early captured Queen Victoria's imagination: she was enraptured by India. At the Great Exhibition in 1851, she had received gifts from the East India Company and even the Koh-i-nor diamond was the property of the British Crown. She began employing Indian servants, one in particular, Abdul Karim, known as the Munshi, virtually taking over John Brown's place in her household. In the 1890s she added the impressive Durbar Room to Osborne House, its splendid fretted plasterwork being part of the decoration devised for it by Rudyard Kipling's father, who was principal of the School of Art at Lahore in India.

She would dearly loved to have visited India, but such a long trip was considered too risky for a women of her age: she was nearly 60 when she became Empress of India. The Prince of Wales went on her behalf and Ireland remained the only country of the Empire outside Great Britain that she visited in her long reign.

For Victoria's subjects, as for the Queen herself, India could, to some degree, be experienced at home, anyway. The spices and teas of

THE IMPERIAL ORDER OF THE CROWN OF INDIA, PROBABLY BY GARRARD.

"NEW CROWNS FOR OLD ONES!" A CARTOON FOR *PUNCH* BY JOHN TENNIEL IN WHICH DISRAELI OFFERS VICTORIA THE IMPERIAL CROWN OF INDIA.

RUDYARD KIPLING BY WILLIAM STRANG.

India were already claiming a place in the British diet, and were joined later in the reign by large imports of oriental goods, the finest of which found their way to stores like Liberty in London, which stocked furniture, textiles and ceramics from India, China and Japan.

Although for the vast majority of the British the Empire was of little consequence for most of the century, there was, at least from the time of the Great Exhibition, an undercurrent of awareness of the Empire at home. Queen Victoria and Disraeli had speeded up the popularization of it in the 1870s. Then came people like the writer Rudyard Kipling, born in India, and always retaining strong Imperialist beliefs, who wrote what people thought were Indian stories but which were, in fact, an interpretation of India by a European. Edward Elgar, with his *Pomp and Circumstance Marches*, perhaps better epitomized the feeling of grandeur and imperialism which, with Britannia at the helm, Queen Victoria and Benjamin Disraeli had helped create.

The Poet Laureate of the 1890s, Alfred Austin, appointed in 1896 on the death of Tennyson in 1892, was perhaps the most jingoistic of them all. A follower of Disraeli and ardent supporter of Imperialism, his simple odes to Britannia and the Empire may never have been taken seriously by his contemporaries, but they did help the terrific cross-fertilisation of ideas and the feeling that nothing could be put back where it belonged because the changes were here to stay that was a characteristic of the age.

The Imperial Dream Turns to Disaster

The conquest of Africa would prove to be the greatest test of the strength of the imperial idea. Britain's conquest of large parts of Africa south of the Sahara was the most bloody and costly in human terms of all the campaigns undertaken by British Imperialism. It was in Africa, towards the end of the century, that Britain and other European states competed with one another to gain control of the vast and potentially hugely wealthy continent. While the Dutch Boers in southern Africa fought against the British, Uncle Leopold's son, Leopold II, reinstated slavery during Belgium's colonization of the Congo and France, Italy and Germany were each trying to grab other corners of the massive continent.

Queen Victoria's personal view in the 1870s was that Gladstone was insufficiently committed to Africa. She was also determined that Britain should not leave black people in the southern part of the continent to be ruled by the Dutch. The first conflict between the British and Dutch in southern Africa was in 1881, when the small British force there proved no match for the Boers.

Far to the north, the Sudan was another zone of conflict. Here, in 1884, General Gordon, a distinguished soldier from the Crimea who had mapped the source of the White Nile, was sent to Khartoum to quell threats of a holy war between Muslims and Egyptians. Britain already had a presence in Egypt and Gordon's job was to rescue the Egyptian soldiers, but he quickly got into difficulties and, despite a relief force being sent, was killed in Khartoum in 1885.

The following year gold was discovered in the Transvaal in southern Africa, then in Boer hands. Britain was determined to get control of this potential wealth and to keep it out of the

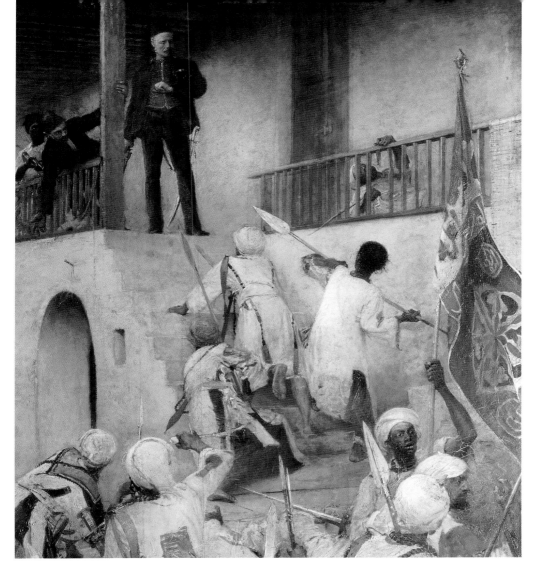

GENERAL GORDON'S LAST STAND AT KHARTOUM BY W.G. JOY.

hands of the Dutch and the Germans who, under Kaiser Wilhelm, Queen Victoria's grandson, were making bellicose noises in the background. By 1899 there was war between the Boers and British in South Africa; an early Boer victory prompted the Kaiser to send a congratulatory message to President Kruger; Queen Victoria was outraged and refused to let her grandson visit her in England.

Britain began pouring thousands of troops into South Africa, including many from the "white colonies". Queen Victoria could not understand why black and Asian soldiers were not also mobilised to fight for Britain. The army commanders, aware of the Boers' attitude to the native black population, explained to her it would be dangerous for them.

In 1900 the tide turned. The relief of Ladysmith and victories at Kimberly and at Mafeking (which was reported to the Queen by it commander Robert Baden-Powell). caused great rejoicing in Britain, and in the Royal Household. Victoria did not live to see Britain's final victory in South Africa, which came in 1902, the year in which Empire Day was first celebrated. But she was well aware of the dreadful losses suffered by her soldiers. British losses and casualties far outnumbered those endured by the Boers. Nearly 6000 British men had been killed and 23,000 injured, to end the days of imperial jingoism.

A COMMEMORATIVE FAN
OF THE BOER WAR.

Chapter 11 Queen of all her People

The fiftieth anniversary of Queen Victoria's accession to the throne of Great Britain and Ireland fell in June 1887 and marked a significant point in her life and reign. She had now served her country for thirty years without the support of Prince Albert and although she still wore black to mark her loss, court mourning had long since been relaxed. There was no doubt that she had matured and left behind her the long period of seclusion that had followed Albert's death.

Now 68, Victoria was strong and in relatively good health; indeed, she had lived a longer life than many of her subjects did and was, once again, confident in her public role as sovereign and her private one as mother, grandmother and great-grandmother. The silver anniversary of her accession had passed with little comment, since it fell a few months after Albert's death, when she was sunk in grief-stricken misery. Initially, Queen Victoria had not wanted to mark her Golden Jubilee either, but the Prince of Wales persuaded her otherwise and as 1887 progressed it became a year of celebrations not only in Britain but around the Empire.

The family continued to take up much of Queen Victoria's attention as more grandchildren and great-grandchildren were born; to them she was the kind and adorable "Gangan". Photographs of her in old age with her grandchildren sometimes reveal a white-haired lady with a huge smile on her face. This refreshing countenance was not often seen, partly because it was very unusual then to photograph someone smiling. Even the difficult Wilhelm in Germany adored her, though this did not prevent him often making political moves that outraged her. Grandchildren and great-grandchildren were always welcome in Queen Victoria's homes and nurseries were kept equipped, often with items that had been used by her own children when they were small.

Princess Marie Louise, Lenchen's daughter, was impressed by the lack of arrogance in her grandmother. Once when Queen Victoria unveiled a statue of herself, the young Princess suggested that she must feel very proud. "No, dear child, very humble," was the reply. She remained a caring person to members of her household and did not allow younger family members to take advantage of her staff. Throughout her life, if she was disenchanted by a family member's behaviour, she rarely addressed them to their face about their conduct, choosing instead to avoid confrontation by writing to them. Prince Albert had used the same practice many years before, when he

A RARE PHOTOGRAPH OF A SMILING QUEEN VICTORIA WITH PRINCESS BEATRICE, PRINCESS VICTORIA AND GREAT GRAND-DAUGHTER ALICE.

QUEEN VICTORIA PHOTOGRAPHED ON AUGUST 16, 1887

Le Petit Journal
SUPPLÉMENT ILLUSTRÉ
Huit pages : CINQ centimes

SAMEDI 11 AVRIL 1891

La Reine d'Angleterre en France
(PROMENADE A GRASSE)

QUEEN VICTORIA
VISITS GRASSE WHILE
HOLIDAYING IN THE
SOUTH OF FRANCE.

resolved rows with his wife by writing to her.

Even supporting a daughter or grand-daughter going through the trials of childbirth was not too much for the Queen and she was present at several births, providing Princess Beatrice with much support when she gave birth to the youngest four of the Victoria's thirty-five grand-children. When her dead daughter Alice's daughter, Victoria of Battenberg, was pregnant Queen Victoria insisted she should come to England and be cared for by her grandmother. Here, in a great act of female solidarity, never forgetting her own experiences of childbirth, Queen Victoria sat through the night as her grand-daughter went into labour. She mopped her forehead, held her hand and comforted her as she watched the delivery of a baby great-grand-daughter, Alice, who in time would become mother of the present Duke of Edinburgh.

Although, essentially, Queen Victoria was constitutionally very strong and in remarkably good health, despite being overweight for her height, as she aged she developed some hypochondriac tendencies. These were well recorded by Sir James Reid, who joined her household at Balmoral as a young doctor in August 1881. He was liked by the Queen, who thought him more than able to do the job as he spoke fluent German, learnt during his time at medical school in Vienna, so that he was able to deal with her German relations.

He recounted Queen Victoria's preoccupation with indigestion and flatulence, which he put down to an over-indulgence in the rich food she enjoyed and suggested she eat more sensibly. This she refused to do and would then complain of further gastric pain and heartburn; it was left to Dr Reid to find a remedy. Her knee gave her constant problems, which Reid diagnosed as rheumatism, and she also suffered from painful backache, which was sometimes

relieved by massage. But she was not to be outdone by ailments and resented being exhausted. As she recorded in her journal on March 6, 1887, "Feel very tired and exhausted, being really much overdone; and fell asleep in my chair, after tea – a very rare thing for me."

She was not so tired that she could not travel, however, and in the spring of Jubilee Year she went on her usual holiday abroad at this time of year, travelling to the South of France. In her household travelling with her were both her secretary Sir Henry Ponsonby and her doctor, James Reid. An excursion to the monastery at Aix-Les-Bains introduced her to the Chartreuse distillery, where the monks made the delicious liqueur of the same name. Here, they received the royal party and in the cells introduced the Queen to a young, 23-year-old English priest. He was overwhelmed by her presence as she looked around the tiny room in which he had lived for the past five years; she was moved by how contented he was and remarked that it was unusual to find someone so. The visit ended with the Queen drinking some of the strong liqueur and arriving home "somewhat tired".

Queen Victoria's tastes and pleasures remained simple throughout her life, despite Prince Albert's attempts to educate her in the more cultured mode of the European intellectual world from which he had come. Tennyson was still a favourite poet and she liked to read light novels, having found the works of George Eliot difficult – and, possibly, too much in favour of women's suffrage for her taste. Her correspondence continued with Vicky in Berlin, where life was very troublesome and Bismarck was beginning to cause problems. Having amassed, in her long reign, hoards of gifts from all around the world, she started to compile an inventory of them all and, when there was time, she painted or knitted.

The British government in 1887 was Tory. Mr Gladstone's Liberal government had fallen and he resigned in July 1886, to the Queen's great relief. The new Tory Prime Minister, Lord Salisbury, had, as Viscount Cranbourne, been Secretary for India in 1874, and was opposed to Irish Home Rule. The Queen's favourite Prime Minister, Disraeli had been made Earl of

Beaconsfield in 1876, and thus went to the House of Lords. He had resigned as Prime Minister in 1880 and died, to Queen Victoria's great sadness, the following year.

The relationship between Queen and Prime Minister was now much more relaxed than it had been with Mr Gladstone as Queen Victoria continued her regal responsibilities, working through her boxes, writing letters, signing documents and giving her ministers much valuable advice from her long experience in the role. Although affairs at home and within the Empire took up much time, events within Europe, as other states were beginning to become industrialized and more powerful, also concerned her. The question of Ireland, with successive governments wrestling with the problems of Home Rule, caused politicians and the Queen much anguish.

were made around the country with the aim of erecting a memorial to it. Queen Victoria thought it would be inappropriate to have yet another memorial to Prince Albert or a statue of herself so she approved a scheme for the setting up of homes for orphaned children, the sick and infirm as a fine way of honouring her Jubilee.

She also particularly approved of the idea, supported by Florence Nightingale, for the Queen's Jubilee Nursing Institute, to be founded using £75,000 collected by women throughout the country. The Jubilee Nurses pioneered the new role of the district nurse as well as promoting the need for trained midwives.

Celebrations of the Jubilee began in the Empire early in 1887. In February, the Earl of Dufferin wrote to the Queen describing the two days of festivities which took place in Calcutta:

The Golden Jubilee Begins

Sir Henry Ponsonby had been making plans since 1886 for the Jubilee celebrations, the central event of which was to be a ceremony at Westminster Abbey, where her Coronation had taken place, on June 21. Jubilee collections

(the people) are PASSIONATELY fond of *pyrotechnic* displays, and on the 16th they were shown FIREWORKS far *superior* to any they had ever seen before. The principal feature was the outline of your Majesty's head, traced in lines of fire, which unexpectedly burst on the vision of the astonished crowd. The likeness was admirable, and caused an enormous shout of pleasure and surprise …

THE ROYAL ARMS JUBILANT IN JUNE 1887 BY TOM MERRY.

OVERLEAF: "QUEEN VICTORIA'S JUBILEE GARDEN PARTY" BY FREDERICK SARGENT.

About 30,000 Indian and European children watched this firework display and enjoyed other festivities which took place in Calcutta, Madras and Bombay.

At home, Queen Victoria travelled the country, touring towns and cities were she was usually met with rapturous welcomes. Occasional anti-monarchist outbursts were put down to "the Socialists or Irish".

In March she went by train to spend a day in Birmingham. At Small Heath Park 20,000 children lined the road and sang the National Anthem as she passed. All the narrow streets of the city were lined with people and decorated with flags and bunting. Queen Victoria, while concerned by the cramped housing conditions, was delighted at the numbers of poor and working-class people who came out to cheer her, noting that "Though the crowd were a very rough lot, they were most friendly, and cheered a great deal."

She was received at the Town Hall and was thankful that her voice rang out clearly above the cheers. Accompanied by the mayor, she passed under an enormous arch made by Birmingham's brass-workers to demonstrate their skills and another made of fire escapes which had been erected by the Fire Brigade; some of the men stood at the top of it. She passed King Edward's Grammar School where the pupils addressed her, then laid the foundation stone for Birmingham's new Law Courts and, finally, returned to the railway station to board her train, arriving back at Windsor at seven in the evening. She was particularly impressed by the people of Birmingham, whom she had hitherto regarded as radical and, while she thought their living conditions harsher than those in Liverpool, she was delighted that their "enthusiasm and loyalty should have been so great."

For a tour through the East End and City of London she was accompanied by Lenchen, Beatrice and Liko. On the route from the City they called at the Albert Docks and saw the boys from one of Dr Barnardo's homes, dressed in sailor suits, waving Union Jack flags at them. Dr Barnardo had opened ninety homes for destitute children, mainly in the East End where there was much poverty. While training to be a

doctor he had worked in a ragged school where he became aware of the appalling conditions faced by hundreds of children. He founded his first juvenile mission in 1866 and by 1899 his homes were chartered and part of the National Incorporated Association for the Reclamation of Destitute Waif Children.

During this East End and City tour Queen Victoria paid her first visit to the Mansion House, the official home of the Lord Mayor of London. Here they were received by the Lord Mayor and Aldermen of the City, and had tea. The Lord Mayor's eleven-year-old daughter presented her with a bouquet of geraniums made up in the shape of the red cross and dagger, the insignia of the City. The royal party finally arrived at Paddington in the evening and were back at Windsor by half-past eight, exhausted, but satisfied once again at the loyalty of the people.

On May 19, five days before her 68th birthday, Queen Victoria received a telegram from Vicky in Berlin, conveying the distressing news that her husband was very ill and asking that Dr Mackenzie, a specialist throat surgeon, be sent to examine Fritz immediately. Two doctors in Berlin had diagnosed the possibility of a malignancy in a small lump in his throat and Dr Mackenzie was the only doctor capable of operating on it. In those days it was common not to reveal to a patient the severity of a medical condition, especially if it was cancer, and Vicky and her family decided to tell Fritz his loss of voice and the surgery were nothing to worry about. Queen Victoria, however, was especially worried for him and the anguish felt by her daughter reminded her of the last days of Albert's illness.

Celebrations for the Queen's 68th birthday took place at Balmoral, Victoria's first visitors being her devoted daughter Beatrice, with her toddler son who brought a bunch of lilies for Gangan. Other presents were laid out, as was customary, on "my present table in dearest Albert's room, and such a lovely quantity of things I received!" The day was spent surrounded by children, grandchildren and great-grandchildren – and hoards of presents, not just for her birthday, but for the Jubilee too.

QUEEN VICTORIA IN THE GOLDEN JUBILEE GARDEN PROCESSION DRIVING THROUGH PARLIAMENT SQUARE AFTER THE SERVICE IN WESTMINSTER ABBEY.

To mark the occasion Queen Victoria gave out Jubilee Pins to all her family and staff and in the evening she had a special dinner with her Household. It was all very different from the eighteenth birthday she had spent at Kensington Palace, nervously anticipating the death of King William IV and contemplating her future.

Further news from Berlin was not good as there was debate between Dr Mackenzie, who announced that the removal of the lump had revealed nothing sinister, and the German doctors, who said Fritz was very sick and too ill to travel. But the party did finally arrive from Berlin in time for the Jubilee celebrations, which began in London on June 20.

Banquets and a Great Procession

Queen Victoria began the day of June 20 at Windsor, had breakfast at Frogmore and travelled by train to Paddington, accompanied by Beatrice and Liko. There they boarded a horse-drawn landau and drove to Buckingham Palace via Edgware Road and Hyde Park. Already crowds were beginning to line the route to wave to them. At Buckingham Palace family members had gathered, including King Leopold II of Belgium, Duke Ernest from Coburg, Crown Prince Wilhelm and his wife Dona from Berlin and many of her grandchildren; among the other guests were the King of Saxony, Rudolph of Austria, the Queen of Hawaii, princes from Siam and Persia, princes and maharajahs from India, and "Dr Tyler with two Indian servants he has brought over for me, two fine looking men handsomely dressed in scarlet and white turbans": Queen Victoria's infatuation with India would now be realized in Britain.

There was a lunch party in the large Dining Room, which Queen Victoria had not used since 1861, when Albert died. Later in the afternoon she was joined by Bertie, Alexandra and the King of Denmark, who was probably the only person there who had attended her Coronation. An enormous dinner party in the evening was followed by a ball.

On the morning of June 21, as she watched the crowds outside the Palace, Queen Victoria was reminded of the day she and Albert had opened the Great Exhibition in Hyde Park. Vicky's daughter, Princess Victoria of Prussia, summed up the public mood when she wrote "For fifty years my grandmother had ruled over her people with a kindliness and a graciousness that found a quickening answer in their hearts."

As the procession left Buckingham Palace for Westminster Abbey, the carriages, filled with family and invited guests, sparkled with their jewels, colourful clothes and uniforms in the bright sunshine. One carriage contained twelve Indian officers; another her three sons and five sons-in-law. There were nine grandsons and grandsons-in-law riding together; and three from among her daughters, daughters-in-law and grand-daughters all together. At 11.30 a.m., still wearing her customary black dress and bonnet, Queen Victoria, accompanied by Princess Alexandra and Vicky, left the Palace in a gilded open carriage drawn by six horses, at

THE MENU FOR JUBILEE WEEK.

the pinnacle of the procession. Equerries accompanied them on horseback and Liko wore an English uniform for the first time; Fritz, too, looked very well. The crowd roared with excitement and adoration as this great pageant rode by. Princess Victoria of Prussia described it many years later:

My MOTHER, too, was *warmly* welcomed by the people, who have always been greatly DEVOTED to *"Our Princess Royal"*; but I almost think that my FATHER'S welcome was one of the *heartiest* of all on that day of UNIVERSAL REJOICING. He was dressed in the white uniform of the Cuirassiers and wore his eagle helmet. Riding on his horse, his noble figure towered above the princes … a typical knight of the fairytale days ….

The procession passed up Constitution Hill, down Piccadilly and through Trafalgar Square to the Embankment and so to Westminster Abbey. Here, Queen Victoria was met by the Archbishop of Canterbury and Dean of Westminster. Her family preceded her inside and, to the sound of the National Anthem followed by Handel's *Occasional Overture*, she walked slowly up the nave.

In the Abbey, she sat, as she had done "quite ALONE" forty nine years earlier at her Coronation. But this time she was to write "alone (oh! without my beloved husband, for whom this would have been such a proud day!) where I sat 49 years ago and received the homage of the Princes and Peers." She enjoyed the service, especially the tributes paid to Albert, and was most moved at the end when all her children and grandchildren and their husbands and wives came up to kiss her hand.

After the service, the procession made its

way slowly back to Buckingham Palace, arriving later than anticipated due to the huge numbers of people along the route. Lunch was served very late, at four in the afternoon. Afterwards Queen Victoria watched a march past by the Bluejackets and then went to the small Ballroom where presents were given to her – a beautiful piece of silver plate from her children, a cup from the Belgians and an arrangement of exotic feathers placed around her monogram from the Queen of Hawaii.

Another huge dinner party followed in the evening. Wearing a dress with silver embroidered roses, thistles and shamrocks on it and her diamond jewellery, Queen Victoria listened to toasts and speeches in her honour and went to bed hearing the noise of the crowds celebrating outside singing *God Save the Queen* and *Rule Britannia*. The following day was spent with further celebratory meals and the bestowing of Jubilee medals on her guests.

At the end of it all, Queen Victoria remarked at how grateful she was to have been at the centre of such attention, but saddened by the absence of those who were unable to be with her. The next four weeks were a whirlwind of garden parties, reviews, laying of foundation stones and dinners for Queen Victoria and when she got to Osborne in mid-July there were more events, including a review of the troops at Spithead. Around Britain and the Empire, celebrations were held, sermons preached and prayers said for the life and achievements of Queen Victoria. The National Anthem was sung in Sanskrit and photographs were taken and circulated, for the first time, of any royal pageant. There were many souvenirs of all kinds produced to mark this unique occasion.

By February 1888 Fritz's condition had deteriorated. He had just been operated on when his own father, the Emperor, died. Now Fritz was the Emperor Frederick III of Germany, and Vicky his Empress. In April Queen Victoria, accompanied by Beatrice and Prince Henry, went to Europe, spending a few days in Florence before going on to Berlin to see her daughter and son-in-law.

In Florence the royal party enjoyed lamp-lit processions, marches and bands performed in their honour. Queen Victoria was presented with an album of photographs to commemorate the visit and they all had a tour of the paintings in the Uffizzi Gallery. From Florence, Queen Victoria travelled by train to Berlin. She crossed the Alps at Innsbruck and arrived in Berlin on April 24, where she was met at the station by her daughter and grandson.

At Charlottenburg Palace she found Fritz desperately ill and was very worried for her daughter, spending much time comforting her. Queen Victoria also took the opportunity to meet the German Chancellor, Otto von Bismarck, before returning to England; neither enjoyed the meeting and their distrust of one another was soon apparent.

QUEEN VICTORIA
WITH HER RECENTLY
WIDOWED DAUGHTER,
EMPRESS VICTORIA
OF PRUSSIA.

through, and *don't mind it*. I am anxious that all should go smoothly, that I write thus openly in the interests of both.

The new Kaiser and his Chancellor, in their desperate urge to make Germany industrially powerful, would become formidable figures on the stage of late-nineteenth-century European history, which perhaps Queen Victoria recognized: her concerns about her grandson's lust for power had been repeatedly aired.

The Queen's Munshi

Queen Victoria was delighted at the entry of Indian servants, especially Abdul Karim, into her Household in her Jubilee year. Her ability to embrace people of all races, from all over the world, into her life was uncommon in her time, especially when British Imperialism was advocating the perpetuation of white rule.

Abdul Karim was a handsome 24-year-old when he arrived in England in June 1887 and almost immediately was filling a leading role in Queen Victoria's household and life. Ever since she had been proclaimed Empress of India, she had felt considerable disappointment that she was unable to visit the country, and she remained enraptured by the exotic nature of Indian life and society. She quickly became enchanted by Abdul Karim. He taught her Hindustani and introduced curries into her menus, and by 1889 had persuaded her that the role of waiter was too lowly for a man who had been a clerk, or "Munshi", in India.

Victoria promoted him to the position of clerk and gave him the title of "The Queen's Munshi". Like John Brown before him, he quickly became closely involved with all aspects of her work, advising her on Indian affairs. So enraptured was she by him that she commissioned a portrait of him from the artist von Angeli. Even the clothing of her Indian servants had to respect the orient and tweed suits were ordered with long, Indian-style jackets and trousers to wear at Balmoral; at Osborne they used their customary Indian clothes with bright sashes and turbans.

Fritz died on June 15, having been Emperor for only a few months. Victoria's grandson, Wilhelm, was now Emperor – or "Kaiser", for Wilhelm certainly preferred the German form of the title. On hearing of Fritz's death, Bertie immediately went to Berlin to be with his sister and reported her anguish back to his mother. Although Queen Victoria was in the perfect position to offer the new head of state much valuable advice, she chose not to tell him how to do his new job. Instead, she concentrated in early letters to him on expressing her concerns about her daughter, often recalling her own experiences of grief. There was never any mention of his now being Kaiser:

DEAR WILLY,
… *Mama* does NOT know I am WRITING to you on this *subject*, nor has she ever *mentioned* it to me, but after talking it over with UNCLE BERTIE he *advised* me to write DIRECT to *you*. Let me also ask you to bear with poor MAMA if she is sometimes *irritated* and *excited*. She does not mean it so; think what months of agony and suspense and watching with broken sleepless nights she has gone

Queen Victoria's family and Household became increasingly angered, not only by the Munshi's close involvement with the workings of the monarchy, but also by the presence of other Indian servants in the Household. Their attitude appears today to be blatant racial prejudice and ignorance of another culture.

Things came to a head when the Munshi's turbaned head was spotted at the Braemar Highland Games and members of the Household refused to dine with him on a royal holiday in France; representations were made to the Queen, who was furious and refused to have anything to do with such despicable behaviour. Determined to protect all her Indian servants, especially the Munshi, she ignored all the complaints and would not have them spoken to in any demeaning way.

The Munshi's rise was always viewed jealously by those around him and when, in 1894, Victoria made him The Queen's Indian Secretary, with his own staff, there was widespread dismay. Many refused to recognize his friend Rafiuddin Ahmed when he arrived; though this man was eventually dismissed, efforts continued to uncover more about the Munshi's true background. All the Viceroy of India could find in the way of new information was that the Munshi's father was a prison apothecary in Agra, not a doctor, as had been

claimed. Queen Victoria refused to accept any of the claims from her household and politicians that the Munshi was a liar, cheat or any other of the demeaning ways she heard him described. In time, little evidence could be found to substantiate his detractors' claims and Queen Victoria, with her advanced anti-racist views, was probably right to ignore them.

Queen Victoria's infatuation with India did not stop with the Munshi and her Indian servants. For years she had been frustrated, when at Osborne, at the lack of a room large enough to hold grand receptions in, but she held back from extending the building because it would have meant spoiling Prince Albert's Italianate facade. All large summer events at Osborne were held outside under tents. Finally in 1890, she plucked up courage to pursue her dream and, like her uncle King George IV, decided to build her own Indian Pavilion.

On a space behind the existing Pavilion Wing and interconnected with it, the enormous Durbar Room was built. Princesses Louise, and Beatrice and Prince Arthur all contributed to the design and regretted afterwards that they had not paid more attention to making the exterior fit in with Prince Albert's original design. Nevertheless, the interior became a fantastic and exotic Indian-style palace.

Queen Victoria commissioned Indian craftsmen to make the decorations vital to its success. Bhai Ram Singh from the Mayo School of Art in Lahore designed plaster moulds for the ceiling, which was then cast in a type of papier maché by the London firm of G Jackson, and the white, plaster walls were framed with teak. Symbols of India incorporated into the design included Ganesha, the god of good fortune, and a peacock, which took 500 hours to craft; the dining chairs were designed by Rudyard Kipling's father who, at the time, was principal of the School of Art in Lahore.

The whole room became a marvellous evocation of India for Victoria as, somewhat incongruously, the exotic east came to the Isle of Wight. She thoroughly enjoyed her new room, which was used for parties and dinners as well as Christmas celebrations, when the now customary fir tree would be placed next to the present tables.

ABDUL KARIM, "THE MUNSHI" ATTENDS QUEEN VICTORIA.

Chapter *12* Sixty Years a Queen

On September 23, 1896, nine months before her Diamond Jubilee, Queen Victoria's reign reached an extraordinary point: she had reigned for longer than any English monarch before her. Thirty-five years earlier, when Prince Albert died, the possibility of reigning and living for even a year without him had seemed to her inconceivable. But, despite her years of mourning, she had survived and was now regarded with great fondness by her family, household and most of her people. Where Victoria and Albert had given the new middle classes aspirations of a happy family life, Queen Victoria in her later years became like Britannia on the pinnacle of a mighty, wealthy empire.

Her last decade was marked by more sadness and deaths. Her great friend, the Poet Laureate, Alfred, Lord Tennyson, died in 1892 and her faithful and patient secretary, Sir Henry Ponsonby, in 1895. Then in the Diamond Jubilee year her cousin, Princess Mary of Teck, whose daughter had been engaged to Bertie's eldest son, Albert, also died. Members of her Household died and others retired, some having given her sixty years of loyal service. John Meakin had woven the Queen's stockings for sixty years and Ann Birkin, her hosiery embroideress (born in 1816, three years before Queen Victoria), had embroidered the royal initials on to them ever since the Accession. In 1892 the ageing Mr Gladstone returned as Prime Minister and once again tried to pass an Irish Home Rule Bill . Once again, he failed and a general election in 1894 returned the Tories and Lord Salisbury as Prime Minister. Gladstone died in 1898 at the age of 89, having served in the House of Commons for 63 years .

The loss of staff and friends, however difficult and sad, was outweighed by more tragic, personal losses which befell Queen Victoria in the last decade of her reign. On January 14, 1892 Bertie's eldest son, Albert Edward, Duke of Clarence died suddenly of pneumonia, shortly before he was due to marry Princess Mary of Teck. Queen Victoria was terribly upset and greatly concerned for Bertie and Alexandra. The heir was now their second son, Prince George, and speculation quickly spread as to whether he would marry Princess Mary. Two months after Prince Albert Edward's death came news of the death of Alice's husband Louis, Grand Duke of Hesse-Darmstadt.

By this time, Princess Beatrice and her husband Prince Henry (Liko) were very much a part of the Queen's household and she had become very involved in the lives of their four young children. Liko was a lively character who, like many young men before him, had begun to find the interminable evenings spent at court rather tedious. In December 1895 he joined the Ashanti Mission to the Gold Coast of West Africa, partly to aid the British reclaim the area from the French and Germans, but also as an escape from the monotony of domestic life.

Beatrice, although anxious, knew that for his own self-esteem he had to go; the prospect of excitement was very great, but Queen Victoria, who had come to depend upon him, was aghast and concerned that he might not cope with the climate. Barely a few weeks had passed before Beatrice received the news that he had a fever and only days later, on January 22, 1896, he died of malaria. Beatrice was devastated. She had four young children, the eldest of whom was only 10 and the youngest, Maurice was, at five, the same age she had been when her own father died. Once again mother and daughter supported one another, as they had done for most of Beatrice's life, this time the mother comforting the daughter in her grief. Arrangements were made to bring Liko's body

FOUR GENERATIONS –
THE BAPTISM OF PRINCE
EDWARD ALBERT OF
YORK (LATER EDWARD
VIII), WITH HIS FATHER
THE DUKE OF YORK
(KING GEORGE V),
GRANDFATHER THE
PRINCE OF WALES (KING
EDWARD VII) AND GREAT
GRANDMOTHER,
QUEEN VICTORIA,
PHOTOGRAPHED BY
W&D DOWNEY.

back to England and Queen Victoria attended his funeral at Whippingham Parish Church and watched her stoical daughter in her grief, so very different from the way in which she herself had behaved many years before. But Beatrice, the youngest of her children, was probably the one most personally affected by having lived with a grieving mother.

Life brightened a little when granddaughter Alix, Alice's daughter, and her husband, Tsar Nicholas II, arrived from Russia to visit Victoria at Balmoral. The buildings in Ballater were decked with bunting to receive them. Alix adored her grandmother but Victoria was wary of the Tsar and tried hard to engage him in conversation. On his return to Russia Nicholas reported that the visit had been very boring.

The wars and skirmishes on the continent of Africa were proving to be great tests for the European powers. Queen Victoria remained determined that Britain should win in the conflict with the Boers in the south, partly out of Imperial pride, but also due to the prospect of wealth from the newly discovered gold and diamonds.

The Boer War was a dreadful conflict with which to end the century and it defined for Queen Victoria her relationship with her grandson, Kaiser Wilhelm. His congratulatory telegram to President Kruger in South Africa after the failed British-backed Jamestown Raid of 1895 so angered Victoria that she refused to allow him to visit her. When the Kaiser visited the Isle of Wight for the next Cowes Regatta he stayed on his yacht moored in the harbour at Cowes and did not visit the Queen at Osborne House. He was, though, well aware of his grandmother's age and constantly asked Dr Reid to keep him informed of her health and any apparent deterioration in it.

Prince George, now the heir to the throne after Bertie, did marry his late brother's fiancée, Princess Mary of Teck, which brought some happiness to the catalogue of recent deaths. The birth of their son and Victoria's great grandson, Edward, the future King Edward VIII, in 1894 enlivened Queen Victoria, who enjoyed posing for photographs with him, his father and grandfather to show the four generations of the dynasty.

The Diamond Jubilee

It was decided that the Diamond Jubilee celebrations should not be on the same grand scale as those of ten years earlier for the fiftieth anniversary. Victoria was now quite frail and Kay Stanniland has revealed that her dresses had been shortened considerably, suggesting that the Queen had shrunk by about 4in (8cm); the clothes from this period reveal she was 4ft 7in (1.42m) high and her waist measured 46in (117cm).

She was also very sad, especially after the death of Liko, and feared the prospect of endless parties, receptions and a lengthy and arduous celebration in Westminster Abbey. She felt it would all be too much for her. Instead a smaller, but nevertheless grand, celebration was planned for St Paul's Cathedral in the City of London. Even so, as the historian Jan Morris has pointed out, the event was still regarded as a celebration of the Empire's success and strength, and the apex of Britain's role as an Imperial power as much as it was mark of the Empire's affection for its ruler.

Congratulatory messages rolled in from Britons living in the Empire informing Queen Victoria of how important news and photographs of her and the family were to those living in distant parts, some of whom had never

QUEEN VICTORIA AT THE DIAMOND JUBILEE CELEBRATIONS HELD ON THE STEPS OF ST PAUL'S CATHEDRAL ON JUNE 22, 1897.

been "Home", for they were reminders of the "Mother Country".

In March 1897, Victoria went on her annual trip to the South of France, but the holiday failed to refresh her and in the weeks leading up to the Jubilee Queen Victoria was rather depressed and lethargic. She did, however, bestow a baronetcy on the ever-faithful Dr Reid.

On June 22, 1897, she set off from Buckingham Palace in an open-topped landau for St Paul's Cathedral, where a thanksgiving service was held on the steps outside because she was too frail to climb them into the great building. Afterwards, she was driven along packed streets full of cheering crowds, passing Mansion House and crossing London Bridge, then along the south bank of the Thames and across Westminster Bridge to Parliament Square and then to Buckingham Palace. There was much celebration, waving of union jacks and purchasing of souvenir mugs and plates. The *Illustrated London News* and other journals reported the events and church services giving thanks for Queen Victoria's sixty years on the throne were held around the world.

The Dawn of the Twentieth Century

By the end of the nineteenth century, if the British had much to give thanks for, so did other countries. The changes brought about by industrialization were no longer limited to Britain, and other countries, notably Germany and the United States, were enjoying their ben-efits and revenues too. In both these countries people were inventing new, often smaller, machines which would nevertheless be just as revolutionary as the railways and enormous mill engines which had transformed Britain.

When Alexander Graham Bell had perfected the telephone and demonstrated it to Queen Victoria at Windsor she initially failed to recognise its potential, but by 1899 had become an avid user of it; she also used one of the new Remington typewriters which were changing the craft of the writer. The phonograph was a new invention in the 1890s, making listening to music at home possible and in 1896 Mr Marconi arrived in London with his ideas and equipment for making the wireless. Queen Victoria and her family were given an early demonstration of the new process of moving pictures. Illumination was no longer to be by gas but electricity.

In the 1890s the motor car became more than just a possibility and the days of the horse-drawn carriage neared their end. In 1897 the first annual meeting of investors in a new auto-mobile company, Daimler and Co., was held in London. Otto Daimler had designed one of the first horseless carriages in Germany in the mid-1880s and from 1895 was manufacturing motor cars in Britain. The first cars to appear on the streets of London were little two-seaters made by Benz and imported from Germany. In 1900 the Prince of Wales bought three Daimler cars. Not content with the telephone, Alexander Graham Bell in 1898 began to experiment with flying machines. A new age was coming in with the new century.

Chapter *13* The Final Years

Sadness and frailty marked the last years of Queen Victoria's life. She had become physically very weak and walking was difficult: a lift had been installed at Osborne so that she did not have to climb the huge flights of stairs. While her mental capacity was undimmed, her eyesight was failing because of glaucoma and even spectacles, worn very late in life and never in public, did little to stay the onset of partial blindness. Princess Beatrice read state papers to her and wrote out her replies, but all decisions remained with the Queen. Extra strong black ink was ordered so that she could read her own handwriting and her journal entries continued until January 6, 1901, a few days before her death. Her Lady-in-Waiting, Marie Mallet, read to her, usually books with a depressing subject matter to match her mood, which was clouded by the recent deaths.

It was, however, the dreadful news concerning two of her own children which brought permanent gloom to these last years. In early December 1898 she learnt that Vicky, in Berlin, was seriously ill and found it almost impossible to acknowledge, even to her journal, the diagnosis of cancer of the spine. These two women, who had corresponded for nearly fifty years, ever since Vicky had gone to live in Berlin, were exceedingly close and Queen Victoria never forgot that Princess Victoria had inherited many of Prince Albert's qualities and intelligence.

Two months after Vicky's diagnosis, in February 1899, Affie's son, Young Alfred, died of tuberculosis. When it had become apparent that Prince Albert's brother, Duke Ernest of Saxe-Coburg, would die childless, Affie, who had been in the Royal Navy since he was 14 years old, was named heir to the House of Saxe-Coburg. Ernest died in 1893 and Affie duly became Duke of Saxe-Coburg.

Queen Victoria was deeply upset at the loss of her Saxe-Coburg grandson so soon after the death of Albert, heir to the British throne. She was also very worried about Affie's own health; he had not been well for some time and by the summer of 1900 his condition was causing great concern. Throat cancer was diagnosed and a week later he died. At the age of 81, and now very frail, she had to cope with the grief and loss of a third child and the prospect that her eldest was also going to die. Then, in the autumn, another grandchild, Prince Christian Victor of Schleswig-Holstein, died in southern Africa. All this time she continued her correspondence with Vicky, who she knew was dying. The two women, who were so close, both tried in their letters to rally one another, but underlying their written words was the reality that they both knew their ends were near.

For someone who had spent many years of her life dominated by death and mourning, it is surprising that, apart from the building of the Mausoleum at Frogmore, Victoria did not make any funeral plans for herself until 1897. In a break with tradition, which was evident in her actual funeral, she insisted that there should be no black. Influenced by Hindu attitudes to death and by the Roman Catholic use of white, she announced that white and gold drapes were to be used with minimal pomp and ceremony and was anxious that the Indian and German members of her Household should be included in the funeral procession. As planned forty years earlier, she would finally rest next to Albert at Frogmore. Unknown to her family, she also asked her dresser to place certain personal items beneath her in the coffin; these included jewellery and photographs from all periods of her life.

Because of her physical frailty, Queen Victoria decided that a spring holiday in

France would be difficult in 1900. Instead, she visited Ireland and spent a glorious few days in Dublin. The summer of 1900, her last, was spent at Balmoral, but she was not well and did not get her old pleasure from Scotland. Christmas at Osborne was not very enjoyable either, as she could hardly see the sparkling Christmas tree and celebrations in the Durbar Room.

In the early days of 1901 Queen Victoria's health deteriorated further; she was depressed and almost completely bed-ridden. Sir James Reid noticed a deterioration on January 15. This was followed by a stroke two days later and she became very confused, beginning to drift away. Her children and grandchildren were summoned to Osborne to be with her for her final days. The Bishop of Winchester also came and the local vicar from Whippingham, which would have pleased her as she had never wanted him to feel left out.

The Kaiser, who had become very concerned about her health, left his own sick mother, who was by now too ill to travel, to attend his grandmother's final days. A few hours before her death Queen Victoria managed to embrace her eldest son and heir, and whispered his name.

He was distraught at her impending death and was no doubt full of trepidation about his future. During her last hours, the Kaiser and the doctor supported her head. Her family surrounded her as she gradually drifted away. She died in the early evening of January 22.

The press had been made aware of the Queen's condition and were waiting around the gates outside the house, eager for news. Bulletins were given to them stating that the Queen was in decline so that they might prepare the nation. Finally, they were given the news they had been waiting for: the Queen had died at 6.30pm on January 22, 1901. They rushed down to Cowes from where their London editors were telegraphed with the news.

Britain and the world were stunned; Queen Victoria of Great Britain and Ireland, the "Grandmother of Europe", Empress of India and longest-serving monarch had gone. For sixty-three years she had reigned over an era unique in British and world history. For many of her subjects she had been "there" all their lives. The Prince of Wales, now King at the age of almost 60, sent telegrams to the Prime Minister, the Lord Mayor of London and other dignitaries:

QUEEN VICTORIA ON HER DEATH BED.

VICTORIA LYING IN STATE AT OSBORNE.

My *beloved mother*, the QUEEN, has just passed away surrounded by her children and grandchildren.

Prayers where said for the Queen and sermons preached in places of worship throughout the Empire. The sermon preached by the Rev. Hensley Henson, Canon of Westminster Abbey, in the Abbey on January 27, was typical:

... The QUEEN has *reigned* so LONG, that hardly anybody remembers any other SOVEREIGN: she has entered into the *national life* so FRANKLY and with such winning SYMPATHY that we all feel personally *bound to her* by some special link, over and beyond our civic duty ... We can scarcely yet realise the greatness of the void in the national life caused by the death of the Queen ... One result of the prominence and publicity of the great is the enhanced power for good or evil of their example. A corrupt court is a centre of corruption: an evil monarch is a national calamity. We can measure the influence for good which the pure life and ordered Court of Queen

Victoria have had on English society during her long reign! Every clergyman, philanthropist, social reformer has had, these sixty-three years past, an ally, a sympathizer on the Throne of this country ...

For many, she was undoubtedly perceived as a great mother figure and a provider of security and safety. Rabbi Isidore Harris of the West London Synagogue even equated her life and achievements with those of King David:

... On his ACCESSION to the *throne*, he found a *kingdom* distracted by CIVIL *dissension*, and as *small* as it was WEAK. He left behind him a strong and UNITED *empire* which stretched from the borders of *Egypt* to the foot of *Lebanon*, and from the *Euphrates* to the *sea* ... She entered upon her kingdom at a time when not England only, but all Europe, was seething with political discontent, when the throne, so far from being "broad based upon her people's will" [Tennyson to the Queen] and everlastingly rooted in the popular affections as we see it today, was beset with manifold dangers ...

QUEEN VICTORIA'S COFFIN ON BOARD THE *ALBERTA* CROSSING THE SOLENT FEBRUARY 2, 1901.

The Funeral

Preparations for Queen Victoria's funeral began immediately after her death. Sir James Reid helped her dresser and nurse lift her body to dress it in a satin gown and the Garter Ribbon. Then she was covered with flowers with her wedding veil placed over her face and her widow's cap on her head. It was then that Reid noticed the personal mementoes she had asked her maid to place with her. The coffin lid was sealed, her family oblivious of its secret contents.

The lying-in-state at Osborne lasted for ten

days before the funeral cortège left, on February 2, on its journey to its final resting place at Frogmore. It crossed the Solent from East Cowes to Portsmouth on the Royal Yacht *Alberta*, in what was a very solemn and moving occasion, described by Cissy, Countess of Denbigh:

The DAY was one of *glorious* SUNSHINE…After a while a black *torpedo destroyer* came dashing down the line signalling that the *Alberta* was leaving OSBORNE and from every ship, both BRITISH and *foreign*, boomed out the minute guns…a wonderful golden pink appeared in the sky … Slowly down the long line of battleships came eight torpedo destroyers, dark gliding forms, and after them the white *Alberta*, looking very small and frail … the motionless figures standing round the white pall which, with the crown and orb and sceptre, lay upon the coffin. Solemnly and slowly, it glided over the calm blue water … giving one a strange choke, and a catch in one's heart as memory flew back to her triumphal passage down her fleet in the last Jubilee review … Silently … the cortege passed away into the haze … leaving behind … sadness which it is impossible to forget.

From Portsmouth, the cortège went by train to Victoria Station and across London in a two-hour military procession, which included the new king, Edward VII, the Kaiser, and thirty-eight princes. At Paddington the procession

THE FUNERAL PROCESSION PASSING THROUGH LONDON ON ITS WAY FROM VICTORIA STATION TO PADDINGTON.

THE *ROYAL SOVEREIGN* LOCOMOTIVE WAITING THE ARRIVAL OF THE COFFIN AT PADDINGTON TO TRANSPORT IT TO WINDSOR.

boarded the train to Windsor. There were two more breaks with tradition; from Tudor times state funerals of monarchs had taken place at night, but this one was in daylight. At Windsor station a horse bolted so the royal naval guard of honour had to drag the coffin on its gun carriage to the castle.

The funeral in St George's Chapel was attended by members of the Royal Houses of Europe, all related to Queen Victoria. Memorial services were held concurrently throughout the Empire. After the service the coffin was placed in the adjoining Albert Memorial Chapel, which Queen Victoria had created as a shrine to her late husband. It remained there for two days before being taken, as was her wish, to the Royal Mausoleum at Frogmore, to be placed in the sarcophagus at the side of her beloved Albert.

Meanwhile, in Berlin Vicky battled with her cancer, wracked with pain and taking morphine. The new Queen, Alexandra, visited her and her sister Helena went to stay with her. She finally died on August 5, 1901, six months after her mother.

THE FINAL JOURNEY: THE CORTEGE LEAVING WINDSOR CASTLE FOR BURIAL AT FROGMORE.

Epilogue

After Queen Victoria died and was laid to rest alongside her beloved husband, a gigantic memorial to her, designed by Sir Aston Webb, was erected at the top of the Mall outside Buckingham Palace. Her successors, all of them her direct descendants, have continued to reside there, having a clear view of the memorial from the palace's ceremonial balcony. Victoria's son, Bertie, king at the age of nearly 60, chose to be called Edward VII. His great-granddaughter ascended the throne as Elizabeth II in 1952; she had married Philip Mountbatten, the great-grandson of Victoria's daughter Princess Alice. Although Edward VII sold Osborne, the Royal Family still enjoy life at Balmoral and spend more time at Windsor than Buckingham Palace.

During Queen Victoria's long life she reigned over a country undergoing unprecedented industrial, technological and social change, most of which she was well able to embrace. For her, personally, the changes brought about during her lifetime must have seemed enormous. Born in 1819, the daughter of a Hanoverian Duke, she was very much a child of the Georgian upper classes and was oblivious to much that was happening outside a small area of London, riding in horse-drawn carriages and dependent upon messengers on horseback to deliver letters. By the end of her life the first automobiles were seen on the streets of London and she was an eager user of the telegram and telephone. Railways had transformed people's lives and she had her own royal train.

Photography, used by both Victoria and Albert from the 1850s, made her reign and her Royal Family the first to be pictured in detail, and the mass-market newspapers which were another innovation of the age were kept supplied with a steady stream of images of them. Suddenly, the Royal Family, its behaviour and way of life

familiar to the mass of the population, became something to be emulated rather than despised, as Victoria's immediate forbears had been. Throughout her reign, there were republican demands for the abolition of the monarchy, especially if it was deemed too expensive or not doing its job, but Britain never reached the brink of revolution as other European countries had done in the nineteenth century.

Perhaps Queen Victoria's greatest legacy was to give the monarchy a stability and continuity that had been lacking in the years of the Hanoverian sovereigns who had ruled before her accession, thus ensuring its future. Her grandfather, King George III, had been mad during the last decades of his long life and her two uncles, King George IV and King William IV, had both lived scandalous lives with numerous inappropriate women. Where mistresses and illegitimate children had been acceptable, Queen Victoria introduced a puritanism influenced by Prince Albert's Lutheran beliefs. The couple's devotion to one another, their nine children and a way of living based on a strong and happy family life and a clear morality had an effect on all levels of society.

Victoria insisted on undertaking her job as sovereign as dutifully as she could. She managed, in the beginning with Prince Albert's guidance, to evolve a good relationship between monarch and parliament, quite different from that which had existed before her. As governance was more firmly placed with parliament and no longer practised at the whim of the monarch, so, during her reign, governments themselves became more answerable to the electorate, which became increasingly more representative through the passing of two Reform Acts during her reign. Although Victoria had disagreements with several of her prime ministers and, it has been observed by some, was

VICTORIA IN 1900 WITH FOUR OF HER GREAT GRANDCHILDREN.

THE QUEEN'S ROOM
AT OSBORNE.

THE QUEEN'S ROOM
AT OSBORNE.

maybe not entirely aware of the full implications of being a "constitutional monarch", she did leave actual governance to her prime ministers. It can only be surmised what would have happened if Prince Albert had lived: he may have wanted a greater political role for his wife and, consequently, for himself. Without him Queen Victoria was initially lost, although she did regain her dignity and public confidence after a solitary decade. She returned to public life in time to put a stop to republican demands, at a period when republics were being established elsewhere in Europe.

Queen Victoria brought a caring and compassionate nature to her job as the ultimate leader of the nation's military forces. She was immensely distressed by reports of illness, death or killing among troops serving abroad. Money would be sent to grieving widows of soldiers and sailors, visits were made to sick and injured soldiers returning from the Crimea and the battlefields of the Empire, and she instituted the Victoria Cross as a medal for outstanding, personal bravery, regardless of rank.

Above all, she was an extraordinarily unbigoted person, easily making friends with people regardless of their race or class. She married Prince Albert, a foreigner mistrusted by many British parliamentarians and the upper classes, she formed a close relationship with the Highlander John Brown, a man socially beneath her, and in her later years she did not hide her feeling for her Indian servant, Abdul Karim.

These were remarkable qualities for a woman of her status in the time in which she lived.

Queen Victoria was a complex character, bound to her duty as monarch and even in her darkest and most troubled times determined to carry on; only once did she threaten to abdicate, when Russia threatened to seize Egypt in 1877. She was shy and yet confident, enjoyed unsophisticated tastes, as shown in the days she spent roaming the Highlands at Balmoral, and yet with her wealth could spend thousands of pounds on jewellery. A loveable matriarch to her family and country, she could be extremely outspoken to her eldest son and to the Princess Royal about her eldest grandson, the Kaiser, whose character traits she regarded with unease.

The Victorian era saw social unrest and change as never before and the Queen's husband was a catalyst in bringing together many of the designers, engineers, innovators, artisans and manufacturers of the day. His greatest achievement, and one of the highlights of the reign, was the realization of the Great Exhibition and the greatest tragedy for the monarch was Albert's early death.

The term "Victorian", derived from the Queen's name, conjures up an age of tremendous themes: industry and work, invention and innovation, design and manufacture, entrepreneurship and capitalism, wealth and poverty, urban populations and wealthy middle classes, empire and imperialism. Then there are the distinctively Victorian styles and forms in architecture, engineering, manufacturing, fashion and literature. The latter, wonderfully represented by the work of Charles Dickens, the Brontës, George Eliot, Mrs Gaskell and others, developed a unique way of describing the terrific social and personal upheavals of the age.

The landscape of Britain changed irredeemably during the reign as architects and builders erected mills and factories, railway stations, viaducts and tunnels and masses of homes for the population as it changed from being predominately rural to mainly urban by the end of the century. Throughout Britain and the Empire Victoria and Albert villas, streets, roads, squares, pubs, gardens, towns, states, waterfalls, rivers, lakes and mountains were named after the Queen and her Consort.

Massive changes in attitudes to public health emerged from the mid-century with Owen Chadwick's report on public sanitation and Florence Nightingale's experiences nursing in the Crimea. Sir William Jenner discovered the difference between the typhoid and typhus viruses and the roles of hygiene and bacteria in the transmission of disease and infection became much better understood. Dr James Simpson's work with the use of ether and chloroform in the quest for anaesthesia enabled the Queen herself to make a great legacy to women when, by making public her use of chloroform at the birth of her last two children, Beatrice and Leopold, she made it acceptable for women to demand pain relief during childbirth. In her Golden Jubilee year the Queen was delighted at the establishment of the Queen's Jubilee Nurses' Foundation which made the new district nurse and midwifery services available to more women.

Education and welfare were major issues in the Victorian age. Legislation to change employment practices and education acts meant that by the end of the century children were attending school and no longer worked long hours in factories. Education no longer remained the domain of the wealthy as ragged schools, educational foundations for girls, working men's colleges, public libraries and charitable foundations were formed.

The Empire reached its zenith in the last decades of Queen Victoria's reign. Undoubtedly, blood was spilt and atrocities committed during its acquisition and the generations of British rule. But democracy was introduced to colonies when they devolved from Britain, and fair systems of justice and law were established, education introduced for all and poverty was relieved wherever possible. Out of the Empire grew today's Commonwealth, still a force for law and justice in most of the countries of the old Empire.

The largest country of the Empire, India, whose last Viceroy was Queen Victoria's great-grandson Louis, Earl Mountbatten of Burma, gained independence in 1947, 99 years after the Mutiny which hinted at its possibility. Hong Kong was returned to China in 1997 after protracted discussions about the nature of democracy for its citizens. Britain is now firmly placed politically within Europe, and has become a cross-cultural country with many immigrants from former imperial colonies, who brought with them cultures which have enriched many towns and cities. Their integration has not always been easy and maybe Queen Victoria's example, enthusiasm and capacity for accepting everyone, oblivious of race, religion or class, has been missed.

At times the Victorian era is viewed with nostalgia as Victorian values – family, a strong moral code and a wealthy and powerful empire – are seen as aspects of life we have lost. Life has changed considerably in the century since the death of Queen Victoria, so it is perhaps important to remember that for an enormous number of people the scale of disruption in the nineteenth century was also considerable, as well as being arduous, dangerous and uncertain. Victoria's age was as remarkable as the Queen herself, profoundly influencing and irrevocably changing the lives of everyone then and since.

UNVEILING OF THE MEMORIAL TO QUEEN VICTORIA OUTSIDE BUCKINGHAM PALACE.

KING GEORGE III = CHARLOTTE OF MECKLENBURG-STRELITZ

Adolphus
Duke of Cambridge
1774–1850
= Augusta of Hesse-Cassel
1797–1889

KING GEORGE IV =
1762–1830
Caroline of Brunswick
1768–1821

Frederick
Duke of York
1763–1827
= Frederika
Princess of Prussia
1767–1840

KING WILLIAM IV
1765–1837
= Adelaide
Princess of Saxe-Meiningen
1792–1849

Edward
Duke of Kent
1767–1820
= Victoria
Princess of Saxe-Coburg
1786–1861

George
Duke of Cambridge
1819–1904

Mary
Adelaide
1833–97
= Francis of Teck

Charlotte
Princess of Wales
1796–1817
= Leopold of Saxe-Coburg-Saalfeld
1790–1865

QUEEN VICTORIA
1819–1901
= Albert Prince of Saxe-Coburg-Gotha
1819–1861

Victoria (Vicky)
1840–1901
= Frederick
German Emperor King of Prussia (Fritz)
1831–88

Albert Edward (Bertie)
Prince of Wales KING EDWARD VII
1841–1910
= Alexandra
Princess of Denmark
1844–1925

Alice
1843–78
= Louis IV
Grand Duke of Hesse-Darmstadt
1837–92

Alfred (Affie)
Duke of Edinburgh & Saxe-Coburg-Gotha
1844–1900
= Marie Of Russia
1853–1920

William II (Willy)
German Kaiser
1859–1941
= Augusta of Schleswig-Holstein-Augustenburg

Charlotte
1860–1919

Henry
1862–1929

Victoria
Vicky of Moretta
1866–1929

Sophie
1870–1932=
Constantine, King of Greece
1868–1923

Alfred
1874–89

Marie
1875–1938
= Ferdinand
King of Rumania
1856–1927

Victoria Melita
1876–1936
= Ernest of Hesse

Albert Edward (Eddy)
Duke of Clarence
1864–92

KING GEORGE V
1865–1936
= **Queen Mary**
1867–1953

Louise
1867–1931

Victoria
1868–1935

Queen Maud of Norway
1869–1938

Victoria of Hesse
1863–1950
= Louis of Battenberg
Marquess of Milford Haven
1854–1921

Elizabeth
1864–1918
= **Grand Duke Serge of Russia**

Irene
1866–1953
= **Prince Henry of Prussia**
1862–1929

Princess Alice
1885–1950
= **Prince Andrew of Greece**
1882–1944

Louise
= **King Gustave of Sweden**
1882–1973

George
Marquess of Milford Haven

Louis
Earl Mountbatten of Burma
1900–1979

Edward VIII
Duke of Windsor
1894–1972
(Abdicated 1936)
= Wallis Simpson

KING GEORGE VI
1895–1952
= **Lady Elizabeth Bowes Lyon**
b.1900

Henry
Duke of Gloucester
1900–74
= **Lady Alice Montagu Douglas Scott**

George
Duke of Kent
1902–42
= **Princess Marina of Greece**

Prince John
1905–1919

Prince Philip Duke of Edinburgh
b.1921
m.Princess Elizabeth
(Queen Elizabeth II)

Prince William
1941–1972

Richard
Duke of Gloucester
b.1944
= Birgitte van Deurs

QUEEN ELIZABETH II
b.1926
= Prince Philip
Duke of Edinburgh
b.1921
Son of Prince Andrew of Greece

Princess Margaret
b.1930
= Antony
Earl of Snowdon
div. 1978

Alexander
Earl of Ulster

Lady Davina Windsor
b.1977

Lady Rose Windsor
b.1980

David
Viscount Linley
b.1961
= Serena Stanhope

Charles Patrick Inigo Armstrong-Jones
b.1999

Lady Sarah Armstrong-Jones
b.1964
= Daniel Chatto

Charles
Prince of Wales
b.1948
= **Lady Diana Spencer**
1961–1997
div. 1996

Anne
Princess Royal
b.1950
= (1)**Captain Mark Phillips**
div. 1992
(2)**Commander Timothy Laurence**

Andrew
Duke of York
b.1960
= Sarah Ferguson
div. 1996

Edward
Duke of Wessex
b.1964
= Sophie Rhys-Jones

Prince William
b.1982

Prince Henry (Harry)
b.1984

Peter Phillips
b.1977

Zara Phillips
b.1981

Princess Beatrice
b.1988

Princess Eugenie
b.1990

Samuel Chatto
b.1996

Arthur Chatto
b.1999

FRANCIS FREDERICK OF SAXE-SAALFELD-COBURG

Sophia
1778–1835

Ernest I = (2) **Princess Marie**
Duke of Saxe-Saalfeld-Coburg of Württenburg
1784–1844   1799–1860

Victoria = (1) Emich Charles
1786–1861   **Prince of Leiningen**
1763–1814

Ferdinand
1785–1851

Leopold I = (1) Charlotte
(Later King of the Belgians) **Princess of Wales**
1790–1865   1796–1817

(2) Louise of Orleans
1812–50

Ernest II
Duke of Saxe-Saalfeld-Coburg
1818–93

Charles Leiningen   Feodore
1804–1856   1807–72

Helena = Christian
(Lenchen)   **Prince of**
1846–1923   **Schleswig-Holstein**
1831–1917

Louise = **Marquis of Lorne**
1848–1939   **(Duke of Argyll)**
1845–1914

Arthur = Louise
Duke of Connaught **Princess of Prussia**
1850–1942   (Louischen)
1860–1917

Leopold = Helena
Duke of Albany **Princess of**
1853–1884   **Waldeck-Pyrmont**
1861–1922

Beatrice = Henry (Liko)
1857–1944   **Prince of**
Battenberg
1858–1896

Christian   Albert   Helena   Marie
Victor   1869–1931 Victoria   Louise = Aribert
1867–1900   1870–1948 1872–1957   **Prince of Anhalt**
1864–1933
(div 1900)

Margaret = **Crown Prince**   Arthur   Victoria Patricia = **Admiral**
1882–1920   **Gustave of**   1869–1931 1886–1974   **Sir Alexander**
Sweden   **Ramsay**
1882–1973

Alice = Alexander   Charles
1883–1981   **Prince of Teck**   Edward
Created Earl   1884–1954
of Athlone   =Victoria
1874–1957   1865–1970

Ernest = Victoria Melita   Frederick   Alix = Nicholas II   Mary Victoria
of Edinburgh   1870–73   1872–1918   **Tsar of Russia**   1874–78
(div 1901)   1868–1918

Alexander = Irene Denison   Victoria Eugenie = **King Alfonso**   Leopold   Maurice
Marquess of   1890–1956   **Queen of Spain** **of Spain**   1889–1922 1891–1914
Carisbrooke   1887–1969   1886–1941
1886–1960

Olga   Tatiana   Marie   Anastasia   Alexis
1895–1918 1897–1918 1899–1918 1901–1918 1904–1918

6 children

Family Tree

Edward = Katherine Worsley
Duke of Kent
b.1935

Princess = Hon. Angus Ogilvy
Alexandra
b.1936

Prince Michael = **Baroness Marie-Christine**
b.1942   **von Reibnitz**

George = Sylvana Tomaseli
Earl of st Andrew
b.1962

Lady Helen = Timothy Taylor
Windsor
b.1964

Lord Nicholas
Windsor
b.1970

Lord Frederick
Windsor
b.1979

Lady Gabriella
Windsor
b.1981

Columbus Taylor   Cassius Taylor
b.1994   b.1996

James Ogilvy = Julia Rawlinson   Marina Ogilvy = Paul Mowatt
b.1964   b.1966   div.1997

Edward   Lady Maria Windsor   Lady Amelia Windsor
Baron Downpatrick   b.1992   b.1995
b.1988

Zenouska Mowatt   Christian Mowatt
b.1990   b.1993

Flora Ogilvy   Alexander Ogilvy
b.1994   b.1996

Chronology

1800   Act of Union between United Kingdom and Ireland passed.

1815   Napoleon defeated by British and Allies, commanded by Duke of Wellington at Waterloo. First Corn Laws introduced.

1817   Death of Princess Charlotte, daughter of the Prince Regent, in childbirth.

1818   Marriage of Edward, Duke of Kent, to Princess Victoria Leiningen of Saxe-Coburg in Germany.

1819   Return of Duke and Duchess of Kent to Britain for the birth of Princess Alexandrina Victoria on May 24 at Kensington Palace and her baptism on June 26. Birth of Prince Albert to Duke and Duchess of Saxe-Saalfeld-Coburg.

1820   Death of Duke of Kent on January 23 and of King George III on January 29. Accession of Prince Regent, King George IV.

1821   *Manchester Guardian* founded.

1825   First locomotive ran from Stockton to Darlington.

1828   Marriage of Princess Victoria's half-sister Feodore. Foundation of Royal Free and University College Hospitals.

1830   Death of King George IV, accession of his brother King William IV. Princess Victoria first in line to the throne. Liverpool to Manchester railway line opened.

1832   Parliamentary Reform Act passed. Sheffield Royal Infirmary founded.

1833   Abolition of slavery in the British Empire. Monopoly of trade with China lost.

1834   Feodore's visit to Kensington Palace. Viscount Melbourne made Prime Minister, followed by the Duke of Wellington in November and Sir Robert Peel in December. Houses of Parliament devastated by fire. Transportation of the Tolpuddle Martyrs. Royal Institute of British Architects founded.

1835   Royal family stays at Ramsgate with Uncle Leopold and his new wife Marie Louise. Lord Melbourne returned as Prime Minister.

1836   First visit to London of Prince Ernest and Prince Albert of Saxe-Coburg.

1837   Death of King William IV on June 20, accession of Queen Victoria. Queen Victoria visits Brighton. Whig Party's majority reduced in General Election. Sound transmitted via cable laid from Euston to Camden in London.

1838   Coronation of Queen Victoria, June 28. London to Birmingham railway line and Euston station opened, Great Western line from Paddington to Maidenhead. Anti-Corn Law League established by John Bright and Richard Cobden in Lancashire.

1839   Resignation of Lord Melbourne. Second visit of Prince Ernest and Prince Albert. Queen Victoria proposes to Prince Albert. British defeat of the Russians at Kabul in First Afghan War. East India Company involved in Opium War against China.

1840   Marriage of Queen Victoria and Prince Albert, February 10. Prince Albert made president of the Anti-Slavery Society and the Royal Fine Art Commission. Birth of Victoria, Princess Royal, on November 21. Existence of slums noted by the Select Committee on the Health of Towns.

1841   Birth of Albert Edward, Prince of Wales, on November 9. Death of Sir David Wilkie, Court Painter. Franz Xavier Winterhalter appointed. Second Tory administration formed by Sir Robert Peel after the General Election. Photographic reproduction with calotype achieved by William Fox Talbot.

1842   Two assassination attempts made on Queen Victoria and Prince Albert in May and June. Garden pavilion in Buckingham Palace built at Prince Albert's request. Queen Victoria and Prince Albert make their first railway journey on the first "royal train". Their first holiday in Scotland. Retirement of Baroness Lehzen from the Royal Household and her return to Germany. Felix Mendelssohn invited by Queen Victoria to Buckingham Palace. Chinese defeated by British. Hong Kong ceded to Britain. East India Company now a quasi-British governmental department. Royal Commission into Mining changes legislation governing the hours and conditions of women & children in mines. Similar changes effected in the textile mills by the Factory Act. Edwin Chadwick publishes his work on the Sanitary Conditions of the Labouring Poor. Ether first used as an anaesthetic for surgery and tooth extractions. The *Illustrated London News* , the first paper to use engravings, first published.

1843   Birth of Princess Alice on April 25. Queen Victoria and Prince Albert visit the Isle of Wight. Queen Victoria the first British monarch to make a State visit to France since Henry VIII. Prince Albert appointed president of the Society of Arts. William Gladstone made Minister of the Board of Trade. First Christmas card designed by Henry Cole. Theatre Act passed, allowing theatres to sell refreshments on the premises.

1844   Death of Prince Albert's father, Duke Ernest of Saxe-Coburg, in February. Birth of Prince Alfred on August 6. First co-operative shop opened by a group of workers in Rochdale. Poor Laws passed, including one allowing mothers of illegitimate children to claim maintenance from their fathers. First "ragged schools" set up by Lord Shaftesbury to provide free education to the poorest children.

1845 Osborne estate purchased, foundation stone for new building laid by Queen Victoria. Prince Albert tskes Queen Victoria to the Rosenau. Irish Potato Famine begins. *The Conditions of the Working Class in England* written and published by FriedrichEngels. Passenger railway journeys organized by Thomas Cook .

1846 Birth of Princess Helena on May 25. Parliament gives £20,000 for improvements to Buckingham Palace. Corn Laws repealed, Sir Robert Peel forced to resign, Lord Russell Prime Minister.

1847 Queen Victoria bathes in the sea for the first time. Lionel Rothschild becomes MP for the City of London. The Communist League formed by Friedrich Engels and Karl Marx. Samaritan Free Hospital for Women founded. Women allowed to become students at London University. Dr James Simpson discovers ether as a pain relief. Presbyterian Church of England Foreign Missions Committee set up.

1848 Death of Lord Melbourne. Birth of Princess Louise on March 18. Balmoral purchased. First Royal Command performance at Windsor Castle. Plans drawn up for the Great Exhibition by Prince Albert and the Society of Arts. Public Health Acts passed to improve sanitation and public health. Abdication of Louis Phillipe of France, who then came to England. Chartist rally held at Kennington Common. The *Communist Manifesto* published by Marx and Engels. W H Smith granted permission to sell books and newspapers in stations in London.

1849 Family portrait by Winterhalter hung in Osborne House for Queen Victoria's fortieth birthday. Assassination attempt on Queen Victoria. Queen Victoria and Prince Albert visits Ireland for the first time. Death of Dowager Queen Adelaide, widow of King William IV. Victoria Station opened in London.

1850 Birth of Prince Arthur on May1. Brighton Pavilion sold by Queen Victoria and purchased by the town for £60,000. Work begins on the Swiss cottage playhouse at Osborne. Death of Sir Robert Peel. Cardinal Wiseman made first Roman Catholic Archbishop of Westminster. Death of Louis Phillipe. First public libraries opened. North London Collegiate School for girls opened in Camden Town by Frances Mary Buss. Death of William Wordsworth. Alfred, Lord Tennyson made Poet Laureate

1851 New wings of Osborne House completed. Great Exhibition opened in London on May 1, to which Thomas Cook organized tours. Closing ceremony held on October 15. National Census carried out. Sound transmitted from London to Paris via undersea cable. Baron Paul Julius von Reuter's first news agency opened in London. Publication of first edition of *Household Words* by Charles Dickens.

1852 Death of the Duke of Wellington. Earl of Derby made Prime Minister, followed by the Earl of Aberdeen in December. *The English Woman's Domestic Magazine* published by Sam Beeton. South American Missionary Society founded.

1853 Birth of Prince Leopold on April 7, chloroform used by Queen Victoria. Work begun on the Balmoral estate. Russian invasion across the Danube. Turkey declares war on Russia. Act passed in an attempt to further restrict the use of child labour. Marriage of Napoleon III to Eugènie. Smoke Abatement Act passed for the Metropolitan Area.

1854 Foundation stone laid at Balmoral in September. France and Britain declared war on Russia, leading to the Crimean War. Tennyson writes *The Charge of the Light Brigade*. In September, Sebastopol besieged.

1855 Royal Family move into Balmoral. Crown Prince Frederick of Prussia visites Balmoral as a suitor to Princess Vicky. Poplar Hospital for Accidents founded. Victoria and Albert acquire the large yacht *Victoria and Albert II*, and use it to make a state visit to France. Victoria appalled at the condition of wounded soldiers in Chatham Hospital. Lord Palmerston becomes Prime Minister. Russian evacuation of Sebastopol. Thomas Cook organizes tours to the International Exhibition in Paris. *Daily Telegraph* and *Courier* founded.

1856 End of Crimean War. Queen Victoria awards the first Victoria Cross. Death of Charles Leiningen, Queen Victoria's half-brother, and Victoria, Duchess of Nemours, her cousin.

1857 Birth of Princess Beatrice on April 14. Prince Albert created Prince Consort. Baron Stockmar retires. Napoleon and Eugènie visit England. Art treasures Exhibition held in Manchester, promoted by Prince Albert. Indian Mutiny begins in Bengal.

1858 Marriage of the Princess Royal to Crown Prince Frederick of Prussia in January. Peace proclaimed in India. Earl of Derby becomes Prime Minister. Lionel Rothschild allowed to take his seat in the House of Commons. Christian Vernacular Society for India formed.

1859 Prince Leopold discovered to have haemophilia. Birth of Prince William of Prussia: Victoria and Albert become grandparents. Palmerston made Prime Minister. *On the Origin of Species* by Charles Darwin published. Mrs Beeton's *Book of Household Management* published. Universities Mission to Central Africa founded.

1860 Retirement of Sir James Clarke, Royal Physician, replaced by Dr William Jenner.

1861 Death of the Duchess of Kent in March. Death of Prince Albert on December 14. Funeral held at St. George's Chapel, Windsor on December 28.

1862 Marriage of Princess Alice to Prince Louis of Hesse Darmstadt.

1863 Victoria journeys to Coburg and to Rosenau to see Albert's Memorial. Society of Arts inaugurates the Albert Medal. Death of Baron Stockmar. First underground train runs between Bishop's Road and Farringdon Street in London. Thomas Cook's package trips to Switzerland begin.

1864 Birth of Albert, son of the Prince and Princess of Wales.

1865 Death of Leopold, King of the Belgians. John Brown made "The Queen's Highland Servant". Birth of George, son of the Prince and Princess of Wales. Death of Lord Palmerston. Earl Russell made Prime Minister. Movement for Women's Suffrage begins. Telegraphic cable laid from England to India. Death of Mrs Beeton in childbirth. China Inland Mission set up.

1866 Earl of Derby made Prime Minister. Telegraphic cable laid across Atlantic. Dr Barnardo founds his first juvenile mission.

1867	Effigies of Queen Victoria and Prince Albert made by Carlo Marochetti for the mausoleum at Frogmore.
1868	Prince Albert's remains placed in the mausoleum. Foundation stone laid for the first school of nursing at St Thomas's Hospital by Queen Victoria and Florence Nightingale. Benjamin Disraeli becomes Prime Minister, followed by Gladstone in December. St Pancras Station built. Introduction of the hotel coupon by Thomas Cook.
1869	Holiday party sent up the Nile by Thomas Cook.
1870	Small crown commissioned by Queen Victoria for her own use.
1871	Prince of Wales taken ill with typhoid.
1872	Assassination attempt on Queen Victoria in St Paul's Cathedral. Death of the Queen's sister, Feodore.
1873	Death of Princess Alice's son, Friedrich Wilhelm, from haemophilia.
1874	Marriage of Prince Alfred, Duke of Edinburgh to Marie, the Tsar's only daughter. Disraeli made Prime Minister again.
1875	Major share-holding in the Suez Canal gained by Britain.
1876	Queen Victoria made Empress of India. Memorial statue to Prince Albert unveiled in Kensington Gardens. Disraeli made a peer, with the title Earl of Beaconsfield. Invention of telephone by Alexander Graham Bell.
1877	Abdication threatened by Queen Victoria following the attempted invasion of Egypt by the Tsar of Russia.
1878	Death of Princess Alice on December 14, the anniversary of Prince Albert's death. Engagement of Prince Arthur, Duke of Connaught to Princess Louise Margaret, daughter of Princess Louise and Prince Frederick of Prussia. Second Afghan War.
1880	Resignation of Disraeli;. Gladstone becomes Prime Minister.
1881	Death of Disraeli. First of the Boer Wars.
1882	Marriage of Prince Leopold to Princess Helen of Waldeck-Pyrmont.
1883	Death of John Brown on March 27. Birth of Alice, daughter of Prince Leopold and Princess Helen.
1884	Death of Prince Leopold, on the anniversary of John Brown's death. Marriage of Victoria's granddaughter, Victoria of Hesse-Darmstadt to Prince Louis of Battenberg.
1885	Marriage of Princess Beatrice and Prince Henry of Battenberg. Lord Salisbury becomes Prime Minister.
1886	Gladstone Prime Minister again, but resigns. Lord Salisbury becomes Prime Minister.
1887	Celebrations for Victoria's Golden Jubilee, beginning on June 20. Arrival of Abdul Karim from India.
1888	Crown Prince Frederick becomes Emperor of Prussia and Vicky, Empress in February. Queen Victoria visits Berlin, meets Bismarck, the Chancellor. Emperor dies on June 15 and Queen Victoria's grandson Willy, becomes Kaiser.
1889	Abdul Karim made "The Queen's Munshi".
1890	Durbar Room added to Osborne House.
1892	Deaths of Prince of Wales's son, Albert Edward, of Princess Alice's husband, Louis of Hesse-Darmstadt and of Alfred, Lord Tennyson. Gladstone returned as Prime Minister.
1893	Death of Duke Ernest of Saxe-Coburg.
1894	Marriage of Alicky, Princess Alice's third daughter, to Tsar Nicholas of Russia. The Munshi made "The Queen's Indian Secretary".
1895	Death of Sir Henry Ponsonby. Jameson Raid in South Africa defeated by the Boers. Daimler begins manufacturing motor cars. Lord Salisbury becomes Prime Minister after Tories win General Election.
1896	Death of Princess Beatrice's husband, Prince Henry (Liko), from malaria. Visit of Tsar Nicholas II and Tsarina (granddaughter Alicky) to Balmoral. Alfred Austin appointed Poet Laureate. Marconi arrives in London with equipment to make a wireless.
1897	Queen Victoria's Diamond Jubilee. Service held outside St Paul's Cathedral.
1898	Death of Gladstone. Alexander Graham Bell begins to experiment with flying machines.
1899	Death of Young Alfred, Prince Alfred's son, from tuberculosis. Queen Victoria becomes an avid user of the telephone. Second Boer War.
1900	Queen Victoria visits Dublin. Death of Prince Alfred in the summer, followed by Queen Victoria's grandson, Prince Christian of Schleswig-Holstein. Three Daimler cars bought by the Prince of Wales.
1901	Victoria suffers a stroke at Osborne House on January 17 and dies on January 22. Her daughter Vicky, Dowager Empress of Prussia, dies in Berlin on August 5.

Bibliography

Allison R & Ridell S (ed)
The Royal Encyclopaedia Macmillan 1991
Bigham C
The Prime Ministers of Britain 1721-1921
John Murray 1929
Bradbury M (ed)
The Atlas of Literature
De Agostini Editions 1996
Briggs A
Victorian Cities Penguin Books 1980
Victorian Things Penguin Books 1990
Victorian People Pelican Books 1965
Buckle G E (ed)
The Letters of Queen Victoria Series Vol 1.
John Murray 1930
The Letters of Queen Victoria Vols 2 & 3.
John Murray 1908
Canadine D
Class in Britain Penguin Books 2000
Carey J (ed)
The Faber Book of Reportage
Faber & Faber 1996
Chesney K
The Victorian Underworld Pelican Books 1972
Colley L
Britons: Forging the Nation 1707–1837
Pimlico 1994
Cook C
*The Longman Companion to Britain in the
Nineteenth Century 1815–1914*
Pearson Education 1999
Cumming, V
*Royal Dress: the Image and the Reality
1580 to the Present Day* B T Batsford 1989
Darwin C
Voyage of the Beagle Penguin Books 1989
Davies N
Europe Pimlico 1997
Dewhurst J
Royal Confinements
Weidenfeld and Nicholson 1980
Dickens C
*Gone Astray and other Papers from
Household Words* Dent 1980
Dimond F & Taylor R
*Crown and Camera, The Royal Family
and Photography 1842-1910* Penguin 1987
Donnison J
*Midwives and Medical Men: A History of
the Struggle for the Control of Childbirth*
Historical Publications 1988
Duff D
Victoria in the Highlands
Frederick Muller 1968
Ellis R
Who's Who in Victorian Britain
Shepheard-Walywyn Ltd 1997
Esher, Viscount (ed)
*The Girlhood of Queen Victoria: A
Selection from Her Majesty's Diaries
between 1832 and 1840* Vols 1& 2
Fair Play (pseud)
*The Marriage of the Queen to Prince Albert
of Saxe-Coburg. A Letter to the People of
Great Britain* John Murray 1840
Fletcher B
A History of Architecture Athlone Press 1961
Fraser G F
Textiles in Britain
George, Allen and Unwin 1948
Freeman M
Railways and the Victorian Imagination
Yale University Press 1999
Fulford R (ed)
Dearest Mama Evans Brothers 1968

Gernsheim H & A
*Queen Victoria, A Biography in Word and
Picture* Longman 1959
Greville C F
The Greville Memoirs Vols I-VIII.
Longmans, Green and Co. 1896
Harris Rev I
*Sermon Preached at West London
Synagogue following the Death of Queen
Victoria. 25 Jan 1901*
Hensley Canon H
*On the Occasion of the Death of Queen
Victoria of Blessed Memory. Sermon
preached in Westminster Abbey*
Macmillan 1901
Hill C
Reformation to Industrial Revolution
Penguin Books 1992
HM Queen Victoria
*Leaves from the Journal of Our Life in the
Highlands* Smith, Elder and Co.1868
*More leaves from the Journal of a Life in
the Highlands* Smith, Elder & Co. 1884
Hobsbawm E
Industry and Empire Penguin Books 1990
The Invention of Tradition
University Press, Cambridge 1992
Homans M & Munich A
Remaking Queen Victoria
Cambridge University Press 1997
von Horn J
*Memoir of the Approaching Marriage of
Queen Victoria* I. J. W. Southgate 1839
HRH Princess Marie Louise
My Memoirs of Six Reigns Evans 1956
Hudson D
The Royal Society of Arts 1754-1954
John Murray 1954
Luckhurst K W & Lloyd C
The Quest for Albion
Royal Collection Enterprises 1998
Longford E
Victoria R.I. Pan Books 1966
Mayhew H
London Labour and the London Poor
Penguin Books 1985
Menkes S
The Royal Jewels Book Club Associates 1985
Morgan K
*The Birth of Industrial Britain: Economic
Change 1750-1850*
Addison Wesley Longman 1999
Morris J
Pax Britannica Faber & Faber 1998
Newhall, B
The History of Photography
Secker & Warburg 1982
One of Her Majesty's Servants
The Private Life of the Queen
C Arthur Pearson 1897
Pevsner N
*High Victorian Design: a Study of the
Exhibits of 1851* Architectural Press 1951
A History of Building Types
Thames & Hudson 1976
Pevsner N & Bradley S
London 1: The City of London
Penguin Books 1997
Pevsner N & Cherry B
London 3: North West Penguin Books 1991
Porter R
The Greatest Benefit to Mankind
Harper Collins 1997
Priestley J B
Victoria's Heyday Book Club Associates 1974

Ranger T (ed) & Hochschild A
King Leopold's Ghost Macmillan 1999
Reid, M
Ask Sir James Hodder & Stoughton 1987
Shannon, R
Gladstone: Peel's Inheritor 1809-1865
Penguin Books 1999
Gladstone: Heroic Minister 1865-1898
Penguin Books 2000
Small H
Florence Nightingale: Avenging Angel
Constable 1999
Smith P
Disraeli: A Brief Life
Cambridge University Press 1999
Staniland K
In Royal Fashion Museum of London 1997
Strachey L
Eminent Victorians Penguin Books 1986
Queen Victoria Harcourt Brace 1921
Sutton A & Carr R
Tartans, Their Art and History Bellew 1984
Tannahill R
Food in History Penguin Books 1988
Thompson E P
The Making of the English Working Class
Pelican Books 1979
Towler J & Bramall J
Midwives in History and Society
Croom Helm 1986
Tyler Whittle M
Victoria and Albert at Home
Routledge & Keegan Paul 1980
Turner M
Osborne House English Heritage 1989
Victoria, Princess of Prussia
My Memoirs Eveleigh Nash and Grayson 1929
Warner M
Queen Victoria's Sketchbook Macmillan 1979
Weintraub S
Victoria John Murray 1987
Albert: Uncrowned King John Murray 1997
Wigman A T
*An Empire's Lamentation. Sermon Preached
at Collegiate Church of St Mary The Virgin,
Port Elizabeth, 2 February 1901*
Wild A
The East India Company Harper Collins 1999
Wilson C A
Food and Drink in Britain Penguin Books 1984
Wood A
Nineteenth Century Britain 1815-1914
Longman 1982
Zeepvat C
Prince Leopold Sutton 1998
Ziegler P
Melbourne Collins 1976

The Crown Jewels Historic Royal Palaces
Agency 1996
Frogmore House and The Royal Mausoleum
The Royal Collection, St James's Palace 1998
*Great Exhibition of the Works of Industry of
all Nations, Official Descriptive and
Illustrated Catalogue* Vols 1, 2, 3. Authority
of the Royal Commission, Spicer Brothers
1851
Haemophilia 3 (Suppl. 1) Blackwell Science Ltd 1997
A History of Cable and Wireless (CD) Cable
and Wireless Plc 1995
Illustrated London News various
The Times various
Windsor Castle Official Guide
The Royal Collection, St James's Palace 1997

Index

Acknowledgements

Many people have provided information in the writing of this book. In particular I wish to thank:

HM The Queen for permission to consult the Royal Photographic Archives at Windsor Castle and the curator Frances Dimond, Susan Bennett the Curator at the Royal Society of Arts, Elizabeth Duff, Dr Anne Green, Sarah Larter, Mandy Little, Pat Maloney, Geoffrey Munn at Wartski, Alfie Vickers, Amelia Rowland, Dr Clare Taylor, Eunice Wilson, the staff of The British Library, The London Library and The Public Record Office. Finally to my family who coped with my absence as I became increasingly involved with Queen Victoria – George, Madeleine and Flora Kessler and Mavis Jaffé.

Picture Credits

The publishers would like to thank the following sources for their kind permission to reproduce the pictures in this book:

AKG London 3, 9, 11,14, 32, 44–5, 74, 167t, 173, /Erich Lessing 71; Anti Slavery International/William Taylor 62; Art Archive 31, 35, 63t, 86, 113b, 133r, 153t, /Dagli Orti 170, /Eileen Tweedy 120, 122, 143 t, 152, /Eileen Tweedy/Gordon Boy's School, Woking 157t, /Eileen Tweedy/London Museum 157b, /Private Collection 166; Bridgeman Art Library/Bourne Fine Art/Private Collection 23, /Bradford Art Galleries and Museums 36–7, /British Library, London 20t, /British Museum, London 30, /Christie's Images, London 177, /Christie's Images/Private Collection 135, /Christopher Wood Gallery, London 28, 56, /City Museum and Art Gallery, Plymouth, Devon 167b, /Crown Estate 48, /Fine Art Society, London 4, 27, /Fine Art Society, London/Private Collection 112, /Forbes Magazine Collection, New York 72, 84, /Guildhall Library, Corporation of London 67, 98, /Maas Gallery, London 49, /Manchester City Art Galleries 65, /Museum of London 24, /New College, Oxford University 16, /Philip Mould, Historical Portraits Ltd, London 39, /Private Collection 51, 60, 123br, 123bc, 150, 161, /Roy Miles Esq 70, 90, /Stapleton Collection/Private Collection 92, /Trades Union Congress, London 66, /Victoria & Albert Museum, London 43, 46; Carlton Books/London Library 110, /E Swinglehurst 102; Cheltenham Ladies' College 108t; Christie's Images 13, 116–117, 143 bc, 143 br, 145 br, 146, 149 t, 155 t, 162–3; Corbis 121, 168, 182, /Bettmann 61, /Hulton Getty 64, 107, 124, /National Gallery, London 22; Hulton Getty 6–7, 8, 12, 19cl, 19cr, 29cr, 50b, 60t, 76t, 76b, 78, 79, 82, 85, 99, 101, 105, 106, 109, 115, 127, 128b, 130, 134, 138, 140, 141, 142t, 149b, 151, 158, 165, 172l, 174, 176, 178b, 179t, 179b, 180, 183, /Rischgitz 111t, /Roger Fenton 119; Illustrated London News 68; Mary Evans Picture Library 17, 18cl, 18t, 34, 47, 53, 55, 63b, 87, 89, 91, 92t, 94, 100, 108b, 111b, 113t, 128t, 131, 139, 142b, 144-5, 148, 153c, 154, 155b, 156, 160, 169, 178t, /ILN 58, 77, /Punch 69; Museum of London 20b, 25, 52; Public Record Office 50 t; Rex Features 38 bc; Science & Society Picture Library 83, 93, /National Museum of Photography, Film & TV 3; The Royal Archives, © 2000 Her Majesty Queen Elizabeth II 29 cl, /Caldesi 21 tr, /Antoine Claudet 126, /Roger Fenton 95, /Ghemar 21c, /W E Kilburn 73, /Horatio Nelson King 133; Thomas Cook Archives 103; Topham Picturepoint 26, 54, 132, 159; V&A Picture Library 2, 38t, 40, 80-1, 96, 172r.

Every effort has been made to acknowledge correctly and contact the source and/or copyright holder of each picture, and Carlton Books Limited apologises for any unintentional errors or omissions which will be corrected in future editions of this book.